SOLDIERS

SOLDIERS

an obituary for Geneva
by Rolf Hochhuth

Translated by Robert David MacDonald

GROVE PRESS, INC., NEW YORK

To the memory of Erwin Piscator

CONTENTS

EVERYMAN

The earth is a temple, in which a Mystery
play is enacted. It is childish and spiteful,
ridiculous and certainly somewhat
gruesome.
> —Joseph Conrad, *Letters*

I gave my ballet a comic character, as I had
the feeling, I ought to make some
allowance for the war.
> —Nijinsky, *Journal*

CHARACTERS

Dorland, a theatrical director
His son, a Flight Lieutenant in the RAF
The Sculptor
An actor, who is to play an RAF Staff Officer
An actor, who is to play a Polish Captain
A West German Colonel ⎫ *played by the*
An American Colonel ⎭ *same actor*
A High Court Judge
A Japanese Professor
A French General
A Russian Military Attaché
A Policeman
The ghost of an Air Marshal of a Bomber Command

Autumn, 1964; one hundred years after the signing of the first Geneva Convention; in the ninetieth year of the life of Sir Winston Churchill; a quarter of a century since Hahn's announcement of his first splitting of the atom and Hitler's entry into Prague and Warsaw, and ten years since the explosion of the first hydrogen bomb relegated America's membership in the International Red Cross to the realm of black humor.

Bright moonlight on the steps of the roofless ruin of St. Michael's Cathedral in Coventry. In November, 1940, German bombers attacked the center of the British aircraft-engine industry, creating a memorial to Hitler by reducing the cathedral to ashes and killing 380 civilians. The ruins of the cathedral have been preserved, and the new church, consecrated in 1962, stands beside them.

The years have romanticized these ruins, much as the brush of Lyonel Feininger might have done, transfiguring the blitzed Gothic wall, which takes up the whole of the back of the stage, dematerializing the fire-stained sandstone and lending it a sort of idealized transparency. The sole indications that the ruins are a product of our own times are a huge scaffolding, behind and overtopping the ruined thirteenth-century façade, and the SCULPTOR's *squat hut to the left and in front of it. A bit of the new cathedral in its scaffolding, a characteristic element of the architecture of the twentieth century, should always be visible behind the original.*

In front of the Gothic façade, with its glassless windows and doorless doorways, stretches an open space that takes up most of the stage, loosely broken up by a few very broad, shallow steps (the remains of the old cathedral steps), and one or two dressed blocks of sandstone from the old and new buildings—the only properties necessary for the prologue.

At the start of the dress rehearsal of The Little London Theater of the World,* *which is being staged, as other plays have been, in the ruins, this setting disappears. The next day's centenary celebrations are to be held here, and at the moment an orchestra is rehearsing. While the curtain is still down, one can hear constantly repeated, obstinately rehearsed passages from either Britten's*

---

* The German, *Das Londoner Kleine Welttheater,* was derived from Calderón's *El Gran Teatro del Mundo,* as taken from the Latin, *theatrum mundi.*

War Requiem, *composed for Coventry, or the first movement of Bruckner's* Ninth Symphony.

That this is in no way an Overture is soon clear from the disrespectful hammering of two STAGEHANDS *and the* SCULPTOR'S *chipping away at his statue—two silhouettes in the low-built hut, visible by the meager light of an unshaded lamp. All the visible happenings, like the audible, should have a "workshop" character.*

Everyman *no longer ponders, as he did in the play of 1529, "on fleshly lustes and his treasure," but has become a soldier, much as the "rich man" of Pieter Dorland and Hans Sachs was transformed, after 1550, by various writers into the more-or-less-Christian knight whose deeds were measured and judged before his death by the standards St. Paul laid down for those who bear the sword. In an age of general conscription and the use of bombs and rockets primarily against the defenseless, a man's conscience is exposed to its most violent ordeals during his years of military service.*

The fact that as a bomber pilot he had become one of the textbook sinners of his time has spurred DORLAND, *the theatrical director (this vanished name has been given him since it was probably that of the author of the first* Everyman *play), who is fatally ill, to take action.*

The "good work" that is to redeem him, during the time left to him to draw up his earthly reckoning—and there is no other—is his adaptation and production of The Little London Theater of the World. *This play, he hopes, will foster the idea, both among his own generation, his enemies, his fellow-pilots from the Second World War, and his son's generation, that the Convention regarding aerial warfare drafted by the Red Cross for the protection of cities should be given the status of international law. All Geneva's efforts so far have been sabotaged unanimously by the military leaders of the civilized nations. The draft submitted to the representatives of eighty-five countries in New Delhi in 1957 disappeared into the filing systems of the bureaucrats. Conventions exist regarding both naval and land warfare—but none so far regarding aerial warfare. A hundred years after the first Geneva Convention, it is thus possible for the defenders of civilization to plan in the certain knowledge that even such an action as the destruction of Rotterdam (carried out in 1940 by Kesselring's second air fleet with all the unpretentious moral feeling of a kidnapper) was not actually "illegal"* . . .

And so—perhaps—this production of DORLAND's, *on the occasion of the centenary of the Red Cross, may also serve as a requiem for Geneva.*

The man who commissioned this obituary from him in the name of the Coventry Festival Committee is the SCULPTOR, *one of the artists working on the new cathedral.* DORLAND *has known him for many years. Nevertheless, this figure inhabits the twilight zone of allegory, like the stranger who appeared as the messenger of death to Mozart in 1791 to commission a requiem. That September the composer wrote: "The vision of that unknown stranger is ever before my eyes. I see him entreating me, urging me and impatiently demanding the work . . . I feel it, my condition tells me my hour is come: I must die."*

DORLAND *learned this, quite simply, from his doctor. But Mozart also soon saw that he was dealing with a "real" (though what apparition can be more real than that of Death?) and quite unmysterious messenger from a musical patron: this in no way prevented him from seeing the commission as one for his own requiem. For when two or three are gathered together in his name, Death (so much more reliable in this than God) is always of the gathering.*

It does not therefore matter whether this Everyman *play is staged as "reality" or as a dream: persons and places in a trial of conscience are precisely as real and actual as we suppose and admit them to be to ourselves. Here* DORLAND, *using the motifs of the traditional* Everyman, *seeks out his companions for guidance and justification: whether his conversations with the Air Marshal, breeding his roses, or with his son, planning the annihilation of cities, or with the* SCULPTOR *are taking place now, at the moment of the performance; or whether they took place a year, a week ago and he is now simply remembering; or whether he is now only thinking of holding them: memories, plans, projects, self-interrogations, actions—this is immaterial.*

This view has dictated the construction of the prologue. The setting is freed from restrictions of space and time. The composition is subject to the paths followed by the dialogue, not the other way around. It should be as supple as conversations can be, particularly conversations with oneself, and all the more calm in consequence —almost static. ("Walking is undramatic," warns Chaplin, the most physically "possessed" actor of all.) At most, if need be, a veil—a gauze curtain—exists now and then between DORLAND *and the still living or already dead figures of his "stocktaking." The prose, where rhythmic, should, even where it becomes almost scannable verse, be spoken prosaically: It looks to the verse form simply as a breakwater against those moments—so often unavoidable in drama—when feeling wells over and becomes a cataract. The yardstick should be the coldest definition of all, formulated, typically enough, by a Romantic, Victor Hugo: "Le vers, c'est la forme optique de la pensée."*

Two STAGEHANDS *are nailing a broad white banner with a red cross on it to the façade of the burned-out cathedral. Not only are they quite unperturbed by the orchestral rehearsal which is taking place in the ruins: they actually enjoy disturbing it. They take the ladder, and, more particularly, their beer, over to the right; one holds up the other end of the banner, the other nails it up. We can now read the inscription, in black:*

1864 First Geneva Convention 1964

From the right, five men appear, picking their way across the front of the stage. First comes a British High Court Judge, in full-bottomed wig, buckled shoes, silk stockings, and robes, all in the bizarre black of the Cromwellian era. Two officers follow behind him. One is DORLAND's SON, *a Flight Lieutenant in the RAF. The other is a Colonel in the West German Air Force. He is in dress uniform but wears no greatcoat, so that one may see his medals. Earned between Guernica and Leningrad, they have, however, lost their primal stain, the swastika—now erased, much as the names of the twelve thousand Jews who fell for Germany in the Great War were erased from the war memorials in Hitler's Germany.*

These men are followed, with some difficulty, by a Japanese civilian on crutches. The hair on one side of his head has been permanently burned off and his scalp is covered with various colorful scars. He is a professor who, as Nagasaki's most-photographed and publicized cripple, has been traveling to congresses like this, albeit in vain, for the last twenty years. Last to come is a dapper little Frenchman in a red-and-gold General's cap.

JUDGE (*the first to cross, or clamber, over the ruins; stopping*):
It's roped off here—we're lost. Orchestra rehearsal.

GERMAN (*pointing at the ruins*):
    Aren't they rebuilding this part?
JUDGE (*while the* STAGEHANDS *still hammer away*):
    No—we are preserving the *ruins*.
    The new cathedral is going up next door.
GERMAN: Were you already officiating in Coventry—when it was
    . . . er, then?
JUDGE: When it was destroyed, you mean? Good gracious!
    Twenty-four years ago? No!
    At the time I was "officiating"—ha ha—in the infantry.
    Listen—we must separate those two.
    I *said* we shouldn't drink before dinner.

The voices of the FRENCHMAN *and the* JAPANESE *can be heard even before they themselves can be seen.*

FRENCHMAN (*almost shouting*):
    Demagogy—ah, oui. I maintain: demagogy!
JAPANESE: Remove your arm: I do not require assistance.

The FRENCHMAN *now enters slowly, backward, as he is helping the* JAPANESE *all the same. The* JUDGE *and the* GERMAN *have already retraced their steps in the direction of the disputants, whose quarrel continues as the* JAPANESE *hobbles in, stubbornly rejecting the little General's help.*

JAPANESE: No doubt of it—you are all agreed,
    all military men, no matter what their country—
    just like New Delhi seven years ago, now here—
    all are agreed to accept the Red Cross draft
    only to make it disappear—this congress is a farce.
FRENCHMAN (*explaining to the others*):
    I did not say that at all—I only said:
    I find it demagogic of the Red Cross
    to bring us officers to Coventry of all places,
    the scene of *Hitler's* crime,
    to shackle our consciences to these civilians.
    Naturally we are all sorry about the civilians:
    but are officers for this reason
    utterly to forgo attacks on cities?
    It is demagogy!
    It must be permitted to bomb aircraft factories,
    even if, mon Dieu, a church is burned as well.

JUDGE: You can hardly blame Geneva, General,
  for not hawking their air war convention
  in *Geneva,* but in a town that was bombed
  precisely because no such convention exists.
GERMAN (*trying to be diplomatic*):
  Even civilians must see that, Professor:
  In the rocket age, you know,
  cities are the most effective targets.
FRENCHMAN: Try yourself to hit a tank—with a rocket.
  Tanks move, towns stand still.
JUDGE: Just as they did for Herr von Braun:
  Even in those days he contrived to kill
  three hundred cinema patrons with a single rocket,
  in Antwerp.
GERMAN: We officers are here in Coventry
  so that the Red Cross
  shall be made conversant
  with strategy, *realistically,*
  not the other way around.
  The Red Cross . . .
JAPANESE (*losing his self-control*):
  In your mouth it is a dirty joke.
  You well know the Geneva Convention is annulled
  when *it* must be made "conversant" with
  your plans for the destruction of cities
  and not the other way around.
FRENCHMAN: We can always leave Coventry, we officers,
  if we are not welcome.
JUDGE: Let us look for our supper, gentlemen.
GERMAN: As my French friend said:
  We officers of every country are prepared
  to leave, to leave first thing tomorrow morning—
  the Russians and the Americans as well.
FRENCHMAN: Correct—if they are going to insult an airman's
    honor.
  We will leave the congress, all of us,
  if they are calling our *honor* into question.
JAPANESE (*drily*): Where is it found, in men?
FRENCHMAN (*angrily*): Please?
JAPANESE: Where is your honor?
  One knows exactly where a woman's is.

FRENCHMAN (*screaming*): I do not permit this remark . . .

JAPANESE: I only asked—while I was attaché in Berlin,
   I read a German author, Lichtenberg . . .

GERMAN: Ah yes, our writers—terrible!

JAPANESE (*quickly*): Oh, a classic, have no fear: He writes,
   "That refined honor possessed by woman
   is situated about half an inch from the arse hole."
   Mon général, where is it situated in us men?

FRENCHMAN: In better days I would have challenged you.

JAPANESE: In better days I would have been capable of shooting
       back.
   However, since officers have equated it with their *honor*
   to bomb civilians, like myself in Nagasaki—
   myself and forty thousand of my neighbors—
   I can, alas, no longer shoot at *them*.

The FRENCHMAN *leaves the stage ostentatiously. The young* DOR-
LAND *sees his father coming and raises a hand in greeting.*

JUDGE: I *said* one shouldn't drink before dinner.

DORLAND *appears before them; the orchestra delivers itself of a
plangent phrase. The director comes quickly through the ruined
archway and unintentionally goes for the two strangers.*

DORLAND: What is that orchestra doing still rehearsing?
   (*To the two* STAGEHANDS, *who are also getting ready to leave:*)
   Where is the first act? Go in and set it up.
   They were to be through by half past eight.
   Hello, Peter.
   (*Pointing to the banner:*)
   And let's have some light on that.

While the two STAGEHANDS *are going off through the ruins with
their ladder and tools, the* JUDGE *has been vainly trying to get a
word in. Now, with ironic politeness, he says:*

JUDGE: Excuse me, we did not mean to cause a disturbance.
   Just trying to find a way out, to get to the Red Cross dinner.

DORLAND: Oh please, make as much disturbance as you like,
       the more the merrier.
   Straight through the ruins, then left, Hotel Leofric.

JUDGE: Thank you so much.

Assisting the PROFESSOR, *he goes out the same way as the* STAGE-HANDS. *The inscription on the banner is now illuminated, as* DORLAND *had asked.*

SON: 'Evening, Father.—Before we go to the dinner—
  can I introduce my Wing Commander, Oberst Weinmüller
  from Germany?
DORLAND (*replying amiably to the other's salute*):
  How practical, Herr Weinmüller, to have *you* lead the German
    delegation:
  It means my son can get leave as well,
  to see my offering tomorrow.
WEINMÜLLER (*modest to the point of shyness: he uses, as Vice
  Air Marshal Bennett did in his memoirs, the word "visit" to
  mean "incinerate"*):
  I don't know, Mr. Dorland, if *I* am quite the right man;
  you will have read, some newspapers are critical
  because I was among those who visited Guernica and Bel-
    grade.
DORLAND: Precisely why you can speak tomorrow—like me—
  when the Red Cross submits the draft
  for an Air Warfare Convention to the military.
  Has it a chance this time?

WEINMÜLLER *next uses the words* (*in quotes*) *of the professor
who, in 1955, spoke of "a vision" when he maintained that today
"Man has ceased to be the measure of all things. The new measures
have not been created by the humanities, nor by the humanist
tradition, but by the physical sciences and their technical application."*

WEINMÜLLER: No, "we must try to live with the bomb.
  The only solution to the problem lies
  not in international conventions for the humanization of war
  and the protection of the civil population . . .
  but in a policy which will prevent the outbreak
  of a war, under whatever circumstances . . ."
DORLAND (*coldly*):
  But there has *been* war ever since Korea, Colonel.
  How can you possibly still talk
  of a policy to *prevent* war?

[*Another quotation from the same world historian and visionary gushes from* WEINMÜLLER's *lips pleasantly, like warm water from a bath tap, accompanied by slight movements of his pear-shaped behind. He uses the word "progress" even in this connection, quite without irony, as if he too was being paid by a technical college.*

"The technique of war also is making progress with the aid of technology and industry. It is inconceivable in today's industrial society and urban landscape that the new armies should wage war in the manner of Frederick the Great or von Moltke, in which connection one must also point out that . . . the inhabitants of the areas of operations . . . suffered considerably."

DORLAND (*now hostile, and with a tired and sick man's irritability, which* WEINMÜLLER, *characteristically enough, fails to notice*): But that is precisely why the Convention for Land Warfare was created. Why is there none for air warfare? Whether the inhabitants happen to be caught up, however seriously, in a war —or whether, as today, they are the primary target: There is a difference. And were not Moltke's rapid victories achieved purely by the encirclement of the *armies?* The shelling of Vienna did not provoke Sadowa, nor that of Paris the capitulations at Sedan and Metz. And as for your King: At Kunersdorf, when he sacrificed half his men, and his adversary more than a fifth of *his,* first of all, the suffering of the neighboring villages was numerically not comparable to the losses among the combatants, and secondly, it would have had as little influence in the counsels of the sovereigns as the burning of native huts has at the White House. And what of us, Colonel —did the bombing of cities bring victory one step nearer for you in Germany and us in Britain? You know quite well— it delayed it.

WEINMÜLLER (*almost cheerful now*): But—excuse me please, neither you nor we had at the time the atom bomb.

DORLAND: Exactly. We have it now—and so, thank God, have our opponents. The Rosenbergs have done as much for the world as Henri Dunant. It is fear alone creates a conscience—in all of us.]

Grateful for the chance to escape, he points to where a STAGE MANAGER *is signaling from the rear of the stage.*

> Excuse me: I have myself to play the pilot
> I was twenty-five years ago:
> I must go and find my lost youth.
> Your banquet is waiting—a blessing on the feast.

The COLONEL *salutes, piqued.* DORLAND's *remark about the Rosenbergs has caused the expression on his face to crack, like a stone thrown through a mirror. Along with most of his comrades, this ex-mercenary of Hitler's has never found it hard to discount the idea that treason* can *be more admirable than holding the front for the creator of Auschwitz and facilitating, year in, year out, the persecution of his victims.*

WEINMÜLLER: Auf wiedersehen.

Exit with DORLAND's SON.

> DORLAND *paces out the length and width of the ruins, counting quietly to himself. In this manner, he arrives at a point upstage left where the* SCULPTOR *is working from a low scaffolding at his larger-than-life-size draped statue. The statue, what can be seen of it, is reminiscent of the Epstein St. Michael at Coventry. The* SCULPTOR, *in a white smock and a flat cap, is bearded like Ernst Barlach, with the same sad, shadowed, outlaw's eyes. His voice, however, is relaxed, amused—like his first words:*

SCULPTOR: Well, Dorland—how is it?
DORLAND: No pain. Morphine is kind.
> Tell me about the angel—coming on?
SCULPTOR (*covering up the figure*):
> The face was giving me trouble—not any more though.
> I'm giving him yours.
DORLAND: The face of a master-bomber!
SCULPTOR (*as* DORLAND *laughs uneasily*):
> Angels *were* sinners before they were made messengers.
[DORLAND (*digressing*):
> How can you still do it, you painters and sculptors: Angels!—
> it's an art, keeping up this naivety.
> You chip the figure of Death out of stone too, well and good;
> death lives amongst us (he does indeed).
> But angels?]

SCULPTOR: Angelos—it means no more than messenger.
Whom the message comes from . . . [just suppose
the idea of such a figure; call him, if you like,
a spirit provoking the questions
which the world's markets withdraw from circulation.]
Each time we speak—another speaks within us.
What kind of man is he, who is no different
from his own outward appearance?

DORLAND (*ironically*): Agreed—but ever since mankind forfeited
belief in a last judgment—
no angel has been able to save him from this:
"The sun is vanished, and the earth as well!
no light of reason shows mankind the way
to find it once again . . . this world is quite
used up, when man shall ever seek for new ones
amongst the planets, though he sees that all
dissolves in pieces, all coherence gone."

[SCULPTOR: What's that from?

DORLAND: Robert Burton, in sixteen-twenty—something.
No . . . ever since I started on this piece,
each time that I have sat down at my desk
I have asked myself in vain:

*Unlike the Burton quotation, the phrase of Kierkegaard's comes
out not as if he was quoting, but as an integral part of what he is
thinking.*

Who I am, how I came here, what this thing is
they call the world, what my part is
in this vast undertaking—and, if I
am forced to take part in it,
who is the director of it?
(*Provocative:*)
I would dearly like to tell him a thing or two.

SCULPTOR: Such as? No! You were quite right, when you cut out
the character of God the Father from your version
of the old Theater of the World.
He only distracts us from our own responsibility.
That is why religious men are so seldom humane;
they forget, in all their babble about God,
that there has never been more than one way to Him:
to treat one's fellow-man as being in His image.

DORLAND (*irritated*): Are you saying that because you know
 how many fellow-men I have not so treated?]
 I usually write by the open window.
 My desk is so placed that the dark glass
 of the window, in front of the gray wall,
 reflects my own image—depressing.
 Each time I look in that black pane of glass,
 I see the portrait of the pilot.
 How easy it must formerly have been . . .
 to live, to kill,
 as easy as for the medieval Everyman:
 One laid one's charge on God—and died, discharged.
 Today—today, the only partner left for us is Death.

Death appears.
 The light on the SCULPTOR *and his statue suddenly goes off. Be-*
hind DORLAND—*and the orchestral rehearsal has helped to prepare*
this moment, to add shadow to the very definite substance of the
projected photograph which now appears, gigantic as the ruined
wall—the picture of a dead woman sitting in a Dresden street, her
skull mummified by the firestorm, which has, inexplicably, not
touched her hair.

 Pause. DORLAND *and the picture alone.*

 DORLAND *has his back to the picture of the dead woman—it is,*
however, all he sees. He speaks as if he were still speaking to the
SCULPTOR, *who is no longer to be seen.*

 Since you commissioned this work from me,
 this image shows through, like a water mark,
 on every sheet of paper that I write on.
 On the second attack on Dresden,
 there happened to me something which
 seldom happens to us today, and which tomorrow
 will, for the men who fire the rockets,
 simply not be possible.
 I had to see, to *touch* what I had killed.
 Because of icing up I had to bale out
 over the last scene of my crime . . .
 And when the Dresdeners finally cut me free
 from my parachute (they let me hang for a day
 screaming among the rafters of a cinema) . . .

they had not come to lynch me.
When they had got me,
they, the swine, forced me, the swine,
two weeks on end, to drag with my bare hands
the cooked and quickly rotting corpses
from cellars, gardens, houses,
and off pavements, cooked soft with the heat,
to one of the five pyres in the Old Market.
This woman—was the first.
This woman sat there, where the heat had thrown her down,
the blast of the firestorm all around her—
eyes and flesh melted away,
only the bridge of the nose, inexplicably,
was still covered with skin,
as if fireproofed.
And her hair had been preserved . . .
(*He loses himself in the picture, murmuring, overpowered.*)
First my victim, now my persecutor, and—soon to be—my
    image.
Horse carts brought in the heaps of dead—
some of the dead were swollen up, the size of horses—
my job was to unload them,
and to lay them in layers.
Many of the bodies, naked or in rags,
were shorter than the logs on which we heaped them to be
    burned.
Always just five hundred bodies—then the flamethrower.
—The Germans had of course a practiced hand
at funeral pyres; first of all for books,
then, by logical progression, for men,
the sequence Holy Mother Church formerly laid down for our
    guidance . . .
These hands, high above many cities,
released the target flares—and later . . . soon
I wiped them clean
(though with what right?) on the body of a woman.
I even brought a child into the world.
(*Loses himself in the picture again.*)
Hands . . . nothing—one sees no trace of all this on them.
How our skin *disguises* us.

Death, or the image of the dead woman, fades, finally to vanish,
and DORLAND *remains on the forestage, his gaze turned in upon*
himself. The light returns, making the SCULPTOR *visible once*
more. Turning to him, DORLAND *says:*

> That my own son should now be in a Bomber Command,
> playing out "war games" under German officers . . .

SCULPTOR: An amiable fellow enough, your son's NATO boss.

DORLAND: Like all of them—all very nice to meet, but . . . the
    compromise-German.
    When they are beaten, they are the ones
    who manage to think up the term vice-champion.
    Germany—vice-champion of two world wars and one world
    cup.
    Over there, the other day,
    twenty years after the surrender
    (which was, after all, unconditional),
    I saw on the TV weather maps
    the old eastern provinces marked as German territory.
    Four times every day every schoolboy is misled to hope
    that it is Poland's duty alone to pay for the German.

SCULPTOR: A people goes to war, to partition its neighbor
    for the fourth time in a century and a half.
    That that people, *as a consequence,* is itself partitioned
    seems to them the greatest outrage in history.

[DORLAND: Alternatively: this people would incorporate into itself
    all Poland, along with the Crimea, Belgium, and the Ukraine.
    Result: one sixth of their own land is taken from them.
    And not one of them is struck by the thought
    that it is a logical consequence.]

SCULPTOR: Let them plant atomic mines
    all along their frontiers, if they want to.
    At least no one will go on taking them seriously
    when they bleat about how "this frontier must go."

DORLAND: The first time I saw Colonel Weinmüller was on the
    box;
    he was telling the press why
    that atomic maniac had been made Chief of the Bonn Army.

DORLAND'S *nightmare is now embodied in the person of the* COLO-
NEL, *who mounts a plinth in the pitch-black background, from*

*where, flooded with light, he speaks in a direction of what one may
assume is a horde of journalists. He is wearing glasses, but no
cap and no medals, and he carries documents and a newspaper.*
DORLAND *and the* SCULPTOR *have disappeared—it is dark and
empty where they stood.*

COLONEL WEINMÜLLER *is blond, bland, and dry, like a sweet
German biscuit. He is trying to efface himself, as he has good
reason to do here in Coventry, although—as a Düsseldorfer—
hardly enough to warrant quite such pious meekness as he shows.
He is engaged in training members of the NATO countries to fly
jet bombers at the British air base at West Raynham.*

WEINMÜLLER *knows the runways of every military airfield from
Ireland to Sicily and has stretched his patriotic feelings accordingly to include the whole Western hemisphere. His political hori-
zon—"a soldier is a man who does not notice when he is being
abused"—extends as far as Alaska in one direction but stops short
at the Elbe, which* WEINMÜLLER *has no desire whatever to cross,
in the other. With his knowledge of modern weapons, he loves
peace as if it were his own grandchild. For this reason his being
delegated today to represent the Luftwaffe at the centenary of the
Geneva Convention met with his heartfelt approval. Since he
regards the so-called pre-emptive strike (the name for the annihilation of population centers in the enemy territory) as permissible in an emergency, namely to anticipate and prevent enemy
aggression (however one is supposed to recognize that), his appearance in Coventry is something of a bad joke. This fact, however, he is unable to grasp—Flake called the German "the man
of approximate comprehension."* COLONEL WEINMÜLLER'S *talent
is to be loyal and honorable, qualities which, as we know, were
as hard to combine in the war as they are now. And so he became,
like everybody else, a (Ger)man of compromise.*

*Politically exhausted and morally overburdened, like any man
who had borne arms, but wishing to be reinstated in the post-
Hitler army, he gave at his examination, with the clear gaze of a
liar well-drilled by past history, an affirmative answer to the question, current then, though soon to be done away with: "Do you
approve of the actions of the officers in the revolt of July 20,
1944?" In private, however, much as in Nazi days he might have
repeated a joke about Hitler, he will willingly confide, as a Luftwaffe man, that it is common knowledge that no officer from his*

service (nor from the navy), was able to bring himself to break his oath of loyalty on July 20.

Nevertheless, after hearing an aristocratic superior make frequent mention of a book on the German resistance to Hitler, WEIN-MÜLLER *found it a social necessity, one fine day, to open it. He did this with mixed feelings of interest and suspicion. The book, to be sure, like all the others did not mention, even in the index, the one solitary man who, with a bomb intended for Hitler, actually killed a dozen Nazis. Georg Elser was only a working man with an illegitimate child, and, more suspicious still, a Communist. All the same, against the grain, the book made* WEINMÜLLER *cautious and when, shortly after reading it, he was invited along with other Staff officers to Bonn to attend a parliamentary debate on the action taken by the police against a news magazine, he was prompted by the behavior of the men on the Government benches to ask himself, for the first time, whether that negative assortment had got there simply because the positive had been decimated by rope and ax and gas and on the fields of battle. He had entered the mighty building full of pious feelings about the Government, impressed with the energy with which these civilians had rumbled these journalists, clearly traitors of the worst sort—and now he actually had to look at the Chancellor, and his Secretary of State, at the Home Secretary even. When the Chief began to sweat more than speak,* WEINMÜLLER *made the discovery that position was not the same thing as distinction: that the Bavarian Strauss sitting there was the same age as the Bavarian Scholl would have been had the Munich students' revolt of 1943 not brought him to the scaffold. All this the* COLONEL *told himself, and had to go out into the fresh air. Quite soon, however, he got slightly drunk and regained his peace of mind, saying to himself over his cognac that the military profession not only spared one, it actually prevented one from indulging in the dirty game of politics.*

Avoidance of politics was one of WEINMÜLLER'S *reasons for succumbing, five years after Germany's declaration of utter military bankruptcy, to his inborn compulsion to wear a uniform. The other reason was that as the son of a tradesman with old-fashioned ideas,* WEINMÜLLER *had an instinct for quality and a wide-awake aversion to the new German measure of all things, the car, whose make is now the criterion of the worth of its owner.*

Instead, therefore, of becoming a lotus-eater in the Cockaigne country of the German economy and of allowing himself to be

*branded with the Cross of Merit complete with Mercedes Star,
he fled, already a grandfather despite his youth, into the army,
once described by Hitler's wittiest officer (who had misgivings
about not having emigrated) as "the only way a gentleman can
emigrate."*

WEINMÜLLER *did his service, at considerable risk to his life,
for a salary almost equal to that received (also for service) by
his brother's "gentlemanly" chauffeur back in their native Ruhr.*

*Loyalty and devotion, judged to be requisites in the training of
sheepdogs and subordinates, have made* WEINMÜLLER *and the
British Wing Commander he is working with into officers of
almost unlimited usefulness—if only within the limits of what
they have been taught and now teach others, such as only to attack
and kill the defenseless from the air, never eye to eye on the
ground as the primitive SS and the Feldgendarmerie did. Even
during the war* WEINMÜLLER *found himself unable to suppress the
thought that a direct connection existed between the part he
played in the overrunning of Belgrade one Sunday morning, without war having been declared, and his sister's being burned to
death in the firestorms of Hamburg. But that he himself over
Belgrade or his English friend over Lübeck should personally
have forfeited the honorable name of a soldier, which belonged
to every fighter pilot as much as to the infantryman—the secure
feeling, the result of their all being part of the international "col-
lective" of bombers together has preserved both of them from
entertaining such an idea.*

The COLONEL *has here the tone of a Government spokesman.
He shows signs of that rigid manner he regards as manly and
objective, although his voice still trickles on in its well-oiled
Düsseldorf tea-party accent.*

The structure of this press conference taking place in DORLAND's
*mind shows that the director is remembering worse things than
simply the* COLONEL's *appearance—von Küchler's Prussian-style
order of the day and Kesselring's tubby pathos force their way
into his thoughts as well.*

WEINMÜLLER: . . . and I should like, Ladies and Gentlemen, to
take advantage of this press conference to point out that the
absurdity of such attacks concerning the person of the newly
appointed Inspector General has long been proved: nor have
our Dutch NATO-colleagues raised any objections to his

appointment. Even the Commander of the Air Force in question, Marshal Kesselring, was acquitted after the end of Marshal War—I beg your pardon—the end of the war, of the charge of the burning of the Citadel of Rotterdam, since this action fully respected both articles 25 and 26 of the Hague Convention.

Sensation, expressed, however, only by murmurings and mutterings in the background—abruptly cut off by an order (on a tape recording) in the arrogant tone of a Prussian officers' mess:

TAPE: Resistance in Rotterdam is to be crushed by whatever means: if necessary the destruction of the city is to be threatened and carried out.—Von Küchler, Supreme Commander, Eighteenth Army.

WEINMÜLLER (*as if warding off counter-arguments*):
But—*please*: the Thirty-ninth Army Corps made still another attempt to persuade Rotterdam to capitulate—but when the Dutch finally sent their negotiators, by then, unfortunately—the bomber groups had been ordered into the air and when they tried to stop them—Good Heavens, it was simply fate . . . [that only forty out of the hundred machines recognized the red signal-cartridges and turned back. Fate.] On this point we have the testimony of the Field Marshal's memoirs, in which he explains:

The tape-recording again, this time in a well-fed, cosy, sensual voice:

TAPE: The fact that it is precisely at the most important moments of the battle that the lines of communication may sunder had become for me, as an old soldier, an everyday occurrence.

More murmuring, muttering, bitter laughter, even while the COLONEL *is speaking—but even here the opposition can manage no more.*

WEINMÜLLER (*with a smile like a great cheese, embarrassed*):
I beg your pardon?—I agree, not very happy: "an everyday occurrence." Hardly the happiest phrase to describe an action with such fatal results for nine hundred and eighty citizens of Rotterdam. Indeed no. For those of you, Ladies and Gentlemen, to whom the Field Marshal's argument may have a somewhat too . . . ah, military ring, may I recommend

you to approach the question of the responsibility to the individual in a technological war in a spirit of the highest humanistic detachment. Here I should like to quote from the *Schweizerische Nationalzeitung* some philosophic observations of the West German writer Reinhard Baumgardt. I should like to emphasize that according to my inquiries we are dealing, neither in the case of the newspaper nor of Herr Doktor Phil. Baumgardt, with Communist . . . er, organs.

He gets out a pair of spectacles and three pages of newspaper, fiddling with them as he comments on the quotations, which are given here in italics, instead of as a parody.

WEINMÜLLER: I quote: *Behind the technical machinery of war, the individual can no longer be identified. The causal nexus of action and responsibility has been broken.* [He goes on to say that even the pre-history of the First World War had already shown that—quote—*the human being as an individual had become as invisible as he was insignificant.* His contention is that *what could be inflicted upon human beings would be capable*—I quote once more—*once and for all to overturn the traditional moral and theological categories of guilt and atonement, the belief, still current even now, in the autonomy of the individual.*] And he goes on to say that for us soldiers this is nothing less than an acquittal: *the means of extermination available had finally outgrown the power of human decision.*

(*He puts down the newspaper and continues:*)
Proof of this is provided not only by the margarine factory, but also by the Rotterdam fire brigade, since it can be proved, Ladies and Gentlemen, that no incendiaries were dropped and *nevertheless* over seventy thousand people were rendered homeless by fire. Is Doktor Baumgardt not absolutely correct when he postulates, Ladies and Gentlemen, regarding the technology of war: *the concepts of guilt and innocence sound like rules of behavior from the nursery— literature should be ashamed to go on churning them out?* End of quote. And I should like to express my thanks in the name of all commanding officers to Dr. Baumgardt for branding as obsolete, once and for all, the widespread postwar vilification and accusations of military leaders, for example regarding the Battle of Stalingrad. Herr Dr. Baum-

gardt has confuted the judges and leftist intellectuals who have denounced Field Marshal Paulus and Reichsmarschall Göring as materially responsible for the fatal tragedy. For fate it was, Ladies and Gentlemen. Thus we can read in Baumgardt that it is *precisely the conventional questions about Stalingrad—the guilt of this man or that, that day on which something could still have been saved which was nevertheless lost,* that are *inadequate to the dimension of the war* because these questions provide only *hand-me-down catchphrases for the historical criticism of Philistines.*

For the Doctor maintains it is *only for the sake of rhetoric* that *freedom of choice between good and evil* is still preserved today. The correctness of this is demonstrated by the example of General Graf Sponeck, who, unlike Marshal Paulus, took his stand *against* one of Hitler's orders because he naively supposed himself still free to interfere *as an individual* in historical events.

Herr Dr. Baumgardt could have informed the General at once that it was laughable and absurd still to suppose, in our day, that *the voice of a single highly placed individual is capable of altering a historical situation.* The philosopher makes fun, and rightly, of *the great men, who, even today, are thought to be making history.* Rightly, since Count Sponeck was shot for adhering to this old-fashioned way of thinking: He believed he could act independently, as an individual. Unlike Paulus, who obeyed his orders, he evacuated the Kertsch island to save his men and did indeed save them—but was still sentenced to death by Hitler. If only he had read Baumgardt beforehand! He would have obeyed orders—and survived. For Baumgardt demonstrates precisely in this context how, quote, *inhumanity given power can, in the last analysis, force every individual to cooperate . . . and that man survives,* the philosopher encourages us, *who measures up to the given situation, even at the risk of appearing himself inhuman.* Herr Baumgardt uses, *expressis verbis,* the word *appearing.* That is some consolation.

The higher the viewpoint, the more objective the view one obtains of the situation: It is no longer possible to state definitely whether the blame for the tragedy of Rotterdam should be laid at the door of the German high explosive bombs, or the criminally antiquated hand pumps, still

did anything in the war
where you did not risk your own lives.
It was only later that the cowards came—
the men who fired the rockets on London
sitting as safe as if they'd been pensioned off—
as they do today.

DORLAND (*with a crooked smile*):
On the other hand, no soldier can sink lower
than to justify his own actions
by measuring them against Hitler's.
But I had to do just that, too.
I really found my balance once again,
for the first time, when I came out of prison camp
and saw Hitler's monument, Bergen-Belsen.

At the first mention of Belsen, the light is concentrated on
DORLAND, *leaving the* SCULPTOR *in shadow.*

They were taking me back to England from Dresden,
along the Elbe, via Hamburg,
and in Belsen I saw Montgomery's soldiers
using bulldozers to push the mountains of corpses,
Germany's victims,
into graves each wide and deep enough to hold
a thousand shameful bodies and more . . .
Now I was able to persuade myself—
those families that I had turned to brimstone,
they too had produced murderers for Hitler.
The war was over, I began to live:
I made films, directed plays.
But still now and again . . . a breath of wavering fear:
Figures stood around me, in the night, figures more of dream
        than reality . . .
but—individuals—always.
Oh—as if a host of murdered people
could not look like a single one . . .
the phantoms of the incinerated.
Water under the bridge, shadows eddying in darkness,
they floated past me down the years.

"Water under the bridge"—at these words, the light takes in
DORLAND's SON *who now approaches. He is no longer in uniform,*

mounted on two-wheeled handcarts, used by the Rot
fire brigade, or even of the streams of burning oil
emerged from one of the earlier casualties, the mai
factory.

[In the final analysis, however, Ladies and Gentleme
are not here to talk any more about guilt (I am referri
course, to the Polish guilt in the annexation of Germa
ritory) but about the defense of the Christian West, ar
must all, Ladies and Gentlemen, be delighted at the t
rebuilding of the German ar—— ah, I beg your pardoi
the city of Rotterdam, which has arisen anew, more
proof and more hygienic; and it is the former stroke of
that they have to thank for giving them the incentive to i
radical improvements in their Fire Brigade. Ladies
Gentlemen, thank you very much.]

The light wanders off the philosophizing idiot and before the
time to recover from him, DORLAND *speaks to the* SCULPTOR
they cross the forestage.

DORLAND: And that is where the Red Cross stands today:
The Hague conventions could not protect Rotterdam
—but the man who destroyed Rotterdam,
him they protect!
I consoled myself, just like these Germans,
with aerial photographs, which show no actual people,
never a single one of those individuals
whom our philosopher says "no longer exist" . . .
[*only propaganda can still try and pick out*
individual figures in an anonymous war—
Baumgardt's article of faith.
War is "anonymous"—
it is not individuals, not people with faces
we are aiming at . . . just a "population."
How quickly we get used to it,
how quickly it becomes part of us—
we wear our phrases as we wear false teeth,
living and chewing painlessly,
word-substitutes, teeth-substitutes . . .]
SCULPTOR: But you can say, so can the German—
the Colonel who was here: neither of you

*but in jeans and sweater, dressed to spend an evening at home.
He is carrying a piece of handicraft later recognizable as a model
airplane—though not yet, as he is still keeping to the background
in roughly the same place as the* COLONEL *held his press conference. This initial distance between him and his father, who is
moreover talking about his* SON *as if he were not there, should
show that the conversation which follows is not happening here
and now, but is only being remembered: The half hour from 8:00
to 8:30 on this evening in October, 1964, is only one level, the
external time-level of* DORLAND'S *personal stocktaking.*

DORLAND: Ever since the hospital discharged me as incurable
     [and polite avoidance of the subject
     became one of the social graces in my family]—
     even my son has become domesticated . . .
     I am continually touched by the excuses he finds
     to spend evenings with me . . .
     [collecting something to remember, I suppose.
     Well now, we talk, drink,
     he brings me something to read, and as he knows
     my time is short, my reading must be relevant
     to my last bit of work.]

DORLAND *turns away from the* SCULPTOR, *who is no longer to be
seen. (It is no matter whether he has been speaking to the audience or to the old man.) He turns straight to his* SON, *who goes
on with what he is doing as he speaks with his father, who takes
some printed pages out of his jacket pocket.*

DORLAND: Here's General Baudissin's lecture back,
     —more energetic than our fathers were—
SON: There you are—Bonn shunted him on to us, as a teacher;
     he was still too much the civilian in uniform for them.
DORLAND: But he talks perfectly seriously about
     civilians as targets, and worthwhile only as such;
     with the usual hypocritical proviso, of course,
     that only the East would think in such a way;
     the Russians, who have never waged a bombing war.
SON: Because they never had any bombers before.
     Now they plan just like the rest of us.
DORLAND: All the same, it is a transference well worthy of the
          Germans

to hold the Russians up as potential criminals
of a bombing war—when you have allies in NATO
who wiped out a hundred and thirty-four thousand people
in Tokyo in one night.
[I should have liked to ask this German whether
he imagines that even a barbarian general
like Falkenhayn, whom they called a criminal
in Hindenburg's headquarters
and who "invented" Verdun, the technique of attrition—
does Baudissin believe that Falkenhayn
would still have shaken his hand if he had dared
in 1916 to suggest the immediate extermination of the French
    civilians?
That is dishonorable—
and officers are always carrying on about honor.]
Has your generation lost its *reason*?

SON (*quite without anger, insultingly unmoved and with the good-
natured stupidity that comes of a clear conscience*):
My generation treads in the footsteps of your own.
[You in Hildesheim and Weimar, Herr von Braun in London,
didn't *you* both kill defenseless people, and mean to do it?

DORLAND: Yes—yes, by the end.]
But we needed the war, *and* an enemy called Hitler.
You are sentencing cities with your war games
in time of *peace*.

SON (*shrugging indifferently, because this has gone home*):
Not *one* Bomber Chief was ever accused
at Nuremberg—not one.

DORLAND: One picks up a medal and a noose by the same roadside.
If that is no longer to apply in Europe,
there remains one sin only: having children.

SON (*laughs, as does his father*):
And that you have committed.

DORLAND (*intimate*): Get out of this business, Peter,
    get yourself a decent job, chuck away that uniform. (*He
    takes the model airplane.*)

SON (*weakly*): Father, it isn't a soldier's business
to discuss the technique of war—

DORLAND (*with gallows humor*): No?—Soldiers indeed! Watch out.
A soldier is a man who fights other soldiers;
a pilot who aims at tanks, bridges, factories, dams.

That is not you—as it was not me over Dresden.

SON (*rises*): So what does being a Planning Assistant make me,
    then?

DORLAND (*unaffected, quietly, literally*):
    A professional criminal. Potentially.

SON (*bitterly amused at last*):
    I see—now you're arguing like the Asiatics,
    who lynch the pilots they shoot down.

[DORLAND: You know the Americans only began to build
    prisoner-of-war camps after the Vietcong
    got their hands on some real live American pilots.
    Before, they simply handed the so-called rebels
    over to the South Vietnamese to be murdered.

SON: That you—a Wing Commander with a DFC
    should find *any* excuse for the lynching of these pilots.
    That's what appalls me.

DORLAND: . . . and not this?] Airmen kill civilians
    as if the Red Cross simply did not exist.
    Yet only *minutes* later,
    when they are shot down and fall
    defenseless into the hands of the defenseless
    whom they have bombed:
    then the Red Cross exists all right—for *them!*

SON (*cornered, and therefore stubborn and sure of himself*):
    Very well—let's do it another way:
    Let's not send pilots any more,
    let's just send rockets.

DORLAND (*contemptuously*):
    Oh, to be sure, that was to be expected.
    Since you lost no time in importing Herr Rocketeer von Braun.
    Hitler's vilest instrument, after the gas chamber,
    the unaimed rocket on the population centers.
    How fitting that the man who built
    the launching pads to fire on London
    should also have built the Auschwitz crematoria.

SON (*somewhat subdued, glad of the change of subject*):
    Where is he today?

DORLAND (*shrugging*): Why—do you want to give him a job too?

SON (*quietly*): Father—don't be so angry, I meant . . .

DORLAND (*contemptuously*):

The way you said just now: "We can go about it another
  way,
we'll do it with rockets, instead of pilots" . . .
Has your generation no desire at *all*
to get away from what Hitler bequeathed it?

SON: I admit—your generation saved Europe from the German
  hegemony,
the Jews, the Chinese, the Africans founded nations;
[the Communists rid themselves of Stalinism;
the United Nations are there, if not in practice, at least in
  theory.]
The other day, for three hours
I was looking through newsreels in our archives
of the war in the Pacific, Japanese films as well—
I was horrified at the suffering
of the sailors, and the infantrymen . . .
the ways in which they died . . .

[DORLAND: . . . and how the American army, with no traditions,
  overnight, after Pearl Harbor, even if it wasn't a surprise,
  produced its complement of first-class generals,
  engineers, admirals, organizers—
  as astounding historically as the achievements of Mao.]

SON (*nods*): —the Roosevelt generation puts us all to shame.
All the same, your criticism
that my generation does not protest
against the worst of our inheritance
is rhetoric.
[Do you think you can foist these deceptions about the bomb
  on the world,
worse than the weapons themselves, and expect
us, your children and grandchildren, to get out from under?
How can we?
It is in any schoolbook, as in Truman's *Memoirs:*
The bombs were dropped to save an invasion.

DORLAND: But what *we* didn't know was that Japan
had been making offers of surrender
for months before the bombs were dropped,
but all on the one condition
(which, after the bombs had been dropped, was granted)
that they should be allowed to retain their Emperor.

That the war had to last till the bomb was ready,
to sober up the *Russians:*
you could explain that today.

SON (*laughs and shakes his head*):
Explain? To give the fall from grace
the value of a precedent?
The white man has taught the yellow just how far
the diplomats can be allowed to go, full stop.
Do you believe this lesson will let itself be outdated?
The vivisection of the civilians of defeated Japan
to frighten Stalin: out of date?
You did not bring me up to be especially religious—

DORLAND (*a gesture of regret*):
Only knaves give more than they have got—

SON (*dismissing him*):
Oh—I only meant, one hardly needs to be religious
to feel that such an atrocity must be paid for.
Not by those who suffered it—
nor by those who inflicted it—
but sometime, and to someone,
the nation whose act it was will pay a price.
The Americans would need to be even more arrogant
not to fall over themselves today to think up
newer and newer anti-rocket-rockets . . .
they're more than justified in the fear
that the "Manhattan" project, the name they gave
with a straight face to the first bombs,
may boomerang on them and destroy Manhattan.]
Father—you were the ones who let them do it, through you.
My generation is simply mounting guard,
in case your grandchildren reap the whirlwind.

DORLAND (*gestures, indicating agreement. Pause*):
But you *can't* protect the cities, not with weapons.
Try it with an air war convention.

SON: I'm not so sure that a ban like that
would be adhered to, not like the agreement
not to use gas on the fronts in the last war.
I'm not so sure.

DORLAND (*impatiently*):
"Sure"—the only ones who are sure are in their graves.
Try it! Form an international conspiracy

—of the Red Cross and the officers—
the retired at first—they cannot be dismissed—
against the honorable demands of the governments
that you should "work" with weapons
which don't admit even the *possibility*
of sparing the enemies' towns, or protecting your own.
Yours is the permissive generation—
the one that didn't give a damn.
I had a German company in the theater a little while ago,
doing *Minna von Barnhelm*—one of them told me later
that his father toured in the same play
twenty years earlier, to the officers' mess at Auschwitz.
And he looked at me, this young man did,
as if I ought to pity him
for his father's lack of character.
The thing that absolutely astounded me
was that it had never once occurred to him
that *his* son, after surviving a catastrophe,
might consign *him* to purgatory because
he had quietly accepted that West Germany, unlike France,
should allow its "protectory power" to stockpile weapons,
which, according to Mr. MacNamara's Christmas message,
have the explosive force
of five thousand Hiroshima bombs.
(*Laughs.*)
Five thousand!—The papers said that to *reassure* us.
SON (*cynically and frankly*):
And so it *is*, reassuring, that *they* and
not we, are the number one target for the Russians.
Germany reunited by the H-bomb!
Subtitle: At the furriers', all foxes are equal.
Father, we should be worrying about
who's going to take over Hong Kong, not Berlin.
DORLAND: That is if you worry about anything—
Ah—tasks are always with us, like the poor.
But all your generation has left in it of Protestantism,
is just about enough to try and overtake
the faster car of the driver in front.
SON (*more fiercely*): If you wear a uniform
you don't want to rebel—
DORLAND: Then take it off.

SON: —you want weapons which will keep your enemy quiet.
  You *know* it wasn't the *soldiers*—
  or not in Europe at any rate—
  who began the last war, even.
DORLAND: Quite enough that they should have fought it.
[SON (*seeming older than he is; he finds this hard*):
  —Dad, I think about it too, so do my friends,
  it's just one *knows* so little . . .
  things like the White House being unable to control
  the rise in the price of steel the other day—
DORLAND (*nods*): Oh yes—very good for business it is.
  We none of us object to making money: ergo—
  if people can make money out of making war,
  then war they will make—it's only human,
  particularly if the enemy is not in a position
  to bomb my factory—
  General Motors is as safe as the vault of the Credit Suisse.
  War is not like the theater—
  it's the spectators who take the money.
SON: It is not for us in uniform to break down
  the private ownership in the arms industry.
DORLAND: No. A civil proposal, the most peaceful.
SON: But you read that it is absolutely out-of-date
  to want to nationalize things.
DORLAND (*laughs*): Where? Where does one read any such thing?
  In the only morning paper—except *The Wall Street Journal*
  —that still manages to survive in New York?
  One!
  The idea can hardly be out-of-date over there anyway,
  since it could never have been put into practice:
  not in the only country on earth which even now
  has not produced a Labor Party—
  Roosevelt—the millionaire liberal—
  was constantly pilloried as a "traitor to his class."
  But for the war, his chances of dying in bed
  would probably have been no better than Kennedy's.
SON: But the unions are very powerful.
  Are they content over there
  just to get working hours reduced?
DORLAND (*amused*): If you let the Ford Foundation pay
  for your son's education, it ill becomes you

to encourage him to read up
the anti-monopoly laws for clauses
that would put Mr. Ford behind bars—]

During DORLAND's *last words the light has separated the* SON *from his father. With the shrug of the shoulders so peculiar to many of his age, he indicates his resignation and withdraws, or the light makes it seem so—it does not matter.*

DORLAND *now speaks to the* SCULPTOR, *who can once more be seen working at his statue. It is uncertain whether* DORLAND *has just been telling the* SCULPTOR *about the conversation, or whether the whole thing is taking place in his head.*

DORLAND: [So we argued away, almost like man and wife,
    but] I was never able to get him away
    into some worthwhile job.
    I had been the one who put the idea of flying in his head,
    I was the one who gave him models to build like this,
    mea culpa!

He turns the model airplane he took from his son around in his hand, putting it down after a while.

SCULPTOR (*laughs*): Your fault?—No, it's not. I don't think
    one is guilty of things that just happen,
    only of things one means to happen
    and takes care that they do happen.
DORLAND (*nods*): Like Churchill—
    to save an island without an army,
    look how he kept at them to build
    the long-range bomber and the atom bomb.
    But his final view—when the thing was there and ready,
    he said if God were to make the world afresh
    He should make the atmosphere from an explosive material
    that would destroy everything
    that rose more than a hundred yards off the ground.
    [He reproached himself
    that precisely these two weapons
    had destroyed the thousand-year impregnability of Britain.
SCULPTOR: Matter of course.]—the conquering hero
    who commissioned the "Winged Victory"
    might just as easily have got Nemesis:
    it is the same bit of sculpture in the end.

At the time I was doing my Churchill bust,
he was seventy-seven and still an obsessive monopolizer
of the conversation—fascinating.
Even so, I managed to edge in a question:
might not the First War at least have been avoided?
Oh no—*certainly* not the First, he said;
at bottom everyone wanted it, in every country.
At bottom? The pit is bottomless, and still there.
Our most typical, most permanent characteristic, and our
    most human.
Look at the dancing in the streets in 1914!
DORLAND: Why did no one dance anywhere
    at the beginning of the *last* war;
    not even in Berlin, where they started it?
SCULPTOR: Verdun had not yet been forgotten,
    nor had the depression, nor the gas.
    [But when areas remain too *long* under the pressure of peace
    (like Western Europe after Sedan)
    the calm seems to become as suffocating as a greenhouse.]
    When the dirty work of our two generations is forgotten,
    there will be no medicine against the Urge To Try Again.
    [H. G. Wells, no romantic you'll agree,
    wrote after the outbreak of war in 1914,
    at least the war "relaxed the tension" and that was A Good
        Thing.
    Franz Marc—I knew him—
    before he fell at Verdun, approved the war.
    "Better blood than endless deception;
    the war is as much atonement
    as voluntary sacrifice into which Europe is throwing herself
    to be able to live with herself."
DORLAND (*shivers with disgust, but admits*):
    It's in *Troilus:* "The wound of peace is surety,
    surety secure."
SCULPTOR (*nods*): Because it makes the brain sick:
    Marc felt that the battle only made fact
    of what the earth had long been brooding over,
    because one could no longer bear,
    according to his insane integrity,
    "the lies of European morality."
    Wells' and the Kaiser's generation,

even a man like Trakl,
had *forgotten* that the war of 1870,
although it had been short had also been,
on both sides, considering its length, the bloodiest ever.
And yet this knowledge,
some forty peaceful years later,
had simply become a *bore*.]
Your actors are come hither.

*The orchestra rehearsal, hardly audible for some time, now comes
to a powerful close—the feeling of movement communicates itself
to the characters entering and emerging from the ruins, a* POLICE-
MAN *and several* ACTORS, *half in costume,* HELEN *among them.
(The actor who is to play the* PRIME MINISTER *does not appear
in the Prologue.) The* STAGEHANDS *have already, during the two
preceding conversations, been carrying pieces of the setting for the
first scene into the ruins.*

The actor who is to play CLARK, *the Staff Officer, pushes himself like a wild boar between* DORLAND *and the* SCULPTOR.

ACTOR (*hysterically*):
   Look, I object strongly to this whole recasting business.
   I was engaged to play an Air Chief Marshal, a sort of—
         Nelson!
   ... And at the last minute I am supposed to be
   some wretched anonymous Group Captain or other.
   It's degrading—literally.
DORLAND (*impatient*): My dear ...
   (*he calls him by his Christian name*)
   months back I sent the play to Sir Arthur for comment.
   I offered in writing to cut every word
   that was historically untrue.
   I could not possibly have known that Harris
   would threaten to sue me if I had him in the play.
   [It is unprecedented that a General
   should want to back out of history
   after setting fire to half a million civilians
   in order to get into it.]
ACTOR: I don't see how he can *forbid*
   people to be reminded of his actions.
DORLAND: You don't have to understand the law to fall foul of it.
ACTOR: But it's unjust ...

DORLAND: We aren't talking about justice, but the law—
> I'm afraid they are not one and the same thing.
> There is no judge in the world who is not paid by the state.

ACTOR: Meaning?

DORLAND: Clear enough, I'd have thought. Go and get changed.

The hysteric goes off like a lamb. DORLAND *continues speaking to the* SCULPTOR *just as if they had not been interrupted.*

DORLAND: You remember Churchill's simile?
> The nations are not chessmen, nor puppets
> grimacing at each other as they dance,
> but planets which cannot approach each other
> in space without causing magnetic disturbances:
> If they come too close, even as friends,
> especially as kindred, as the English and the Germans were
> > then,
> sparks begin to fly.
> There comes a certain point—an uncertain one, more likely—
> once gone beyond, the stars are snatched from their courses,
> they collide, and chaos is come again.

SCULPTOR (*with agreement, even if he has another explanation*):
> Cropping the grass peacefully, side by side—everything in
> > Man—
> body, blood, tooth, and claw,
> his constitutional leaning toward tragedy—
> and don't forget the erotic compulsion
> which the terrible outsiders feel to hunt for fame—
> all this he only finds bearable if it does not last.
> Look at marriage—Love without desire:
> one escapes from it into some vice or other—
> the front, a mistress, fast cars—
> only condoned morally because of,
> or proportionally to, the risk involved.
> [(*Laughs.*)
> A bus conductor, a schoolmaster, or a sweep—
> are they supposed to feel patriotic
> before they are allowed to shoot—and be shot?
> The little girl who plays with dolls
> usually gets what she wants later.
> But what boys dream about—way, way beyond
> the capacity of civilization to fulfill.

An Indian chief—denatured, chained to an office desk,
tyrannized for forty-five years by his bank manager . . .
by contrast, how much more honest was the existence
of the policeman they found the other day
who turned out to have robbed a bank.]
Attlee said it is a great mistake
to allow a government to become boring.
[The puddle of human emotions is the spawning-ground of
    aggression:
the rationalizing buffoons who fill eight hundred pages
of documents proving this or that country's sole responsibility
for the First War forget this fact.
The mass, domesticated against its nature,
has an instinct which drives it
periodically to let itself be exploited.
The man we know as the average consumer
becomes the average consumed.
He *wants* to shout Hosannah to the Son of David
on Palm Sunday, and Barabbas on Friday,
he wants to touch the Sacred Shroud,
to go on Nuremberg rallies.
He *longs* to be as grain betwixt the upper and nether
    millstones.]
Why else is adoration ladled out
in exact proportion to the sacrifice demanded?
[It is incredible how long it took
for a Swede to turn up to kill Charles XII—from behind.
Did anyone in Russia ever take a shot at Stalin?
Again and again the French flung themselves
round the neck of a foreigner, a Corsican,
who consumed them to a skeleton
like the Greeks with the playboy Alcibiades.
The Germans let themselves be hacked to bits
by another foreigner
after he had used them as a hatchet first.
The most popular man in England—half American.
When were the sober citizens of London ever keener
than during those nights when Churchill held their city out
as bait to keep Hitler's aircraft away from Dowding's
    fighters?]

It is the *lion tamers* who win elections—legally—
by not hiding the fact that *that* is what they are.
DORLAND (*depressed and disgusted*): Perverse.
SCULPTOR (*in the same manner*):
"Natural"—since we are talking about human nature.
DORLAND: If that is so then history too is like the migration of
      lemmings?
Hundreds of thousands of vole-like creatures
making for the cliffs and throwing themselves into the sea,
to be crushed and drowned . . . might this not be the way
to avoid war as an outlet for the death wish?
[Or does it protect the human race from itself
by reducing its numbers?
SCULPTOR (*quietly*):
Perhaps by reducing its strength by strength:
the ark is lighter now, by fifty-six million passengers
thrown overboard during the last war.
Perhaps society can only absorb
just so much strength, and no more.]
The point of history is to reduce strength through strength.
DORLAND: I see no hope.
[SCULPTOR: One can always hope.
Perhaps what we feel may become instinctive,
the instinct to avoid the big weapons
because they make a tournament like Jutland,
or the Battle of Britain,
no longer possible, but lead straight to the apocalypse.
DORLAND: Then how—is the caged beast to get free?
SCULPTOR: Revolution will take the place of war. I hope—
DORLAND (*disbelieving*): In Europe too?
SCULPTOR: If things go too peacefully, one may hope so.
Just think how automation, in ten years time,
will have taken the work away from the industrial worker.
They won't even need to be hungry to start storing up
      anger—
boredom will do . . . and the whole capitalist system
becomes with every year increasingly grotesque.
But: no one is going to drop a bomb on a town on this
      account.
DORLAND (*with a laugh*):
The first piece of optimism I've ever heard from you.

SCULPTOR: Faith and hope always have to struggle
    against the fact that one knows better—]
    The Voice of America!

He gestures toward the back of the stage where a radio is playing in raucous and successful competition with the orchestra rehearsal. He flees to the shadow of his statue. DORLAND *goes off into the ruins. Before they appear in front of the ruins, we hear the sounds of footsteps, noises, and attempts at speech by two men who, when they do appear, can be seen trying to hold each other up in a brotherly fashion. With an* AMERICAN COLONEL, *who is carrying the radio in his hand, is a rather younger* RUSSIAN MILITARY ATTACHÉ. *Their tongues float like cockleshells on the high seas of alcohol. They forge their way almost to the front of the stage. The* RUSSIAN *hangs back slightly, making repeated but unsuccessful attempts to do up his shoelace. The* AMERICAN *should be played by the same actor as* WEINMÜLLER.

RUSSIAN: Is not vodka, is space.
[AMERICAN: This way—no—that way to the party.
RUSSIAN: State secret, Comrade—I am—I am not—
    the *first* cosmonaut who—damn—since . . .
    has ringing sound in his ears after his flight.
    You have same defect in USA—
    earrings—ringing in ears with your spacemen.
    I am most envying men who carry head simply on neck,
    without need to balance.

He pulls the other back from a certain fall into the orchestra pit.

AMERICAN: Leave go of me—I can bend down O.K.,
    I'll do your laces up—but which one?
RUSSIAN: No—not, rise please,
    the others are coming . . .
AMERICAN (*his cap falling off as he looks for the loose shoelace*):
    They're drunk, man.]
RUSSIAN (*picks up the cap and dusts it, returning it to the* AMERICAN. *Perforce they have to sit down in the road*):
    Balance gone—Halt!—
    Balance taken away. Wish to vomit.
    Not permitted to fly.
    Laboratory is busy with my waters.

Myself no more interesting to research,
my waters only.
(*Tormented.*)
I was man to put Russian flag on moon.
Now—all kaput. And, every evening, like tonight,
there, it grins at me, like backside of God.

The AMERICAN *has put down the radio to give the* RUSSIAN *sustenance from a hip flask.*

Thank you, Comrade, thank you. How sad—brother—
that we cannot be brothers: but—
impossible to wipe out distinction—
under capitalism man exploits his fellow men,
under Communism it is other way around.
[AMERICAN: Politically, Comrade—where the essentials are—
we are agreed, as in the war:
anyone who has ever fought against Germany,
like you, like me,
he just loves that land so much
he's got to have the two of them—right?
RUSSIAN (*laughs in agreement, overtired to the point of tears*):
Is true, is true—only you . . .
my bottle—here: Under capitalism
are bottles—simply getting smaller.
Liter is not what once liter was.]
AMERICAN: Very possible, General, very possible: I'm no
economist,
my brother-in-law though—
he's in the wholesale scrap metal business,
owns the biggest marine graveyard in Boston—he said—
RUSSIAN: Marine graveyard—what things you can own in your
country.

*It should be clear that the music-hall atmosphere here is purely
formal. The facts on the other hand, are incredible but true, and
accessible in the* Frankfurter Allgemeine *of January 13, 1967, or
the* Basler Nachrichten *of February 18, 1967.*

AMERICAN: Ah, the graveyard was no picnic to own for a long
time.
Only three months back my brother-in-law

was forced to sell an obsolete World War II tanker
for as little as two hundred thousand bucks;
it's a disgrace, rock-bottom prices . . .
it's our policy in Vietnam woke up that scrapyard.
My brother-in-law, for the very same ship—
the very same—he gets twice the price.
Four hundred thousand dollars, yup.
[And nickel!—My wife inherited some shares:
her brother got the scrapyard—
nickel is up by 135 per cent!]
War is, yes, well what I mean, it's a social measure:
a *social* measure. Of course, you gotta be careful
and keep it within bounds,
that is to say, other people's bounds for choice.
[The Middle East is always as good an area as any.]

RUSSIAN: But if . . . if your boys . . . ?
Asia is huge—so easy to lose yourself there.

AMERICAN: My brother-in-law volunteered his own son—

RUSSIAN: *For Asia?*

AMERICAN: Well, no, he's still studying—volunteered him to
the CIA at his university. He's fighting on the Home Front
against the anti-social destructive elements
in the student bodies, sabotaging our fight against the poor.

RUSSIAN: Against poverty?

AMERICAN: What?—Fight against poverty, that's right.
You want to get rid of the poor? You gotta feed 'em,
clothe 'em, educate 'em; we're drafting
almost all unskilled workers, unemployed,
colored men, illiterates, and criminal elements like that.
But my God—the way people abuse this!
They arrested a woman in Boston—a chiropodist—
she'd got married in eleven cities to GI's who were
being sent to Vietnam—just for the insurance.

The POLICEMAN—*the* SERGEANT *in Act Two—appears in the
background, hesitating to disturb the conversation of the dis-
tinguished pair.*

We'd have won this war a while back,
but once it's won, my brother-in-law says, he's *through.*

Nobody gets any pickings any more.
We might just as well have hung on to Kennedy.
And above all: the fact we *don't* win,
is all the fault of the press.

RUSSIAN: The press? Ours is never giving trouble.

DORLAND *has appeared behind the* POLICEMAN *and motions to him
to get the strategists away to their dinner. He is just about to go
back into the ruins when someone approaches him energetically,
the actor who is to play* KOCJAN . . .

POLICEMAN (*coming forward, saluting*):
For the Red Cross dinner, Gentlemen?

They stand up, their conversation interrupted. The AMERICAN *has
turned off his radio, which he hands to the* POLICEMAN, *and
straightens his cap. It now appears that he has, by mistake, tied
the* RUSSIAN's *shoelaces together.*

RUSSIAN: Oh.

Before the POLICEMAN *grasps what has happened, the* AMERICAN
bends down and reties them.

AMERICAN: Goddammit . . .

He now points to the Red Cross banner, and claps the POLICE-
MAN *on the shoulder.*

Buddy, that banner—there's one hundred bucks,
two hundred, if you can get that for me,
after the celebrations—
(*To the* RUSSIAN, *as they lurch out followed by
the* POLICEMAN:)
I've got the rope they used to hang General Tojo;
my mother collects art, and things like that . . .

The ACTOR *who is to play* KOCJAN *has meanwhile buttonholed*
DORLAND.

ACTOR: Are we making up tonight? What's the lighting like?

DORLAND *turns and speaks with some impatience to the young*
ACTOR *who is to play* KOCJAN, *who has just spoken to him:*

DORLAND: Haven't you changed yet? Of course, make up.
    You do open the play, remember.
ACTOR (*smiles*): . . . and close it—Apropos,
    could I ask the Professor a question?
    I shan't be late.

He turns to the SCULPTOR, *who is getting ready to go back to his hotel.* DORLAND *goes into the ruins, saying to another* ACTOR: *"Come with me a moment"—they vanish. The* POLICEMAN *also goes with him, trying to get a word with him. The* SCULPTOR *stops as the* ACTOR *speaks to him:*

    My name is . . . I'm playing the Polish Captain.
SCULPTOR (*holding out his hand*): I know.
ACTOR: I wanted to ask you, when you were
    making the bust of Churchill
    did he ever say anything about *Poland?*
SCULPTOR: Often. He used to talk about his terrible struggles in
        1945
    with the Prime Minister who succeeded Sikorski.
    They used to *shout* at each other,
    but Churchill knew in advance
    that nothing he might ever be able to achieve for Poland
    would ever satisfy the Poles.
ACTOR: I read that in Mikolajczyk's memoirs,
    a great admirer of Churchill even so.
SCULPTOR (*smiles*): Like all of us.
ACTOR (*also smiles, frankly, as he is later to do on stage*): Sure.
    Did you never talk to him about Sikorski?
SCULPTOR (*evasively*): [I don't think anyone—
    besides his doctor, Marshal Stalin, and Smuts—
    could ever have made him talk
    about anything he didn't want to talk about.]
    Take the well-meant advice of an old man
    and leave the Poles in peace.
ACTOR: It's only that, having to play this Pole
    I looked for some reading about the General—and found
        nothing,
    nothing at all: in the masses of memoirs
    and biographies to come out of Whitehall
    the death of the Polish Prime Minister
    is simply never mentioned.

The SCULPTOR *is silent under the young man's gaze.*

> Every leading figure has gone into print,
> apart from General Menzies, of course,
> whose report would be for Downing Street alone.

SCULPTOR (*primarily for the sake of saying something, since the
young man is once more looking at him expectantly*):
> That is standard practice: In no country
> is the head of the secret service likely to publish his memoirs.

ACTOR: But—Professor—what is *your* explanation of the fact
> that Churchill, in the final version
> of the one-volume edition
> of his history of the Second World War,
> which is otherwise only very slightly condensed,
> why he should have removed *all* references to Sikorski?

SCULPTOR: Time will remove all our names.
> [Historians simply speed up the process—
> or slow it down. The final version
> does not contain the line and a half
> about the destruction of Dresden either. There's the bell.

ACTOR (*utterly confused, hurries away*): Oh,—thank you.] Yes.

The SCULPTOR *glances irresolutely into the auditorium. The stage
is quiet, the music rehearsal is over. As he prepares to return to
his hotel, the old man once more turns to* DORLAND, *who now has
nothing to do till the start of his dress rehearsal.*

SCULPTOR (*mocking*):
> Group Captain Clark will be no substitute for Harris:
> a bit too easy for you to write
> your touchy father-son relationship with Harris
> out of the play now.

DORLAND (*nods*): Apart from anything else, it's not like me
> to talk to people personally as if they were not
> utterly different from each other.
> Uniforms stop at the neck—that is why
> I have never taken seriously the classic excuse
> of our century of flight from responsibility—
> acting under orders.
> We *did do* it.
> To say: Had I not done it, somebody else would have,

can only lead—as Hannah Arendt explained in the case of
  Eichmann—
to reliance on the crime statistics.
As so and so many crimes are committed yearly,
someone has to commit them, after all,
and so *I* have committed one.

SCULPTOR: I am inclined to suspect, in the case of soldiers
  the uniform is worn just so that they
  may cease to be individuals,
  differentiated from other people,
  personally responsible.

DORLAND (*nods; then*):
  Uniforms only protect us as long as we have them on.
  In hospital I was just wearing the pajamas
  in which I shall probably be buried soon.

His glance is turned in on himself. DORLAND *is once more taking
up his inner conversation with the man who let him become a
murderer—and who has disturbed him, inwardly, ever since he
knew he was going to die.*

  I had countless imaginary arguments with Harris
  lying awake at night in hospital,
  knowing I was inoperable.

The SCULPTOR *speaks his last words, after which the light takes
him away from us, leaving* DORLAND *to his internal struggle with
the monstrous silhouette of the accomplice of his crime.*

SCULPTOR: You were about the same age then your son is now.
DORLAND (*nods; then he is alone in the prison of his memory*):
  They told me that I was to have the *honor*
  of leading the first attack
  on the center of the unharmed city
  we knew to be a refugee collection point.

The second bell sounds; there appears to DORLAND *the most com-
pelling of the interlocutors of the conversations of his dreams;
with a walking stick and a small bulldog, he limps onto the stage,
a stout old man in ordinary civilian clothes, not* HARRIS, *but a
projection of the sick* DORLAND's *mental image of him.*

INTERLOCUTOR: This I have not deserved at your hands, Dorland,
  that you should degrade the bombing-war
  to a theatrical spectacle.

It was I who saw to it you got your DFC in '43,
after you had holed the Eder Dam.
Hitler's munitions chief, Speer, admitted
after the war that six more operations
like Gomorrah and the Nazis
would have been forced to put the shutters up.
I ask you: The Hamburg raids killed forty thousand people;
multiply that by six—but what is that,
compared to the number that actually did die
before the war was ended?
Still, a soldier is the man who is always sworn at;
even when we tried, in 1922—
with the shoddiest equipment imaginable—
to batter a little sense into Iraqi villages—
they took it very sportingly, those who survived—
even those law and order raids were being criticized.
[Tell me, Richard Coeur de Lion, Sir Francis Drake:
I've been reading about them—fascinating chaps.
Why don't you write a play about *them,* Dorland?
Must we bombers . . .
DORLAND: Sir Arthur, the theater isn't a museum.
History only ceases to be academic
when it can illustrate for *us* and *now*
man's inhumanity to man—the historical cliché.
Richard Coeur de Lion—just a handsome suit of armor,
no longer alive and no longer dangerous,
but what you and I did twenty years ago,
has become the A B C of the airmen of *today.*
INTERLOCUTOR (*with a sensitivity that it is difficult to pin down*):
Setting a precedent, making a tradition—
all the more dishonest now to try
from the safety of a narrow-minded peacetime armchair
to make out that that Bomber Command was . . . unnecessary,
as the historical fraternity now do.
Naturally, I have no intention of reading
the four-decker official history
commissioned by the Government: dreadful.]
The nation's gratitude—that fifty-six thousand British airmen
and more than forty thousand from America
died in bombers over Germany . . .
(*He is shaken, so is* DORLAND.)

The men of Fighter Command, each single man
who fell in the Battle of Britain has his name
in a golden book in the Abbey.
But you—*my* men, the dead of Bomber Command,
you can't even find the *number* in Westminster.

DORLAND (*dismayed*): There are so many—too many.

INTERLOCUTOR (*laughs, frighteningly*):
Whom are you trying to convince, Dorland?
The *number* of my dead, they could have written
the *number* there, could they not?
But *our* comrades who were sacrificed would now seem
to be socially *de trop* all of a sudden, eh?
[Anyone who knows me, knows I don't give two hoots
about that kind of thing, but for my dead airmen
it is a slight, that I should be the only Air Marshal
not to be given a peerage at the war's end—
not that it concerned *me*—not for myself—
not in the least.

DORLAND (*agreeing hastily*): I know—

INTERLOCUTOR: Not in the least! In '46, on the first anniversary
of Dresden, I went home to Rhodesia—
it did not affect me in the very least.

DORLAND (*calming*): I know—

INTERLOCUTOR: The most popular Marshal of the RAF,
yet after we had won, the only one
who wasn't given a peerage, not once they realized
that I had followed, to the letter,
the order of His Majesty's Government
to burn the German cities to the ground.]
During the war the P.M. called Bomber Command
a shining spearhead. Today, ha . . .
Five thousand!—Five thousand guests my wife was hostess to,
at Bomber Command—all who had rank and name
were glad to be our guests . . . and overnight,
we bombers were—I don't know—Mélac, Tilly,
Torquemada . . . tcha! the specters at the feast,
the ones whom no one wishes to sit next to.

He totters and sits. DORLAND *bends over him sympathetically.*

DORLAND: Sir—while I was facing an operation,
I could not shake free of the thought

of what our generation has done,
myself, Herr Rocketeer von Braun, the Nagasaki pilot.
You gave me my orders, that thirteenth of February . . .
INTERLOCUTOR: I? Please: passed them, only passed them on.
I was never enthusiastic about Dresden, I . . .
DORLAND: I still ask . . . how does one live
    when, in the pathway of our lives, there lie
    three quarters of a million civilians—
    Germans of course, but Frenchmen,
    Italians, Belgians as well . . .
    the Kesselrings, the von Brauns do not interest *me*.
    No man who did such things for Hitler
    is any sort of partner in our inner stocktaking.
    That is why I have thought of you, Sir . . .
    I wondered what life was like—
    in a rose garden . . .

*Third bell. Huge as the back wall, the projected image of the dead
woman of Dresden appears, seen only by* DORLAND.

    . . . where the Thames narrows, flowing softer now,
    fine furniture, good pictures,
    playing with the dog, the grandchildren,
    avoiding one's club, visiting sick acquaintances . . .
    arranging lead soldiers, all colors, on the window sill,
    the Coronation procession in miniature—
    and over the desk, a reminder of the service—
    the wooden model of a Lancaster.
    Everything said, one's point always carried,
    the memoirs written, published long ago,
    ambition burnt away—yet whether, even so,
    watching the play of flames in the open grate,
    at the sight of a woman in a next-door garden,
    a moment's gaze into the fire—
    as one turns the stem of a wineglass in the hand—
    just once—the length of time it takes to blink—
    one street in *one* city might not come into your mind
    five hundred dead or one—
    images of what we—with impunity—
    gave to our children as their inheritance.

*The image of their deed vanishes as the curtain falls, to rise again
as quickly as possible, as if a hand had snatched it away, to reveal,*

in a blinding white light—the audience is dazzled—the first act. The setting has been built inside the cathedral; we should be reminded of this by the fragments of Gothic ruin visible to the left and right of the setting during the whole of the play-within-the-play.

THE LITTLE
LONDON
THEATER
OF THE WORLD

Three acts for nine actors

THE SHIP
THE BED
THE GARDEN

. . . this belongs among those things which
should not be investigated to the very
end . . .

—Cervantes, *Don Quixote*

THE ACTORS

*The Prime Minister and Minister of Defense of His
   Majesty's Government*

*The Prime Minister and Supreme Commander of
   the Polish Forces*

The Bishop of Chichester

The Chief of the Imperial General Staff

The Paymaster General

The Commander-in-Chief of Bomber Command

A Wing Commander in the RAF

A Captain in the Warsaw Underground Army

A Second Officer in the Women's Royal Naval Service

April–July, 1943

THE SHIP

The Prime Minister . . . wished . . . to
substitute an amphibious operation
against the tip of Sumatra for the
American project of reconquering
Burma by land. The latter . . . seemed
to him like "munching a porcupine
quill by quill!" He considered we
should wait till we got Russia against
Japan. We should then establish air
bases near Vladivostok from which
Japan could be bombed, and, according
to him, we should then sing the
"Ladybird Song" to the Japs:
"Ladybird, ladybird, fly away home,
your house is on fire, and your children
at home!"
—Field Marshal Lord Alan Brooke,
in his diary, April 22, 1943

"Light of light inexhaustible" over the North Sea, early in 1943.
*On the quarter deck of HMS "Duke of York" (as we see from
a life belt), on the way to Scapa Flow. Across the back is projected a wide expanse of smooth sea and cloudless sky.* CHURCHILL
*was to grumble, because of the U-boats, "as I came on deck I saw
an unwelcome amount of blue sky."*

*The actual setting is limited to a semicircular railing running
around the upper part of the stage, with a short flagstaff at the
stern, and a light collapsible wooden chair. Downstage, to the
sides, are two square life rafts, made of wood, rope, and canvas
painted in camouflage colors.*

*The acoustics of the theater will determine whether the ship's
stern here indicated should be turned around, so that the flagstaff,
empty but for a rope hanging from it, faces toward the audience,
so that the longitudinal axis of the "Duke of York" runs from upstage left to the extreme downstage right. An iron staircase (not
a ladder) connects the quarter-deck and the main deck. From the
main deck we can see the bridge, behind, raised above the level
of the quarter-deck just sufficiently for a man to be able to pass
underneath. If this two-storied construction is felt to be unsuitable,
but if a back wall is needed nevertheless as a sound-reflector, a
battleship's four-barreled gun emplacement can be built. The gun
barrels, with their hatches, will then overtop the setting on an
axis, roughly diagonal, left to right, starting upstage and coming
no further than the center of the stage. The anti-aircraft gun which
the "Duke of York" carried on her main deck should be avoided.
All constructions should be green, like the edge of a piece of plate
glass. A cyclorama is recommended, lit from upstage, so that when
we first see the actors they are depersonalized, little silhouettes in
front of the stabbing duck-egg colored light as it floods into the
auditorium—like marionettes in the hands of an unseen director.
This ties in with this old-fashioned attempt to make the boards
of a stage the platform for the* teatrum mundi. *Only later is the light
reduced sufficiently for us to be able clearly to perceive the in-
dividuality of these figures, their characters and gestures.*

The PRIME MINISTER AND MINISTER OF DEFENSE *wears a
peaked cap and a knee-length jacket, navy blue, buttoned up to
the neck. He wears no badges of rank, and is carrying neither
stick nor cigar. He is not a short man, to correct at once the most
common misconception about his appearance. He is above average*

height, though his girth, especially in this costume, makes him appear monolithic.

P.M.—*the abbreviation is taken from* BROOKE's *diaries—has a rough voice and speaks rapidly, perhaps to conceal his lisp. The only times he speaks slowly, and dramatically, are when he employs, to his own considerable satisfaction, his favorite Victorian turns of phrase. Taking his cue from the Kaiser's address to his troops embarking for China, he refers to the Germans, sometimes even in writing, as the Huns, and describes them, not out of sarcasm but as a matter of deep feeling, in an Old Testament fashion, as "the foe."*

His best-loved images are drawn from English history, Gibbon, the animal kingdom, the hunting field, medicine and anatomy— marching on Vienna becomes "a thrust in the armpit of the Adriatic." He delivers them like kicks, violent, casual, genial, brutal, according to choice, but always with relish, even when he is in a black rage, for most of the time it is with relish that he exercises the leadership of this "amazing" war. His depressions are short-lived. If he weeps copiously, it is never for long. "Amazing" is his favorite adjective.

The man who defeated Hitler, and who was himself only to be defeated by the British electorate, announced his comeback, at the age of seventy-two, to his doctor, with the battle cry: "I'll tear their bleeding entrails out of them." Moran notes further about the octogenerian: ". . . when the nation insists on looking to him as the sagacious world statesman . . . his tastes lie in the rough and tumble of the House . . . enjoying every minute of the back-chat. In short, he is still at heart the red-haired urchin, cocking a snook at anybody who gets in the way. . . ." CHURCHILL *could write contemptuously, referring to the warless years, of "the bland skies of peace and platitude."*

A mistrustful fondness is perhaps the feeling which not only BROOKE, *but* BISHOP BELL *as well, show toward the* P.M. *Had the* BISHOP *left a description of how* CHURCHILL *dealt with him, the man of God, it might well have read not unlike Disraeli's letter about Bismarck: "B. ate and drank much, and talked more: Rabelaisian monologues, interminable revelations of things he should never have mentioned, mostly at the expense of the Kaiser and the court, delivered in a sweet and gentle voice, and very refined enunciation, contrasting strangely with the recklessly frank things he was saying, which make one literally blench by their indiscretion and audacity."*

For a statesman, even more than a banker, is flattered now and then at being seen through. . . .

All CHURCHILL's *gestures, unpredictable but calculated, especially those of his small white hands, constantly shaping figures in the air, are products of his words. After half a century's experience in public, the obsessive monologist, who talked rather than wrote his hundredweight of books, is so sure of his ground that even his most unadorned clichés, deservedly derogatory, forced upon him by the occasion, and spat out, such as "that man" or "that man over there" become at once the* mot juste *for Hitler.*

Before he fires off one of his prize effronteries, CHURCHILL *screws up his nose. When enraged he rubs his chin with his fist. His pauses are famous. Both he and his wife divulged how effective a means it was of increasing the tension of a speech to introduce a long pause or an artificial break: the search for his spectacles to read a sentence long ago learned by heart; the nervous hunting through waistcoat and jacket pockets in search of notes for which there was not the slightest need since he had not only dictated and redictated the "speedily improvized" speech six times already at home, but also rehearsed the bon mots with which he was, at the very least, to cast suspicion on the calculated counterarguments of some Hon. Member or other. As he got older, he was in the habit of humiliating antagonists of whose sallies he was himself apprehensive by appearing to be extremely deaf—his hearing was normal—and desperately fiddling with a hearing aid, even asking for a joke to be repeated, which no joke has ever been known to survive. Bismarck, who comes repeatedly to mind when one is dealing with* CHURCHILL, *was capable of such audacities as his reply to Count Schwering when asked what he, Bismarck, had against him, "That you were not killed at Prague." In the same way* CHURCHILL *could say to the Socialist Woodrow Wyatt, with calculated ennui: "Still alive?"*

CHURCHILL, *when he appears on deck, stands alone at first, with his hands far apart, against the railing. His broad back and thick neck make a more effective image of militancy than the* CHIEF OF THE IMPERIAL GENERAL STAFF *in the foreground, standing with his foot up on one of the rafts, to make a note of something.*

BROOKE *uses his notebook a great deal. He is wearing the uni-*

form of a Field Marshal, with a short greatcoat, very light in color, looking like a civilian camel's-hair coat.

BROOKE *lives by Schlieffen's Law: Staff officers have no names. His reserve in the face of irascible temperaments, and the modesty without which* CHURCHILL *would never have stood the sight of him for five years—Montgomery's increasing popularity drove the* P.M. *to excesses of jealousy—both combined to prevent the British from realizing just what it was they possessed in their Commander in Chief. After working with* CHURCHILL *almost every day for five years, he noted: "I feel that I can't stick another moment with him, and would give almost anything never to see him again."*

When, however, four months later, the man whom BROOKE *calls "the greatest war leader of our times, who guided this country from the very brink of the abyss of destruction to one of the most complete victories ever known in history," when this man was defeated at the polls,* BROOKE *would not speak when he came to say good-by, in case he burst into tears.*

Almost ten years younger than CHURCHILL *(here aged sixty-nine) he was exploited almost to death by the older man's volcanic outbursts and dangerous brainwaves. When victory came, he was so used up that he could not even write his memoirs. He became President of the Regent's Park Zoo, and made films of the birds which, with the exception of his family and of the dynamo who nearly killed him, he appears to have loved intrinsically more than his fellow men. Amused or offended observers on his staff used to say that* BROOKE, *who could be abrupt, even arrogant to subordinates, was like a bird himself, and they would imitate his clipped, almost incomprehensibly rapid manner of speaking and his habit of flicking his tongue over his lips, like a lizard. The actor should think carefully about which, if any, of these mannerisms he should adopt.*

The men who mimicked BROOKE *during the war probably never dreamed that their withdrawn, unsmiling chief, who wrote even of his dead enemies as Boches, whom it is hard to imagine visiting a field hospital or talking with one of his men, that this man was himself a first-class parodist, whose diaries, the most colorful and informative of the period, are so caustic that they cannot be published unabridged in our century. His lack of humanity was self-defense. He knew the field of battle too well to allow himself to be involved with the individual whom his orders caused to be thrown onto the fire like a lump of coal. But for the anonymous man in the ranks this disinterest was disconcerting. Perhaps the exhaustion felt by the General, not a robust man, at the end of each day spent with the most robust of men prevented even his imagination, of which* BROOKE *had a great deal, from stretching as far as the front when he wrote in his diary at night. For the* CHIEF OF THE IMPERIAL GENERAL STAFF *was fighting Hitler as well: the greater part of his energies was taken up with pushing through the British Mediterranean strategy in opposition to the American plans for a landing in France—as early as 1942–43—and in the defeating of* CHURCHILL *the strategist. The* P.M. *was capable of holding his fist under* BROOKE's *nose and shouting, red in the face: "Leave me alone with these long-term projects of yours, they are only paralyzing our initiative," or "Have you not got a single General in the Army who can win battles, . . . must we continually lose battles in this way?"*

This armchair strategy of attrition was waged almost every day, usually ending with the complete exhaustion of BROOKE, *the victor; sometimes with the* P.M. *recovering his good humor, and suddenly deciding at midnight or later to see a film together, or asking* BROOKE *to lunch the following Sunday to eat plover's eggs or to look at the latest photographs of the destruction caused in the cities of Nazi Germany, before sending pictures to the Kremlin as morale boosters.* BROOKE *may well have regarded these pictures with mixed feelings out of concern for his daughter, who was living in Berlin, married to von Tempelhoff, a German staff officer from the same military dynasty which produced the mother of General Ludendorff. Sir Arthur Bryant, the editor of* BROOKE's *diaries, which are otherwise so full of family details, apparently finds this fact so painful that no mention is to be found of it.*

In between the sensitive BROOKE *and* CHURCHILL, *no less sensitive, for all his monolithic stance on the deck, oscillates, like the pendulum of a fine grandfather clock,* CHURCHILL's *intimate friend, the physicist* FREDERICK ALEXANDER LINDEMANN. *Since 1942, Baron (after 1956, Viscount)* CHERWELL, *he has been nicknamed, after Richelieu's Father Joseph and Bismarck's Fritz von Holstein, the Grey Eminence of Downing Street. His enemies, a term which includes almost everyone, avoid him or decry him for being a German or a Jew, whichever term seems the more opprobrious to the user. Whether* LINDEMANN *was a Jew, nobody exactly knows. His biographer, Lord Birkenhead, gives us a picture of* LINDE-

MANN's father which recalls one of Rembrandt's Jewish sages. LINDEMANN enjoyed telling malicious Jewish stories. A German he may be called with some justification. First, his mother, although like CHURCHILL's mother, an American, gave birth to Frederick in 1886 in Baden-Baden, a circumstance for which he never forgave her. Secondly, his distinctly well-to-do father hailed from the Palatinate, although he had in youth become a British citizen. Nevertheless, Frederick went to school in Darmstadt, and it was there, in shirts buttoned up to the neck, that he used to play tennis with the Czar and the Kaiser. For the whole of his life his social ambition was to outweigh his scientific, and it was his position in society, not in physics, that he would have to thank for his rise to being the leading wire-puller in those secret committees where soldiers allow themselves to be advised by scientists.

His student rooms were in the Adlon, the most expensive hotel in Berlin; among his fellow students under Nernst were von Born, Einstein, and Henry Tizard. It was in Berlin that he took up boxing. If he looked like losing, he would lose his temper and abandon the rules. Volunteering in 1914 for the British infantry, he was turned down, like Tizard, who was rejected by the navy. In this way the two of them ,in cautious amity, gravitated to the Air Force, and Sir Charles Snow, LINDEMANN's weightiest critic, speaks of their exceptional performance: "Both happened to be . . . abnormally brave, in the starkest physical sense . . . Lindemann, for experimental purposes, deliberately put his aircraft into a spinning nosedive. It was against the statistical probabilities that either remained alive."

After the war, Tizard went back to teach chemistry at Oxford, and campaigned for LINDEMANN's being given a chair of experimental philosophy that had fallen vacant, much to the astonishment of the English academic world, since, as Snow points out, "Lindemann had never been inside an English university."

In 1921, the moment of destiny came for LINDEMANN when he met CHURCHILL. Sensing that the scientists did not consider him a heavyweight, he associated with the nobility. His singular meals began to be laid respectfully before him in the dining rooms of a good many great English houses. He avoided eating, or indeed other contact with flesh of any kind, neither drank nor smoked, and lived chiefly on the whites of eggs, Port Salut cheese, and olive oil. He was not, however, a frigid man; on the contrary, he had a considerable emotional drive. The dislike felt by his colleagues was not caused by his scientific performance, but by his idiosyncratic sense of humor: "I would like to castrate So-and-So, not that it would make any difference to him."

Hardly had Hitler moved into the Chancellery, from where he could give the force of law to his hatred of Jews and intellectuals, than LINDEMANN went to Berlin to invite important scientists, many of whom, like Einstein, had been fellow students, to take refuge from the Nazi persecutions in England. It was not only Jewish professors, or those who had married Jews, who accepted this invitation, with which LINDEMANN, six years before the invasion of Poland inflicted the most decisive defeat of the war on Hitler, a fact acknowledged by none of the history books.

All services must be paid for, and the Western world paid for this immeasurable service nine years later, when her leader, CHURCHILL, accepted LINDEMANN's miscalculation that by destroying the working class areas of the German towns, victory would be brought about within eighteen months.

When one reads that Albert Einstein admired LINDEMANN for being a smooth operator in court politics, "a great man in the Renaissance tradition," one can understand how, in 1940, immediately after CHURCHILL's arrival in Downing Street, the "Prof." managed to jockey his colleague Tizard out of being the senior scientific adviser in government employment, and to secure the position for himself. Even allowing LINDEMANN to be CHURCHILL's "discovery," it was in the summer of 1940 that the Battle of Britain began, and apart from Sir Robert Watson-Watt, the father of radar, no other single man had done as much to bring about this decisive victory as Tizard.

Over the years, Tizard had adapted the invention of radar to its practical military use, thereby laying the foundation for the victory over Hitler's fighting aircraft. Nevertheless, LINDEMANN managed to unseat the man who had once been instrumental in his being made a professor: one should beware of those whom one has placed under obligations of gratitude. From the moment the P.M. accepted LINDEMANN's formula for reducing to ashes the industrial quarters of all German cities of more than 50,000 inhabitants ("middle-class areas have too much space around them and so are bound to waste bombs") and gave the order for it to be used as a major offensive weapon, CHURCHILL defended the Prof. like a tiger against all scientific attacks. Critics of strategic bombing *"were shown out of the room." Anyone who cast any doubt on the effectiveness of the terror-raids*—CHURCHILL *found the expression a good one—even such reputable defense-experts as Tizard, and Blackett, a Nobel Prize winner, was done for. Snow describes how "the faint but just perceptible smell of a witch hunt" created an atmosphere "more hysterical than is usual in English social life."*

In his sixties, insofar as anyone ever saw him without his bowler hat he possessed a head like a gray stone bust of Cicero, of striking malicious, virile handsomeness, with somber brown eyes. Here on deck he is wearing his bowler, along with a thin black overcoat with a white silk lining, striped trousers, and white spats. He holds his head like a cat carrying a mouse. His walk, as so often, betrays more than his face. He moves like a man who knows he has a hundred by no means friendly eyes staring him in the back. His walk is in the highest degree correct, economical.

When he is not talking to CHURCHILL, *his eyes remain half-shut: the impression that he does it to see more, rather than less, clearly is a false one. There is very little that* LINDEMANN *considers worth noticing. It is not curiosity, but an attempt to keep a distance, to repel, that makes him examine every change in the weather with his high-bridged nose.*

Snow, who was repelled by the repressed cruelty which he saw in LINDEMANN, *reports with a sort of admiring repulsion: "He was altogether a bit bigger than life-size. Lindemann, who was not an Englishman but became one, had the fanatical patriotism of someone who adopts a country which is nevertheless not, in the deepest sense, his own. No one cared more about England than Lindemann. . . ."*

And no one did LINDEMANN *care more about than* CHURCHILL. *"A good deal of Lindemann's social progress was snobbish, an escape from inner defeats. But his devotion to Churchill was the purest thing in his life," Snow admits, and he shares the general astonishment at the permanently unruffled affection between the two men, figures as diametrically opposed as one could conceive. David Irving, who has made a study of* LINDEMANN's *posthumous papers, writes of* LINDEMANN's *"typically feminine reaction" on hearing that* CHURCHILL *had entrusted the investigation of all evidence to do with the German rockets to his son-in-law, Duncan Sandys.* LINDEMANN, *till then the* P.M.'s *only personal scientific adviser, was prompted by jealousy and his irreconcilable dislike of Sandys, "to take up a false and unscientific position, which he himself had more and more to recognize as untenable." Apparently, Sandys noticed nothing of* LINDEMANN's *jealousy: he was guided by the principle that "experts should be on tap, not on top."*

Until the day in 1957 when he followed his friend's coffin, CHURCHILL *remained devoted to him, in a way that no man is simply to his Grey Eminence.*

By the railing stands a woman orderly. With her is a Polish captain, in a British paratrooper's uniform; he is hatless. Great Britain had not only by far the greatest number of women in the ranks (in June, 1941, the PRIME MINISTER *reported in a secret speech that he had demanded 170,000 women to replace men in the antiaircraft defenses alone), but she also had women officers, even attached to the staffs. The mechanization of war, the conducting of it by remote control from the switchboard of the administration, has made women, like workers in industry, almost as eligible to be serving soldiers as to be targets for the bombers in the bombed and beleaguered cities. No man anywhere could have given the order for total war without the acquiescence of women to cooperate in it.*

In several British books of memoirs and diaries, women in privileged positions as officers attached to the staffs or the ministries appear as sympathetic background figures. We meet a captain, a member of the Combined Operational Staff, sailing on the "Queen Mary" to staff conferences in America. CHURCHILL, *who always had room in his memoirs for such details, even if not for the mention of the two aircraft crashes (within six months of each other) of the Polish Prime Minister, mentions a WRNS officer who met his private secretary on the homeward voyage from Quebec, and, promptly, as these things will happen on board ship, became engaged to him. Another officer,* CHURCHILL's *daughter, was nearly washed overboard on the same journey as she was walking with one of the ship's officers on the afterdeck: on a zigzag course, the waves are unpredictable.*

Certain of these women were bearers of secrets of the first rank —so that even now they are mentioned, and fleetingly, in very few memoirs; somewhat imaginatively by Duff Cooper, autobiographically by Sefton Delmer, who, after the war, married the daughter of an "Establishment" family—the "Secret Lady" of Leonard

*Ingrams, a banker and a leading man in SO-2. This secret organ-
ization was later led by Major General Sir Colin Gubbins under
the title of Special Operations Executive (SOE) and was responsible "for the organization of acts of sabotage and resistance,
assassination and similar undertakings." One is assured that the
"Old Firm," as the macabre institute in Baker Street came to be
known, was dissolved after the war—and no one can doubt this,
since Sir Colin is now director of a textile firm in Regent Street.*

*HELEN MACDONALD is a Second Officer in the WRNS, a grave,
beautiful woman in her thirties.*

*The Pole is the engineer and secret agent KOCJAN. (We take
only his name and his most impressive feat from Churchill's
memoirs.) He belongs to the small handful of officers and men
who served in the lower ranks, but whom CHURCHILL nevertheless
found worthy of special mention in his history of the "thirty years'
war" of 1914–45.*

*The service this Pole performed for England, for which, as
CHURCHILL mentions with due reverence, he was executed by the
Gestapo in Warsaw on August 13, 1944, was one of legendary
audacity. KOCJAN stole from the Germans the entire component
parts of one of von Braun's rockets, bringing them in a Dakota
from the forests of Poland to England, months before the first
one landed on London.*

*All those Polish patriots who were not, as most of them were,
murdered with calculated savagery during or after the war, had to
be sacrificed by that hemisphere which calls itself "the free
world" to the alliance with Stalin. In this play the figure of
KOCJAN does duty also for that of the emissary of the Warsaw
Underground Movement, Lieutenant Jan Karski, who made repeated journeys across Nazi-occupied Europe to Gibraltar in
order to be able to make reports to, and receive commissions from
London and Washington. He was received by President Roosevelt,
to whom, in the spring of 1943, he brought the news that the
Germans had already, at a conservative estimate, murdered
1,800,000 Jews in Poland alone.*

*KOCJAN and Karski are examples of that phenomenon of our
time, the revolutionary fighter, whom the so-called regular soldier,
with scant justification, denigrates as a "partisan," and who is not,
"as a rule," taken prisoner, but murdered, ostensibly because the
very existence of partisans contravenes the Hague Convention. In
the Eastern theaters of war, this Convention was not, in fact, re-*

*spected even by the "regular" troops, so that the murder of
partisans was perhaps understandable in regions where the partisans themselves made a point of refusing quarter, acting on the
principle of "an eye for an eye, and a tooth for a tooth."*

*Given today's weapons of mass destruction, one may well sup-
pose that the partisan alone will be capable of sparing the child
in the cradle, and that the bomber pilot, who aims at the town,
will, if he is honest, be quite unjustified in demanding to be treated
as a prisoner of war.*

*As the curtain rises, the noise of a fighter escort is heard flying
low over the ship. The sound fades quickly.* HELEN *looks up,*
KOCJAN *looks into the water. He is smoking.*

[KOCJAN (*touching the tackle of the empty flagstaff*):
 I miss the Union Jack—it always meant
 a lot to Poland, now it means everything.
HELEN (*mocking, but kind*):
 All honor to your complicated feelings, Captain Kocjan,
 but we cannot run the flag up for their sake—
 we are lucky enough not to have to steer
 a zigzag course as it is.
 Hoist a flag into the bargain?
 Are all Poles so—romantic?
KOCJAN: Am I? Maybe the realities of life in Poland
 compel us always to imagine, to hope.
 After nearly three weeks, underground,
 hand over hand, through Germany and Holland,
 Belgium, France, and Spain—then to see
 Gibraltar there in front of you . . .
 The English flag means safety—not romance.
 And then, not only that, you send to meet us
 the kindest man on earth, the governor of Gibraltar,
 General MacFarlane, a—wonderful man.
HELEN: After the adventures you have gone through for us,
 surely some hospitality is to be expected.
KOCJAN: That is not the point. MacFarlane is like a father, espe-
 cially to the Poles. He told me that from 1939 till a short
 while ago he was the head of the British Military Mission in
 Moscow, and I know, from Sikorski, that many, countless
 Poles were saved from Stalin's prisons by his own personal
 intervention.

HELEN's *irony is defeated, almost. She is now a little afraid of the
passion in this man, who now, without a break, asks, as if changing the subject:*

> I want now to know why you call
> my feelings "complicated"?
> What is "complicated"? Just a joke?
> Come tonight!

HELEN: No—complicated, complicated means . . .
> unclear, lots of things mixed up together—
> and you know very well I can't come, Bohdan.
> What are you thinking of?
> I am on duty, eighteen hours a day,
> in case he sends for me.
> It's the same with his menservants;
> the only one who's stayed more than a year
> is Sawyers, the one he has now.

KOCJAN (*smiling, but with energy*):
> You're putting me off, Helen!
> I'm not interested in Churchill
> or his manservant. I only asked . . .

HELEN (*cheerful again, without sharpness but quickly*):
> —and I only answered—ten times.
> I cannot leave my cabin. If he wants
> to dictate, I would not put it past him
> to have the ship turned upside down for me
> at two in the morning.

KOCJAN: But—you lock your cabin door.
> He's not going to break it in, and find me there.
> They'll find you over the loudspeaker.

HELEN: Are you always so tenacious?

KOCJAN: What means—"tenacious"?

HELEN (*amused*): In war—a virtue: patient, firm.

KOCJAN: But not a virtue—in love, you think?

HELEN (*mocking*): Careful, careful, just say private life.
> That is enough. Love is for peacetime.

KOCJAN (*gloomy*): Not at all—then it is not so necessary.
> When one is alone—in war—there are ghosts.

HELEN (*also gloomy. Suddenly*): Yes.
> Here is my key—Cabin fourteen.
> But . . . I cannot promise, that—

I am very well equipped—
to deal with ghosts.
KOCJAN: They do not come
where there are two—
HELEN (*pulls her hand out of his and steps back, speaking quickly*):
The Prime Minister.]

CHURCHILL *enters, followed by* CHERWELL *and* BROOKE. KOCJAN
clicks his heels and bows in the P.M.*'s direction.* CHURCHILL, *leaning against the railing, does not notice; nor does he glance up at the fighter escort, which once more approaches and flies over the ship, the deafening noise quickly fading into the distance.*

KOCJAN *withdraws.* HELEN, *all at once the orderly so discreet as to be almost invisible, waits. The moment the fighters are out of earshot, the* P.M. *heads about, like a battleship, in the* GENERAL'*s direction, for all his brooding monumental quality, a nimble antagonist. His right hand rests on his hip so that his shoulders are bowed; in his left hand he holds a telescope. His cap, worn to one side, is placed on a head bent low and thrust forward in a characteristic posture: the man pushing the globe with his forehead. Perhaps his figure and his heavy jowls betray the fact that he is a man of nearly seventy. The face, pink as a ham, wears, as usual, the photogenic expression of belligerence and youthful obstinacy. In comparison with this "entrance," his first words, though not in fact at all amiable, seem as much so as his comment on the ceremonious style of his declaration of war upon Japan: "After all, when you have to kill a man it costs nothing to be polite."*

P.M. (*here anticipating the decision which he in fact took during the sessions of June 22–July 15*):
Codeword Gomorrah
Hamburg or Cologne—depending on the weather.
Harris must ask his weather prophets.
At all events *both* cities, as targets, carry an equal element of
risk.
(*To* CHERWELL:)
A risk it still remains, Prof., and a big one.
That man over there *lives* on the dream of revenge,
of doing to London what he did to Coventry.
I do not wholly share
the Minister of Home Security's anxiety
about the rockets—but what if one night

our own defense system should be frustrated by these tinfoil
strips?

CHERWELL's *voice already has the break of old age, and he speaks
with the over-accuracy of a man who has learned English as a
foreigner; he is older than his years. Before he died, at the age
of seventy-one, he asked someone for a definition of a perfect
machine, and answered himself: One whose component parts all
give out at the same time and to the same extent. He added, "I
am that machine."*

CHERWELL: We are saving men and machines.
Hitler's night fighters will be completely baffled
by the dropping of these strips . . . .

*He brings an envelope out of his overcoat pocket, and with his
supple, tapering fingers takes from it a bundle of paper foil in
strips, backed with stiff black paper, some of which he gives to
CHURCHILL, some to the GENERAL. By way of demonstration he
lets a few of them hang down from his upheld hand. CHURCHILL
does the same.*

This one handful alone will be enough
to give the appearance on the German radar
of a second bomber.
It will take half an hour for the strips to flutter to earth,
and only then will the radar screens
be once more capable of locating individual aircraft.
P.M. (*holding the strips out to* BROOKE):
Brookie—isn't that ingenious—the simplicity:
On every Christmas tree a dozen weapons
to beat the subtlest of the subtle
that science has unearthed—amazing.
BROOKE: For that precise reason, Prime Minister:
this is a two-edged sword:
the first use we make of it will betray it . . . .
CHERWELL: But *not* invalidate it.
BROOKE: Then let us use it first against the rocket sites, Lord
Cherwell.
Not Hamburg, nor Cologne, but Peenemünde.
(*Curt, abrupt, rapid.*)
What if we miscalculate now?
What if the rockets are ready sooner?

What if they devastate the South of England
to such an extent that I can no longer embark
the armies of invasion?

CHERWELL: Sir Alan—the mountain has labored
and brought forth but a mouse:
these rockets do not yet *exist*.
Why at this early stage inform the Germans
that we are on to them?

P.M.: C.I.G.S., do not be so obstinate:
(*He starts fidgeting with the back of the wooden collapsible
chair—a barometer of his temper.*)
Harris will not neglect the rockets, any more
than he will the dams, or Schweinfurt, or Herr Krupp:
But all these single targets are mere pedantry.
[They seem to me like the Americans' Burma Plan:
they are trying to munch a porcupine, quill by quill.]

As CHERWELL *puts the tinfoil streamers back into the envelope,
he speaks impatiently, without pausing.*

You must, of course, Prof., promise the C.I.G.S.
that Hamburg or Cologne will be the prototype
of something quite new,
something to make us sit up, a victory!

[CHERWELL: Harris is doing very nicely as it is.
A year ago, it took a thousand bombers
ninety minutes to unload a mere five hundred tons
over Cologne—we can now drop
the same tonnage from no more than four hundred Liberators,
in a quarter of an hour.

P.M. (*sullen*):
We have already made ourselves a laughing stock
over Hamburg a hundred and seventy-three times:
this time the last sacrament, for good and all.

CHERWELL: Harris reckons we need
a minimum of ten thousand tons
to destroy a maximum of five thousand acres in a built-up area.]

BROOKE: But Sir, the Americans will not fly by night.
They're waiting for their long-distance fighters.

P.M.: Waiting, waiting—are they here to sun themselves?
These daylight bombing runs are criminal—
the Huns can pick them off like clay pigeons.

CHERWELL: Only because they imagine they're hitting industry:
　　　　they are, in fact, *exporting* bombs.
　　　　(*He grins, that is to say, he bares his teeth, but his jaws re-
　　　　main firmly together.*)
　　　　Winston, do something about this nonsense.
　　　　Speak to the President.
BROOKE: Ask Roosevelt for long-range fighters, too.
P.M.: Must I *ask* for everything?
　　　　Do I have to pull the udder off the cow?
CHERWELL: The Americans will provide the second wave,
　　　　the morning after our first attack by night.
P.M. (*while* BROOKE *writes in his notebook*):
　　　　How many?
CHERWELL: Seventy.
P.M. (*angrily*):
　　　　Seventy—magnificent—and us with seven hundred?
　　　　Seventy—for Gomorrah.
[CHERWELL: Harris is putting the Americans on to the dock
　　　　　area.
　　　　With their aim, three quarters of their stuff will go into the
　　　　　water;
　　　　no matter, so long as they
　　　　are a nuisance to the Fire Brigade.
P.M.: Very well then: if our American cousins
　　　　have as accurate an aim as you have told us,
　　　　then let them take care of the Fire Brigade.
　　　　And when does Harris go over again?
CHERWELL: Weather permitting, two nights later—
　　　　the next night he goes to the Ruhr,
　　　　to distract attention.
　　　　Sir Alan, can you not persuade the Americans
　　　　that our new H2-S blind-bombing apparatus
　　　　and the water features of the city itself
　　　　will show them Hamburg on their screens
　　　　as clear as midday?
　　　　They can aim all they want—if they can aim at all.
BROOKE: Maybe, Cherwell, but . . .
　　　　there is resistance in the Eighth Air Force,
　　　　we don't want to stir it up.] Squadron Leader Dorland
　　　　speaks of open discontent, even among the officers.
P.M.: Dorland?

BROOKE: RAF Liaison with the Eighth.

P.M.: Let him fly with them: Gomorrah—by daylight,
and report to me. Orderly!

HELEN (*entering*): Sir?

P.M.: Fix a time when there's a moment free for this—

BROOKE (*to* HELEN): Squadron Leader Dorland.

HELEN (*making a note*): Thank you, Sir.

P.M. (*very uneasy, taking it out on the chair*):
After he's flown on Gomorrah—he must report
at once, to Harris would be best,
and then—no hurry, some Sunday would do—
get him to lunch at Chequers. *Mutiny?* Brooke!

HELEN (*going out*): Yes, Sir.

BROOKE: Forced landing in Switzerland and Sweden, clearly
desertion.
There is an entire fortress crew in Zurich.

P.M.: Do these cowards send home picture postcards?

BROOKE: They are not cowards, Prime Minister:
the Americans recently lost one-fifth of their men in a single
attack.

P.M.: God knows—
though I fear it is no concern of His either—
our own pilots are by now so stoical,
that the only comparison I find for their courage
is the doggedness of the men on the Somme.

[CHERWELL: With all respect. But flying in nineteen-sixteen,
in lath and canvas double-deckers
with spluttering engines, Winston, was no joke either.
Who would have spared *our* feelings?

P.M. But Prof.,—*thirty* times they have to keep their nerve,
before Harris will take them off these operations.
Well nigh as bad as the men in the arctic tankers.]
Helen—to the Minister of Information,
copy to Bomber Command.

BROOKE: May I suggest to British only, Prime Minister?

HELEN *is hardly on stage when he starts to dictate so fast that she
has no time to put away a telegram that has evidently just arrived.*

P.M.: Very well. How are we to prevent the newspapers from
getting hold of reports of the suspicious number of forced
landings made by American bombing aircraft in Switzerland?

Indicate to the newspapers that they are to keep quiet about these reports. Similarly they are not to act on the anti-Russian propaganda which has been appearing in the countless news sheets run by Polish exiles in Britain, following the discovery in Katyn of the mass graves full of Polish officers, until I have taken steps to counteract it . . . taken steps together with General Sikorski to counteract it; full stop. [What have you got there?

Takes the telegram out of HELEN's *hand. She answers quickly.*

HELEN: Just arrived, Sir.
P.M. (*reads the telegram, then turns to the others*):
Ah—the President informs me that
Harry Hopkins' son has been killed.
BROOKE: Is Harry still in the naval hospital?
P.M.: I'm afraid so. Harry did more than anyone
to bring America in with us;
and now his son is dead.
Helen, get Downing Street to have one of those parchment scrolls
inscribed, and sent to Scapa tomorrow for signature.
Text:
Stephen Peter Hopkins. Eighteen years old.
Paragraph:
"Your son, my Lord, has paid a soldier's debt:
He only lived but till he was a man,
The which no sooner had his prowess confirmed
In the unshrinking station where he fought,
But like a man he died."
        Macbeth, last scene.
Then, down at the bottom, "To
Harry Hopkins from Winston S. Churchill."
Date of death.]

HELEN *nods and goes out.*

(*Dreams, but, as always, of facts.*)
Katyn—the gangrene which could poison our
        alliance.
Absurd! to be threatened by any army
devoured by quicklime for the last four years,

their hands behind their backs, trussed up with ropes,
face downward in the mud,
where the revolver bullet threw them,
twelve layers deep.
[CHERWELL (*with a contemptuous laugh, not parting his jaws*):
The stench rises from the graves
so that the age of science—haha—
is not entirely spared the experience
of what the ancients—tsch tsch—knew as *demons*.
The bacteria in the organism of history.]
BROOKE: An army of four thousand dead,
more formidable in their common graves,
than at the heads of their divisions!
P.M. (*beside himself*): I will not *allow* it!
That the Poles in London should even suggest
that the murderer of their officers was—Stalin.
BROOKE (*laughing*):
Sir, that is what public opinion has been saying for *days*.
P.M. (*harshly*): Public opinion? There is no such thing.
There is only *published* opinion.
(*Laughing.*)
Just try telling that to Sikorski,
the noble voivode Quixote of the Sjem!
CHERWELL (*looking around, as if he was afraid of eaves-
droppers*):
You have underestimated *him* already
in your quarrel about the Russo-Polish frontiers.
Sikorski is not just respectable
like any old respectable foreigner,
but like a respectable Englishman.
P.M.: The oracle itself could hardly have been
more Delphic than Stalin in his last letter
—could he not ask, as a friend, that I—I
should make certain substitutions in the membership
of the Polish Government.

Pause. They look at each other.

BROOKE (*breaking out*): I know nothing about politics, Sir—
but this demand is . . .
P.M.: . . . unrealistic, of course. Substitutions!

CHERWELL (*drily*): You think so? Stalin has never,
   in his whole life, made an unrealistic demand.
BROOKE (*against* CHERWELL): Is the Prime Minister of England
   to depose the Prime Minister of Poland?

The PRIME MINISTER, *speechless, looks* CHERWELL *in the eyes.*
CHERWELL *pauses while* BROOKE *goes on.*

   This latest demand is monstrous;
   what are we *not* doing for Stalin as it is?
P.M. (*sober to the point of irony, at the same time thoughtful*):
   Now it is you, Brookie, who are being amazingly
       unrealistic.
   What is the Kremlin not doing for *us?*
BROOKE: Stalin is defending Russia for Russia—not for us.
   [He laughed out loud three years ago when Hitler
   knocked out the second front in France and Scandinavia:
   and now he's crying out for one
   as if he had a right to it.
P.M.: All] perfectly correct, but this as well:
       he is taking
   at least a hundred and ninety German divisions
   off our backs, while we—how many is it, Brookie,
   that we are driving back in the desert?
BROOKE (*humble*): Fifteen, or thereabouts.
P.M.: Hm.
BROOKE (*aggressive*): Sir, if that is too few for you,
   change your orders
   to concentrate our bombers—our elite—
   in the German *interior.*
   (*Vehement, wounding.*)
   What has changed
   since Wavell wrote to me from India,
   at the time when he was expecting the Japs?
CHERWELL (*interrupts, in extreme irritation*):
   That they *didn't:* that's what has changed.
BROOKE: Wavell is right all the same—then as now:
   it cost him three important warships
   and a hundred thousand tons of merchant shipping,
   because he had less than twenty light bombers
   at a time when we were sending

two hundred heavy bombers and more
to attack one single town in Germany.]
Why are we not destroying their hydrogenation plants?
If the Boche has no more gasoline for his tanks
and no oil for his U-boats, he is done for.

CHERWELL: Ploesti? What use was that?
Out of a hundred and seventy American Liberators,
the Germans shot down fifty-four.
Where the Boche makes oil, he fakes fog.

P.M.: And dummy factories: how long were we bombing
Krupp and Borsig before we realized they were cardboard
boxes?

The chair and the C.I.G.S. *come in for some maltreatment.*

Brooke, let us have an end to these objections.
We have not turned our attention to the towns for *fun,* Brooke.

BROOKE: But it is wrong. [First, it was your opinion,
Prime Minister, this war would *not* be, like the last,
a war of armies. There was much to support this view.
But now it has become one nonetheless,
the army has a claim on our bombers.
We know that]
the towns fall when and where the front collapses.
Secondly: Just as the Londoners
first cut their fighting teeth during the German night attacks
so do the Germans now.

CHERWELL: I fear, Sir Alan, you may have omitted to study
the system by which we have so far "Coventrated"
Mannheim and Lübeck . . . .

P.M.: I *have* studied it!
[On my return, I shall expect to hear
that the C.I.G.S. has abandoned his opposition,
which is unusually fruitless—

He goes out, making even his retreat aggressive.

BROOKE, *undismayed by the accustomed outburst, leans expectantly against the life raft, while* CHERWELL *puts on his lecturer's manner, walking with mathematical precision, as an aid to concentration, on particular patches of the floor, as he might pick out part of the pattern on a carpet, the black squares of a tiled floor, certain patches of parquet. Here he walks across the boards of the deck, overstepping the same number each time. He speaks like an experienced Harley Street specialist, cautiously, gently, always with confidence in whatever treatment he prescribes; this time the incineration of Hamburg or Cologne. He is quite innocent of the motives which lay behind Robert Oppenheimer's unforgettable admission about the dropping of his Hiroshima bomb: "We wanted to have it done before the war was finished, and there would be no further opportunity."*

As he walks up and down, talking, his hands, in constant motion, are the only things to escape the self-discipline of a lifetime, though he is not fidgety; the finger tips continually mark the aiming points in what he is saying. He shows the same impatience with his interlocutor as the doctor when a patient asks questions which are not his business, demands a bigger dose, or even disputes a prescription.

Like a Savile Row tailor underpraising his cloth, CHERWELL *is able to make the wildly arrogant understatement about his phosphorus: "It is what it is, Sir!"*

He laughs frequently, a sort of toneless hiss, as if he had a stomach-cramp: what makes him laugh "naturally" is merely the repellent stupidity of all his fellow men, CHURCHILL *excepted. His persecution mania, sublimated in Whitehall into a mania for persecuting other people, he has brought with him onto the ship, and even here on deck, with only the wind to overhear him, he cannot resist turning around apprehensively before speaking of colleagues whom he has played false. His unease shows itself in a repeated and unnecessary taking out of his watch; the double chain—a habit of* CHURCHILL's *he imitates—passes through one of his upper waistcoat buttonholes, with the watch on one end, in the left pocket, and on the other, in the right, a little gold pillbox. A glance at his watch, and he knows when it is time for a pill, or an apple.*

BROOKE (*impatient, irritated*):
　　Lord Cherwell, are you trying to imply . . .
CHERWELL: I imply nothing. All the same—
　　Blackett is still quoting as a statistic,
　　that each ten of our bombs
　　kills point two Germans only.
　　I am not to be made fun of in this way, Sir Alan.

Lübeck already proved, a year ago,
that with one ton of H.E. we could dispose
of two thousand square yards of the city center,
and with one ton of incendiaries, thirteen thousand.
(*Laughs.*)
—Zuckerman "calculated," as he is pleased to call it . . . .
BROOKE: Who is Zuckerman?
CHERWELL: He works with goats. At Oxford.
He pegged his goats out in pits,
the depth of a cellar in an average house,
spaced six, eight, and fifteen yards apart.
And in among them he detonated bombs,
and then complained how few goats were killed.
Conclusion: the blast effect alone is not enough:
ergo, the raids should be called off.
Amazing, the childishness of this conclusion.
Zuckerman overlooked the fact
that *people* will be crammed together:
as soon as the alarm sounds, they will stream
into the cellars.
The tenacity of Zuckerman's goats led him
to a false conclusion: in an open space
a man would have as good a chance as they.

BROOKE *makes a face as if someone were cutting cork with a blunt knife.*

Of course Zuckerman also investigated
blast and splinter effects:
with limitless application, he fired high-velocity steel balls
into rabbits' legs and, once again, *eo ipso*
came up with a negative result.
Since the possibility of death by smoke and fire
cannot by any means be ruled out,
Zuckerman might have done better to examine
the bodies from Coventry for a change.
These bodies showed how many died *directly:*
A, mechanically, from fragmentation,
B, chemically, from smoke, lack of oxygen, etcetera,
C, physically, from the heat with or without actual flames;
and how many *indirectly:*
A, atmospherically, from air pressure and pulmonary collapse,

B, from direct hits, that is to say, falling ruins,
dust, suffocation, and the like,
C, from burning, carbonization, first-degree burns,
monoxide poisoning, hyperoxygenation, etcetera.
Conclusion, Sir Alan: fire is *the* element of our
age, this war is to be won with fire.

*The Grand Cremator has spoken his monologue with precision
but also with rapidity and an impatience with the summarily
marshaled facts; as he spoke, his walk, a built-in pedometer,
regulated his lecture-room manner—now after a glance at his gold
hunter, he begins to peel a small apple. This, so to speak,
"grounds" the nervousness he feels at having to listen to* BROOKE's
*vehement opposition, in his finger tips. As he listens, his eyelids
half close.*

BROOKE (*standing away from the railing*):
    With divisions, Lord Cherwell—and good fortune.
    How is the fire in the cities to paralyze industry?
CHERWELL: Coventry is the example, Brooke—example and proof.
BROOKE: But the aircraft factories in Coventry
    were right in the middle of the old town.
    Coventry is the ideal case, not the pattern.
CHERWELL: You are quite wrong! Krupp is right inside Essen.
    There are aircraft, tank, and locomotive factories
    not far from the center of Kassel.
    It is not unusual.
    Forty per cent of our own aerial missiles and artillery
    are built in the middle of London.
    In Dessau . . .
BROOKE: Quite, quite: where that is so,
    you must demolish the towns.
    But using aiming points.
CHERWELL (*almost weeping with impatience*):
    No, no, Sir Alan, set the place on *fire:*
    The dislocation of the working population,
    the gas, light, and main water—*these* will paralyze industry,
    and only these.
BROOKE (*breaking out*):
    If Coventry is the example, as you say,
    then you must *aim*. The Boche, unhappily,

aimed all too well . . . . A month's halt in production
in the aircraft engine factories . . .

CHERWELL (*considers this, amused, apparently in agreement*):
Vice versa, it was the fire in the city destroyed
the main services. And that alone—
not the bombs on the factories—put the lid on things,
and shut down nine factories besides
that were not hit at all!
But the Germans, whose stupidity exceeds
their brutality even, did not realize this . . .
and since we played up nothing in the press
beyond the incendiaries that destroyed the cathedral,
they did not come again—*sentimental* butchers.
They lament and restore cathedrals to disguise
the fact that they are destroying God.

BROOKE: The burning of the cathedral was no reason
for them not to come again.
More than one of theirs is burning.

CHERWELL (*contemptuous*):
It is, of course, quite possible they have no stamina.
It was just the same, when I used to play tennis
in Darmstadt, with the Kaiser and the Czar.
The Czar was just a good-natured ass—but Wilhelm:
he would have been quite an enemy,
if he had ever had the application.
But he had no patience,
a "tear-away," rather than a talker;
his restlessness let me beat him,
as often as respect permitted.

BROOKE (*laconic*): Hitler is not the Kaiser, Cherwell.

CHERWELL: He needs the momentary triumph all the more.
Think of it, he destroys the radar towers
on his first raid: we patch them up:
he does not come again.
Or: the march on Moscow, before he has
secured Gibraltar or blocked the Suez Canal.
It's the same with Coventry:
A second raid the following night—
and where would our aircraft factories have been?
He might even have managed to create a firestorm.
The panicking force of fire is immeasurable.

Take Rotterdam, for example, where, paradoxically,
no incendiaries were dropped—

BROOKE, *not so much repelled by* CHERWELL's *computer-like mentality, as motivated by the spontaneous feeling of a professional General, to shield even Hitler's army against the "slander" that it was the air arm that decided the battle.*

BROOKE: Tscha! It was Hitler's *tanks* that knocked us flat,
not his Stukas.
But the tanks could have by-passed Rotterdam completely.

CHERWELL *lets it be seen that he is taking pains not to let it be seen that he finds this ludicrous.*

CHERWELL: Sir Alan—all honor to the tanks. But—
it was fire, the panicker, taught the Dutch what fear was
—and brought them to capitulate.
Tanks passing by—panic no one,
except generals.

BROOKE *turns away, only appearing to let the outrageousness of this remark pass him by: for* CHURCHILL *has once more appeared, behind them, unobtrusively, listening loweringly to them, a glass of brandy in his hand.*]

BROOKE: I am persuaded
that industry is only to be put out of action
by our causing widespread fires in the towns,
to dislocate the public services—
P.M.: As in Coventry.
BROOKE: Yes—but the hydrogenation plants
are not in Hamburg *or* Cologne;
nor are the Peenemünde rockets.
I therefore stand by my conviction
that the surprise effect of the tinfoil strips
is not worth wasting on Operation Gomorrah.

The PRIME MINISTER *again takes hold of the back of the chair with his right hand. With mounting anger he spins the chair around, bangs it down, picks it up again, scrapes it along, and finally pushes it quickly from him, as if it were the Field Marshal.*

P.M.: I had expected you would cooperate, C.I.G.S.
As this does not appear to be the case,
let me justify Gomorrah politically:

to render a million Germans homeless—that is a victory:
to puncture half a dozen oil tanks—that is not.

[BROOKE (*sharply*):
Sir, I can only indicate the bitterness in the other services:
Rear Admiral Hamilton has expressed what many are thinking:
If we are to raise Bomber Command to such a power
then they should be fighting the U-boats in the Atlantic,
or in the desert or Russia—but not against civilians.

P.M. (*with a contempt which also shows that the Admiral does
not even merit an objective rejoinder*):
So, Hamilton says that, does he indeed?
Yes: that would be his revenge: he must have heard,
as I meant him to, that I called him a coward
for leaving Convoy PQ 17 defenseless to Hitler's sharks—
and sailing his cruisers away from the danger zone.

BROOKE (*with barely concealed distaste*):
You *know,* Sir, that Hamilton is not a coward.
He warned against sending the convoy out unarmed.
You *know* that he was ordered three times to abandon the
convoy.

P.M.: That will not stop me calling him a coward.
Obedience is the rule—but a man is superior to a rule.
Is Hamilton a German, then?—
to sacrifice his subordinates to an idiotic order
even when he sees it is idiotic?
Or is he an Admiral of the Royal Navy—
who listens only to reason?
Had Nelson obeyed, instead of turning a blind eye
at Copenhagen, he would have lost at Trafalgar.
A man who needs principles and orders,
mistrusts his own strength—
and belongs *in* the ranks, not at the head of them.

BROOKE (*as if he were actually trying to reveal the limits of the
military mind*):
What, however, if Hitler's warships had nevertheless
come out and destroyed Hamilton's cruisers?
In that case you would have had the Admiral
court-martialed for disobeying orders.

P.M.: Of course. A man who exposes his men

to the risk of battle, must expose his own person
to the risk of the court-martial.
When I presume to take upon myself
the leadership of this country,
I declare myself ready to be beheaded
on Tower Hill, if we should lose the war.

BROOKE (*coldly angry*):
But, Sir—coward is one thing the Admiral is *not*.

P.M.: It is not a question of the Admiral—
but of the good it does
to broadcast my comment on him.

BROOKE: But it may wreck Hamilton?

P.M. (*very quietly, but rapidly and with such menace that* BROOKE
is silenced):
Hamilton's obedience has already wrecked
twenty-four out of thirty-six merchant ships.]
Have you anything to add, C.I.G.S.,
regarding Operation Gomorrah,
for which I am now giving the order?

BROOKE: Only that it is superfluous, Prime Minister.

P.M. (*almost speechless with rage*): Thank you.

BROOKE *turns abruptly and goes out, saluting correctly but hastily.*
CHURCHILL *at last leaves the chair in peace, but walks up and
down.*

He understood nothing. He hates me—
things are no longer working between the two of us—
he *detests* me.

CHERWELL: Of course he does nothing of the kind, Winston;
he is a soldier—and jealous of the bombers.
Departmental pride. [Still—
the rivalry of subordinates has its uses:
rivalry in the parts increases the strength of the whole.

P.M.: Where it doesn't weaken it.]
You want to make a firestorm?
Is that not a natural phenomenon, then?

CHERWELL: It can be *produced*.
[Given the right atmospheric conditions.

P.M.: Can *they* be produced?
Are our met. men reliable?

CHERWELL: Only one, his name is Krick,
  an American with the Eighth Air Force.
  Probably a genius, since no professional takes him seriously.
P.M.: Prof., this man must be consulted—Helen!—
  before Sicily too. Helen, the C.I.G.S. . . .

HELEN, *who has entered quickly, thinks she is to fetch* BROOKE, *and starts to go.*

HELEN: Right away, Sir.
P.M.: No, *don't* bring him up here again. Take this down:

HELEN *writes.*

> Before all landing operations consult the opinion of the Ameri-
> can Krick, with the Eighth Air Force, *independently* of our
> own meteorologists. Before consulting him about Operation
> Husky, call his attention to the fact that the *west* coast of Sicily
> is, in my recollection, often subject to surprisingly heavy
> inshore currents, even at the time of year we have in mind.
> Inform him that the storming-craft were so christened in a
> moment of over-enthusiasm, and are not, in fact, proof against
> storms, but extremely light; also that the operations can only
> succeed on condition that a high sea is not running during the
> unfavorable moon period, which could hinder the *punctual*—
> underline—the *punctual* convergence of the various convoys
> immediately prior to the landing. Should Krick and our own
> weather men come to different evaluations of the situation, I
> am to be informed. Prof.—how then do we . . . thank you,
> Helen.]

HELEN: Sir, you wished to receive the Polish Prime Minister
  and Captain Kocjan at five o'clock.
P.M.: Ask them to come out here. . . . Prof., how do we do it?

HELEN *has gone out.* CHERWELL, *the nonsmoker, quickly pulls out a cigar case containing colored pencils, colored chalk, and a slide rule.*

CHERWELL: Bear with me a couple of minutes.
  Essential is a rainfall during the preceding thirty days
  of less than four inches . . . look, here
  is Gomorrah. Here is the city—

On the gun turret, or wherever the setting allows, he draws quickly and with astonishing accuracy, in white chalk, two concentric circles. He speaks with composure, much as BROOKE, *talking about strategy, noted, from Malta, the grotesque phrase: "We also dealt with S.E. Asia . . ." In the other hand he holds a piece of red chalk, which he wields with increasing fervor. He continues:*

> I propose at the outset one and a half million small
> caliber incendiaries, four-pounders; these,
> dropped over the tightest possible area of the old
> town, will cause localized fires, which, in a
> space of time, the duration of which will depend on
> the atmospheric conditions . . .

As he speaks he indicates the local fires by crosses and shades in the whole surface of the inner part of the town, i.e., the whole of the inner circle.

CHERWELL: . . . will coagulate into a single conflagration.
> (*He shades in the inner circle.*)
> Here you have the burning inner city, in whose
> center temperatures of up to eight hundred degrees
> will soon consume not only all the normal
> combustible material, but also—and this is the
> funny thing—the oxygen. Now, as you know,
> all combustion is dependent upon a supply of
> oxygen. Therefore: the rapidly increasing
> need for oxygen in the center of the fire
> results in a *suction draft* on the perimeter,
> which drives the air from the quarters contiguous
> to the city center centripetally toward the
> heart of the conflagration.
> (*He draws arrows, radiating from the outer circle to the center.*)
> These air streams we describe, aptly enough, as
> firestorms. They sweep through the streets, with
> force and a velocity reaching the highest speed on
> our windscale.

P.M.: Force twelve—in a *town?*

CHERWELL: Certainly—comparable to the typhoons
> which rage in the tropic zones—
> we may reckon with a force of more than
> eighty miles an hour.

The Prof. is not yet aware how seriously he is underestimating. Air Marshal Harris reprinted, in his memoirs, a secret German report in which it was stated that the firestorms in Gomorrah reached a force of 160 m.p.h.

"Trees three feet thick were broken off or uprooted, human beings were flung alive into the flames . . . the panic-stricken citizens knew not where to turn. Flames drove them from the shelters, but high-explosive bombs sent them scurrying back again.

"Once inside, they were suffocated by carbon-monoxide poisoning . . . in a crematorium which was what each shelter proved to be. The fortunate were those who jumped into the canals or waterways and remained swimming or standing up to their necks in water for hours until the heat should die down."

> In the center, therefore, a windless furnace.
> On the perimeter, hurricanes—which
> will carry along all those objects,
> [whose stresses and strains are conditioned only
> to the storms usual in our latitudes. . . .]

P.M.: Objects—what sort of objects?

CHERWELL: Animate and inanimate—men, animals, trees, lorries, balconies, roofs, chimneys, and other architectural features.

P.M. (*almost in awe*): All this is—hurled all over the place?

CHERWELL: *Not* all over the place, drawn centripetally toward the furnace.

> A typhoon is not itself a chaos; it merely leaves one behind it.

P.M. (*takes three long, heavy strides*):
> Then let us dot one more "i" for them.
> We shall lift the black-out in London! Helen!
> This report, coming while Hamburg burns,
> will sound the death knell of German megalomania.

CHERWELL (*as if he had a nasty taste in his mouth, while the* PRIME MINISTER *looks at him questioningly*):
> Nothing to fear—Hitler has hardly any aircraft
> left, and if he should attack with rockets, they are
> blind, anyway.

P.M. (*not noticing in his eagerness, that* HELEN *has brought* GENERAL SIKORSKI *on deck*):
> Helen—take this down—ah, later—Hello—

HELEN: The Prime Minister General Sikorski and Captain
    Kocjan—
P.M.: My dear General: I took the liberty
    of asking you up here on deck, because
    Moran had recommended sea air. . . .

CHURCHILL *goes over to the Pole with rough cordiality—handing
his now empty glass to* HELEN. *His darting hand, the flow of words,
the manner, all immediately create a magnetic field which compels
the Pole's arguments like iron filings. The* POLISH PRIME MINISTER
AND SUPREME COMMANDER OF THE POLISH FORCES *is still, in
"the lusty squalor of the twentieth century"* (CHURCHILL's *phrase*),
*of picturesque chivalrous appearance; had he reached a normal
old age, this knight-errant figure would have survived into the
rocket era. The square cap, the short black cavalry cape, the
waisted jacket with the lanyards, the tight fitting knee-length boots,
along with the knightly* courtoisie, *the reserve that escapes, when
it is allowed to, in an undiplomatic directness—all these awake
affection . . . and almost as much pity. His helplessness with the
language* (CHURCHILL *and he could only discuss things in French*)
*would, if we could demonstrate it here, mark him as the loser after
the first few sentences. We soon know the things and the people
he has to struggle with—and will have to struggle with, unarmed,
till the end. One of the men who worked with him, describing
his last leavetaking from* SIKORSKI, *mentions the "expression of
deep worry on his sensitive, manly and still youthful features."*

SIKORSKI (*saluting as he steps quickly forward to meet* CHURCHILL):
    I find it better on deck too, Prime Minister—Good
    morning, Lord Cherwell—Captain Kocjan and I
    would both like to thank you for allowing us to go
    with you to Scotland in your ship.
P.M. (*after shaking* SIKORSKI's *hand, bringing forward the ex-
    tremely shy* KOCJAN):
    Captain Kocjan—young people are more easily seasick than
        us old ones.
    My orderly will take you down to Sawyers later
    and get him to give you a little
    of what the Kremlin provides under the innocent description
    of "our Russian whisky"—a pepper-vodka,
    which tears you apart,

like grapeshot in the mouth, but in the stomach,
oil upon troubled waters.

Meanwhile no one is just standing around—movement is continuous. CHERWELL *has greeted* SIKORSKI, *raising his hat with a smile, bowing formally;* HELEN *has withdrawn;* CHURCHILL *has half-taken* KOCJAN's *arm, which makes the young man feel a little safer, and led him over to* CHERWELL's *chalk drawing, to explain it.*

SIKORSKI *is about to ask* CHERWELL *something—but his answer is obscured by the fighter escort, which once more roars deafeningly over the ship; the noise fades swiftly.*

SIKORSKI: And how does the sea air agree with you, Lord Cherwell?

Since conversation is impossible, they look at each other, and away. Then . . .

CHERWELL: Excellency, oh: the ship is like a monastic retreat.
The sea air, A, brings out one's best ideas
and B, cheers one up.
Only at sea does one notice how completely we have got rid
of the U-boats.
When we came up to Scapa last autumn
we were still having to steer a zigzag course.
SIKORSKI (*smiling*): At which time, as the Prime Minister
had to instruct me, one must not walk
about on deck.
P.M. (*turns to* SIKORSKI):
Excellency, did you know that it is possible
to *create* firestorms? A recipe
for reducing a great city to clinker.
SIKORSKI (*with a gesture of resignation*):
I understand nothing about these things—
we had horses—not bombers.
CHERWELL: We shall see one another at dinner.
SIKORSKI (*saluting*): Until then, Lord Cherwell.

CHERWELL *puts his hat on and goes.* KOCJAN *makes a great effort to listen, as* CHURCHILL *is speaking very quickly. Without a break, even before* CHERWELL *has gone out,* SIKORSKI *asks, naively:*

For which city is this intended,
Prime Minister?
P.M.: Oh, all of them—probably Munich to start with,
the primal cell, the cheery Chicago
of the German gangsters.
I nearly met the man himself in Munich
the year before he became Chancellor:
[Cherwell and I were making a leisurely tour
of the Duke of Marlborough's battlefields:
we went through the Netherlands, passed the Rhine
at Coblenz, and on down the Danube, studied Blenheim—
then, in Munich,]
in the Regina Hotel
we were approached by a favorite
of the "Führer,"
as he called him, a fellow of some charm,
played the piano, and sang all the
English songs I liked very well.
I really ought to meet the "Führer,"
he said, he came there for tea every day.
Well and good. I was curious of course.
Such *application* cannot but be impressive.
However, in the course of conversation I asked:
"Why is your chief so violent against the Jews?"
I asked it without malice.
I still don't understand it, even now.
Next day the pianist appeared alone—
very *piano*—today Herr Hitler
would *not* be there for tea.
We stayed in the hotel for several days—
but never once did Hitler take advantage
of the invaluable opportunity of making my acquaintance.
SIKORSKI: He's making it now—more closely than at the tea table.
(*He points to the diagram of the firestorm.*)
P.M.: His electors are!
Captain Kocjan, I have read your report carefully,
including these apocalyptic . . .
absurdities from Oswiecim and Belzec. The figures!
SIKORSKI: One million, eight hundred thousand Jews
murdered in Poland, already.

Silence.

> It is not only a rumor that
> Hitler has Jewish blood himself.
> Then where does this irrational hatred come from?

P.M.: I have never made a study of hate—quite possibly
because it only needs a rumor to touch him off,
perhaps *because* it is such a primitive object lesson.
I have written ten thousand pages of history—
and now I am contributing a few myself—
and yet with each succeeding year I *understand* it less.
The final conclusions are *so* banal
that the memory of all the sacrifices
and the roundabout ways that led us to and from them
makes one ashamed to give them voice;
that final scene, where pandemonium and world history are
        united
and all is once again made plain, and fearful,
as naive as a fable from Herodotus.
[Whether or not the devil's grandmother
was raped by a Jew when she was a kitchenmaid
is *only* interesting, General,
in that this devil is a danger to the community
and must be got rid of.
This undeniably attractive task
is further lightened for us by Hitler's Satanism:
it spares us diplomatic complications.
All we must do is kill him, stamp him out.

SIKORSKI *is forced to laugh, as is* KOCJAN, *who, though he has understood little, has seen the* PRIME MINISTER's *final demonstration
of "stamping out" his opponent.*]

> But the Polish Underground Army's request
> that we should drop leaflets informing the Germans
> that they will be bombed because they are killing the Jews
> cannot be complied with.
> In the first place, His Majesty's Government
> does not undertake acts of *revenge.*
> Secondly, we cannot lend credence to the propaganda
> of that homicidal lunatic in Berlin
> who says that British pilots are being sacrificed
> to Jewish interests:

Jewish interests today are those of all mankind.

KOCJAN: I will explain this in Warsaw, Prime Minister.
I—I cannot in English explain my feelings
that you personally, and President Roosevelt personally
receive an emissary of the Warsaw Underground Army.
Allow me to say, Prime Minister,
that we all of us in Poland see in you alone
the rock of all our hopes
to raise our downtrodden people from the dust.

The PRIME MINISTER, *moved, slaps* KOCJAN *on the shoulder in rough affection, and turns to* SIKORSKI.

SIKORSKI: Prime Minister—Kocjan has spoken for me as well:
Now more than ever Poland stands or falls
with you!

P.M.: Who talks of *falling?* . . .
Without heroes in the old-fashioned sense, like Kocjan,
who can still carve themselves a *destiny*
out of the automatism of war today,
it would not be possible to make war
as passionately as one makes love—
the only possible way to win it.
One may *count* the number of Polish and British pilots
who decided its outcome in the Battle of Britain.
[Men like yourself, or Lieutenant Commander Esmonde
whose torpedo bombers smashed the Bismarck's rudders
and left her to the Home Fleet's guns—
or the commandos (my hobby) at St. Nazaire
blowing up the lock gates of the largest dock in Europe:
and the Italians—if I may be allowed
to go over to the enemy—
in Alexandria in December. Six of them
laid up two battleships, and blew a tanker to smithereens—
terrible fellows: they *swam* with the time bombs
and clamped them to the bellies of the ships.
We caught two of them in the water
before the explosion, stuck them right down in the hold
of the battleship itself, to make them talk quicker,
but they never spoke, although they knew
they might be blown to pieces.]
How I miss Lawrence of Arabia today.

With him, and his obsession, at the head of a command
and me behind him—the good Lord
would have gathered Marshal Rommel to Him long ago.
Kocjan, where and when do you make your jump?

KOCJAN: Starting at Scapa Flow, Prime Minister, they calculate
that I will jump at twenty-three hundred hours over
the suburbs of Smolensk. And it will still not
be daylight by the time the Dakota comes into range
of the German fighters in northern Norway
on the return flight. But the time and day
of the start I do not know so far.

P.M. (*somewhat impatient*):
How reassuring! Where did our Intelligence pick you up?

KOCJAN: In Spain, Prime Minister. Through Germany,
Belgium and France—the Polish organization
pushed . . . er . . . passed me [from hand to hand.

P.M.: Did you come through Portugal or Gibraltar?

KOCJAN: We flew here from Gibraltar.

P.M.: Taking off from there is child's play: one big detour
to avoid the Bay of Biscay and the Hun fighters, and you're
home.
But landing in Gib.—fearful. The rock.

SIKORSKI: Mr. Churchill—*you* are not the man
to be blown to pieces. And I firmly believe
that courage arms a man better against misfortune
than reason. If not, we Poles
would long ago have given up all hope.
In war the only realist is the man who believes in miracles.

P.M.: Perhaps—only a miracle is not always a blessing.
It is a miracle that that sick man in Germany
has been so weakened by his hatred of the Jews.
I dare not think of how things would have been
had he *not* persecuted the Jews.
When he took power, the physicists of genius,
some two or three apart, an Italian, a Dane,
were all sitting around one table, at Göttingen;
yet purely out of hatred of the Jews
Hitler drove the whole club, gentiles and all,
into the Diaspora. A miracle
that history should in this way have deprived

that haunted, morbid being of the world-shattering—let us
call it:
(*he hesitates*)
grenade, which might one day perhaps . . .
have ordered the destruction of Kiev, or Birmingham.
SIKORSKI (*politely, though repelled by this train of thought*):
But that this one unhappy people must endure
the hate that works to our advantage . . .

The PRIME MINISTER *turns up his nose: once again,* SIKORSKI
*appears to him to be "amazingly" sentimental. Naive as that
philosopher of whom he had never heard—Schopenhauer he
knew, but not Hegel—*CHURCHILL *also finds it reasonable that
the "stratagem of reason" should present such barbaric accounts.*

P.M. (*shrugging*): Mankind never gets something for nothing.
That Hitler the exterminator should dash the victory
from the hand of Hitler the conqueror
and make of his vassals, partisans,
that too is one of the prices.
It is possible that the partisans in Russia
have massacred more Germans than the defenders of Stalingrad.
Hitler's obsession with extermination
is, therefore, for the Russians, as a whole,
a blessing—an immeasurable blessing.
(*With hardly a break.*)]
How did you get this noteworthy information
out of Poland to your British counterparts?
KOCJAN (*with a smile*): Mr. Prime Minister—in my ears—
hiding in my ears—excuse me, I do not know how to say . . .
SIKORSKI: I will translate, Kocjan.
KOCJAN: Mialem w uszach prawie 100 stron sprawozdan
w maszynopisie sfotografowanych na mikrofilmie.
SIKORSKI (*amused*): Captain Kocjan brought your Intelligence
nearly one hundred pages of reports, typed and then micro-
filmed,
hidden in his ears—so much—so small, mmm?
KOCJAN: Tak male jak 6 papier owych zapalek.
SIKORSKI: Incredible—no bigger than half a dozen book matches.
P.M.: If the technicians can do *that,* why can they not yet
find a way for the courier aircraft to *land* in Poland?

Couriers should be flown out. The journey to
Gibraltar is far too hazardous.

KOCJAN: Oh no, Prime Minister: thank you, it went smoothly
taking off from Gibraltar.

P.M.: You misunderstand me: it's not the leaving
Gibraltar was so risky, but the *getting* there.

KOCJAN: Ah, so. But a landing in Poland, in the forest clearings
is very—er, incalculatable,
since we never know,
never exactly know,
how long the Germans will leave a wood . . .
not patrolled, and redirectioning airplanes once in the air . . .
    is . . .

P.M.: I understand. How are the relations
between your Underground Army and the Russians,
and the Polish Communists?

KOCJAN: We have none—or bad ones, till today.
Now they are worse than bad, and worse than none,
since one third of our vanished officers and scientists
were found in Katyn, their wrists tied with Russian ropes.

P.M.: . . . but *German* bullets in their necks.

KOCJAN: Ach, ropes, bullets, they mean nothing—

[SIKORSKI: Hitler and Stalin were business partners. German
soldiers too have been killed in Russia by German
bullets, fired from Russian guns; and Hitler's tanks
first rolled into Russia on Russian gasoline.]

KOCJAN (*imploring*): Prime Minister, Polish nationalists . . .
We will all be liquidated if Stalin
ever enters Warsaw. Liquidated.

P.M. (*noticeably cooler*):
The "if" is strange, Kocjan: who else, pray,
should liberate Poland—if not the Red Army?

SIKORSKI: You hear, Kocjan—the Red Army.

KOCJAN (*shocked, turns to* SIKORSKI):
You have said yes, General? You have said yes to that?

SIKORSKI: You know my orders—no provocation of the Russians.

KOCJAN: We do not provocate not even Polish Communists.
(*Passionately, but moderated by respect, not loud.*)
Stalin is to liberate Poland?
The man who accepted forty-eight per cent
of our country as a gift from Hitler?

[P.M. (*speaking now with dangerous cordiality*):
    You are quite mistaken, Captain Kocjan;
    Stalin had to take Eastern Poland before Hitler,
    or else the German's march on Moscow
    would have been that much shorter.
SIKOSKI: All the same, Prime Minister:
    It was the alliance with Stalin first encouraged Hitler
    to march on Warsaw.
P.M.: No, Excellency—no. Stalin had *no* choice,
    since, to democracy's shame let it be said,
    after we left Prague in the lurch, he could
    no longer trust us to keep our promises to Poland.]
KOCJAN: Prime Minister, while Stalin was still Hitler's crony
    and Britain was alone, voluntarily
    you declared war, to liberate Poland.
    Hitler wanted nothing against England.

The PRIME MINISTER *is at a loss for words, a thing that hardly ever happens: but* KOCJAN, *beside himself now, goes at him tooth and nail.*

    Today, with America beside you
    you let us fall into—slavery.
[P.M. (*gripping* KOCJAN *with both hands, and quieting him down by his friendliness, and his cold blue eyes*):
    Do not make two disasters out of one,
    you Poles: do not even consider fighting Stalin.
KOCJAN: Are we supposed to *laugh,* then, with a man
    who shoots fourteen thousand of our comrades in the neck?]
    General, is Poland tomorrow to be a Russian province?

He laughs, recklessly, but the PRIME MINISTER, *himself only able to keep reason uppermost with an effort, is sorry for him;* SIKORSKI *welcomes* KOCJAN's *plainness of speech, which he could hardly have permitted himself.*

P.M. (*moved. More to* KOCJAN *than to* SIKORSKI):
    It must be said, you Poles, it must be said,
    your Russian campaign of twenty years ago
    was as fantastic in itself as was the victory won
    by the General over the powerful cavalry of Budjonny.
    (*With feeling.*)

Excellency! I have always envied you the fame
of being the last cavalry commander in history.
[A war without cavalry seems hardly worth the fighting.
That, twenty years after I rode in the battle of Omdurman,
three years after Verdun,
that you should have been able to decide the whole campaign
against the Russians on the Vistula on horseback,]
alongside Pilsudski, [squadron to squadron!]

SIKORSKI (*with more resignation than pride*):
That it should be I—who now am to give back
to the Kremlin, the very provinces I conquered—
impossible, Sir.

P.M. (*gloomily*):
You must have known the Kremlin would send a bill,
so pay it, Poland: *now,* with German loot,
that the Kremlin loots from you.
(*To* KOCJAN:)
One should not stick one's neck out, nor one's hopes.
The best war—is the shortest.

SIKORSKI: We have, in the west, two hundred thousand men;
do not deny us the opportunity
to land with you in Trieste,
march through the Laibach Valley to the north,
and free Warsaw. Once Italy is finished, then . . .

P.M. (*unconsciously tactless*): Is it wise—
to knock Italy right out of the war? Only think
how much Hitler has invested in the boot.
Why should we amputate this leg completely?
Let him hobble on it—let it rot until he dies
of blood poisoning. Let him learn how easy
it is for a strong man to come to grief
through a weak ally.

His delight in clinical metaphors has carried him away—he is sud-
denly appalled at what he has just said to his weakest ally, who
has taken the remark as a direct personal reference, which was
not at all the intention.

SIKORSKI (*with a ghost of a laugh, to hide his alarm*):
I wish I could jump over Smolensk at dawn with Kocjan.
(*To* KOCJAN:)
They are worse off at home, but they are—at home.

P.M. (*sincerely*): Excellency, your hour too will come,
the day when Poland has you once again . . .
(*Takes* KOCJAN's *hands.*)
Kocjan, go with God, and do not doubt us.
Now I shall hand you over—Helen!—to my orderly.
(*To* HELEN, *whom he, but not the audience, can see waiting
behind the deckhouse:*)
Where did you find that cat? Show me—

HELEN, *who was about to put the cat down when she was called,
brings it in. The* PRIME MINISTER *holds it, and pats it like a dog,
without interrupting the dialogue. There is the feeling that the*
PRIME MINISTER, *like all men of power and egocentricity, culti-
vates a spontaneous love of animals, regardless of whether it will
be rewarded by the presence of a press photographer—he* likes
*animals: they do not answer back, they are even more easily
trained than his human contemporaries, and—unlike them—are
almost invariably faithful. The* PRIME MINISTER *purrs and mews.*

HELEN: It belongs to one of the crew, Prime Minister—his
mascot.
P.M.: . . . What's your name, then, what's your name . . .
What are you laughing at?
HELEN: They called it after you, Sir.
P.M.: How flattering—a lissome beast.
All babies look like me; the papers say so,
it may nevertheless be true. But a *cat!*
Which? Winston, Spencer?
HELEN: No, Sir. Winnie.
P.M. (*laughs with the others, addresses the cat*):
Winnie—aha, a mascot are you then? . . .
(*He hands the cat to* KOCJAN.)
Then you can bring the Captain luck, today,
before his hazardous flight! I beg your pardon—
have you introduced yourself to Mrs. MacDonald?
HELEN (*quickly*): Yesterday evening, Sir.
P.M.: Take Captain Kocjan to Sawyers and see he gets some of
that vodka.
Make sure, just now, that the Minister President and I
are not overheard, and stay within calling distance.
My good wishes to your comrades, Captain Kocjan: Good-by.

KOCJAN *stands at attention; wishing to salute, he hands the cat to* HELEN. *The cat jumps to the deck.* HELEN *catches it quickly. The* PRIME MINISTER *turns and takes* SIKORSKI *by the elbow.*

P.M.: Watch out—don't let him fall overboard,
   salt water will *not* improve the loyal beast.
SIKORSKI (*with an effort at cheerfulness*):
   Loyal?—cats are not loyal, Prime Minister,
   at least not to human beings, only to home and country.

HELEN *and* KOCJAN *withdraw,* HELEN *putting the red rope across the companionway leading from the bridge to the maindeck. Until they are out of earshot, the* PRIME MINISTER *keeps up the small talk, then suddenly changes his tone, like a slap in the face.*

P.M.: Well—*clever* beasts: to be faithful to what abides.
   Dogs are faithful to men—they have a harder time.
   Does loyalty to one's country then exclude
   that to one's fellow men? *Your* problem, General:
   either you abandon the wishes of your people
   —or you abandon your country. Yes.
   (*Taking* SIKORSKI *by the elbow.*)
   The conversation with Captain Kocjan *appalled* me.
   Prime Minister: the murders at Katyn lie in the past
   and—to quote Stalin—the past belongs to God.

Although SIKORSKI *has been expecting this, he is quite unable to hide his revulsion at this "realism"; his sudden fierce reaction reveals at last how careful he had been to conceal his anger in front of* KOCJAN.

SIKORSKI: The *past?* Sir, three weeks have passed,
   since the discovery of that first grave . . .
P.M. (*his words fall harshly as the clanging of a prison gate*):
   Three *years* since your officers
   were buried there: three *years*. Excellency!
   (*He bangs the chair roughly.*)
SIKORSKI (*beside himself*):
   Four thousand of Poland's fourteen thousand officers
   have been found there, the elite of my officers,
   the great names of Polish science—
   and is the Prime Minister of Poland
   to be forbidden even to *inquire*
   who the murderer is?

P.M.: But since you *know*—
   for *Poland's* sake
   do not ask *now!*

SIKORSKI (*laughs*): All Poland knows it!
   Captured officers, British among them,
   have been taken by the Germans to see the graves.

P.M.: For myself, I am incapable of telling,
   by looking at a man who has been shot,
   who it was that shot him.
   Let the people . . . talk and know better: all that matters
   is that their Prime Minister should declare
   that the investigation of the bodies
   shall only take place when the soil of Poland
   has been swept clean of the German butchers.
   General, I beg of you, make use, make use
   of this one advantage of the fearful carnage
   that Hitler's terrorists have been committing
   for the last four years in Poland;
   that just a *possibility* is left
   that these murders too are theirs—

SIKORSKI: That would be irreparable, Prime Minister; later,
   when . . .

P.M. (*bursts out, then begging*):
   What, General Sikorski, exactly do you want?
   Do you want to write history? Then seek the truth.
   Or do you want to make it? Then it is facts that count.
   The dead are impartial, the dead have time to wait.
   [Concentrate on those of your people who are *living*.
   The truth decides nothing.
   Were the truth simply imperiled . . .
   but it *is* itself the peril.

SIKORSKI: Prime Minister—if the butchering of our officers
   is ever to make sense objectively—

P.M.: There is no objectivity in war.
   There is only an objective.

SIKORSKI (*offended, sarcastic*):
   That is what I meant—I—begin gradually
   to understand English; but I shall never learn
   to speak it correctly too.

P.M. (*only apparently calmer, he has undone the top button of his
   thick coat; he now fingers his shirt collar, to give himself*

air. As was frequently the case, the top button of his shirt is missing; only the tie holds the collar in place) :
Forgive me—Excellency.]

SIKORSKI (*firm, though with an effort*) :
The objective [then] of our investigation
is morally to force the butcher to restore,
by treaty, the eastern half of Poland.

P.M. (*laughing painfully, out of a barely controlled disgust*) :
Morally—force Stalin *morally?*

[*Pause. He is so much at a loss that he even ceases to maltreat the chair. He murmurs, twice, almost inaudibly: "If you can't beat 'em, join 'em." Then:*

Excellency—forgive me, but every schoolboy learns
the foe you cannot conquer, you must court.
The question of what he may have to answer for . . .
We *all* have much to answer for.
The Polish nationalists' hatred of Russia,
their flirtation with Berlin
so long as Berlin was amicable,
was, not to put it any more strongly,
potentially dangerous for the Kremlin.

SIKORSKI: As dangerous as it was for Poland
that Russia signed her pact with Berlin,
at Poland's expense, as always.
But let us speak of today:]
Only so long as Hitler keeps him in check,
can we demand from Stalin
that he respects Poland's prewar frontiers.

The explosion threatens, but is, as yet, to come. What is visible is that the PRIME MINISTER's *disgust at the arguments the Poles have presented a thousand times since 1941 can no longer be politely disguised. At ever shorter intervals he "grounds" the lightning of his anger by banging the chair. He shifts his feet with impatience, when he does not actually stamp up and down; his hands are either rammed deep into his pockets or darting out of them to underline phrases, or as if to cut them up into lengths.*

P.M.: Demand? Here is the picture, General:
What we can *offer* the Kremlin
is the destruction of the Hun in Africa,

and insofar as it is successful, the landing in Italy.
Further, we offer Stalin the burning of the large cities,
and therewith the partial paralysis of industry and German
     morale.
Measure against this, Excellency,
what we are asking *from* the Kremlin:
First, acquiescence in the stoppage of all convoys
till the return of the winter night, one whole half-year;
secondly—and this news is so appalling
I have so far found no way to inform the Kremlin of it—
we must tell Stalin that—this year, as last—
we still cannot land in France.
[SIKORSKI (*uncomfortably*):
     Why, Sir, are you stopping military aid to Russia?
P.M.: Every vessel is needed in the Mediterranean
     and Hitler has despatched the "Scharnhorst" and the "Tirpitz"
     to northern Norway.
     The brute has instinct: his strong point.
     He suspects that it was always my idea
     to land up there . . . and so we cannot get
     any more convoys through the Arctic Sea
     —not in the months of the white nights.]
     Our . . . breaches of contract quite entitle Stalin
     to make a separate peace with Germany.

Short pause.

SIKORSKI: Prime Minister, this concern seems to me superfluous.
     For three months now, since the victory on the Volga,
     no Russian of honor can any longer
     negotiate with Hitler.
P.M.: And if he should grant us the honor
     of allowing the Hun to bleed *us* to death?
     Stalin is losing ten thousand men a day!
     [Three times in a hundred and thirty years
     Russia has saved the West.
     From Napoleon, from Wilhelm—
     yes, I may well be the last man alive
     who has not forgotten that it was the Czar and his armies
     who kept the Germans from the gates of Paris
     by the blood they shed at Tannenberg in 1914—

And now . . . it is the Red Army, Sikorski,
that is wiping out Hitler's divisions.]
Stalin is sacrificing ten thousand men a day.
Whole hecatombs of Russian soldiers lie
paving the roads that lead into Berlin.
For everything the Kremlin takes from Poland,
the Russian soldier will pay Poland back.
What do you want with Lvov
if Stalin gives you Breslau and Stettin?
[We shall give Prussia and Silesia to a people
who will build schools, not crematoria.
It is no matter if it takes the German
two or three hundred years
to understand the logic of this move.
As victors we shall stand guard for Poland—
as long and irksome as need be, until
we are assured the Germans will continue
in that humility with which they, as the conquered,
receive us.
One either has the German at one's throat
or at one's feet—the animal walks upright
only in uniform, not in mufti.]

SIKORSKI: I see only new battlefields that lie ahead.
It is our *own* land we want back again,—and East Prussia,
East Prussia, without having Stalin
sitting on our necks in Königsberg.
[Forever after there will be powerful elements in Germany,
will not forgive the Poles for occupying . . .
the birthplaces of their Silesian national monuments,
Eichendorff and Hauptmann.

P.M.: Eichendorff—who is he?

SIKORSKI (*irritated*): One of their poets.

P.M.: Hm. Then they should have organized
poetry readings there—instead of Auschwitz.
No—that people must go. I say it without hate—
I want merely to balance the books.

SIKORSKI: I hate the Germans,
despoilers of Eastern Europe,
they have driven all of us
into the Kremlin's slaughterhouse.
I *hate* them; but I fear them too.

That, Sir, is why] we must have frontiers that will *last*.

P.M.: The Kremlin wants them too.
And this new frontier on the Oder: that *will* last.
It guarantees the Russians
permanent enmity between yourselves and Germany.
Sikorski, you cannot begrudge Stalin's
laying a sword between you and Germany,
that will abide forever.
Like Alsace-Lorraine—now in France's clutches
and now in Germany's—
for centuries it kept the world secure
from France and Germany's ever making friends.
In the same way, the enmity between
Poland and Germany will insure
that Poland never shall be used again
as the wedge to breach the walls of Russia.
I cannot blame the Russians for this, Sikorski.
When, twenty years ago, Russia lay
trampled in the mud by the Germans,
you Poles did not hesitate to invade her;
eighty years ago you wanted to declare
Kiev itself a Polish city!

SIKORSKI: You are forgetting what the Russians have been doing
to us for centuries. *I* have never thought
the Kremlin would bring anything but harm
to Poland, not before Katyn, not after.

P.M.: I know of no nation on earth that benefits another
beyond the limits of its own self-interest.
Excellency, Stalin's demands are reasonable.
They are reasonable.
All he demands from Germany is Königsberg.
All he demands from Poland are the provinces
she took from Russia—twenty years ago.
Give up Lvov—for Breslau.

SIKORSKI *almost staggers under the finality of this pronouncement.
He leans against the life raft. His voice is weak, and he hides his
emotion under a lack of emphasis.*

[SIKORSKI: Mr. Churchill, *understand* us.
Lvov is the homeland of countless of my soldiers.

What would you say, were someone to demand
the secession of Scotland—

P.M. (*sadly, simply, compassionately*): *We* have a good tank trap.

Pause. He nods to SIKORSKI *without speaking, a movement of the hand, as if to say, "Geography is the decisive factor."*

SIKORSKI (*tormented and unjust*):
Just eighty years ago, the year of the Polish uprising
against Russia and Prussia,
when the leader of the Polish *émigrés* in London
was begging Downing Street for help, *your* predecessor
said: "We are talking about politics, not humanity."
And when *my* predecessor reminded him
that England had helped the Belgians and the Greeks
in their struggles for freedom, Palmerston brushed it aside.
The Dutchman and the Turk had both been weak,
the Russians, on the other hand, were strong.

Transferring his bitterness to the chair, the PRIME MINISTER *walks around the chair and the General, his chin sunk on his chest; one is reminded of a stag rubbing its antlers against a tree.*

P.M.: *One* difference between Palmerston and me:
no one, not even Hitler, has *forced* us
to save Poland, and with her the balance of Europe,
from the hegemony of Berlin.
I am supporting the rebuilding of a strong Poland
at the expense of German territory—
SIKORSKI: I am *afraid* of this compensation, Mr. Churchill.
Our peasants say no chicken costs one dearer
than the one you receive as a gift.
The Polish press in exile in London—
P.M.: Sikorski—please—a statesman
who listens to the press in wartime
instead of making it listen to him!]
To go along with them, *that*—forgive me—
anyone can do.
SIKORSKI: I could demand much from the Polish press in London,
before the mass graves were discovered.
Now my people are demanding a guarantee that—
P.M.: I ask you in the name of our common task—

the overthrow of Hitler—
be silent about Katyn.
Postpone the investigation—I entreat you.
Not in this terrible year.

The PRIME MINISTER *goes over to the* GENERAL, *his hand actually extended, in "entreaty."* SIKORSKI *draws back. He is agitated because of what* CHURCHILL *is demanding of him, more so because he cannot—any longer—grant it. He mutters:*

SIKORSKI: Too late—it is too late, Mr. Churchill.

CHURCHILL *for the first time looks pale and alarmed. He tries to bridge the gap as usual, but cannot, as the Polish General announces formally:*

Prime Minister, I have to inform you officially in
the name of the Polish government-in-exile
that my ambassadors, this morning,
demanded from the International Red Cross in Geneva
a full investigation of the graves at Katyn.

It seems as if the PRIME MINISTER *wants to throw himself at him, to prevent anything further happening. He is holding on to the back of his chair; in his haste he picks up the whole chair, holding it like a walking stick.*

P.M. (*a great cry*): No!—No!—No!

His fury must be directed at something. He flings the chair from him; it flies over to the railing and smashes.
    Silence.
    SIKORSKI *is deeply affected. He would like to say something, but does not dare to.* CHURCHILL *has turned his back on him—now he turns to face the Pole again, but without looking at him, and speaks, with painful composure, articulating the words with unnatural clarity.*

P.M.: The International Red Cross
    is bound to absolute neutrality.
    His Majesty's Government will remind Geneva
    that investigation of the mass graves at Katyn
    cannot be permitted while the forests around Smolensk
    continue to be held by German military units.

He looks up, but avoids meeting SIKORSKI's *eyes. The Pole, to obviate the impossible situation of a Head of State being dismissed, salutes, as if at a graveside, turns without a word, and goes. His walk, earlier that of a cavalry officer, is now stiff and heavy. He goes hesitantly toward the companionway. At the last moment, as he puts his foot on the bottom step,* CHURCHILL *controls himself and speaks quietly:*

Sikorski.

SIKORSKI *turns and makes a gesture with both hands, his arms slack, signifying utter hopelessness.* CHURCHILL *takes a step forward to the waiting man, then—*

We are in the same boat, Excellency.
SIKORSKI (*harder than* CHURCHILL):
What more do you want, Prime Minister?
Poland's elite—in ashes,
ready to shake hands with the murderers . . .
P.M.: Shake hands with me.
SIKORSKI: —ready to give them half of Poland too. Half.
P.M. (*a calculating machine, but sadly, warning*):
Stalin is waiting, either for me to drop you
or for you to break off relations with the Kremlin.
Either way he will no longer need to treat with you, Excellency.
But Hitler hopes that I shall keep you—
to use *against* the Kremlin—
he speculates upon the undermining
of our great coalition.
[Each time you, General, appear in person in the Kremlin,
you remind them of the Red Army's first major defeat.]
SIKORSKI: Am I in your way, or in my country's?
P.M. (*violently, determined that every word that is uttered here and now shall be kept under control*): Rubbish—in the way.
But let us be loyal—
SIKORSKI (*bitterly*): To country or to men?
P.M.: To one another.
You are stabbing me in the back, Excellency—once again.
Now in Geneva, lately in Washington—
contrary to my own denial to the Russians,
you have induced the President
not to discuss the Polish frontier question.

SIKORSKI (*hurt, but playing a high card*): That is *my* loyalty!
Otherwise it would have been better
if I *had* been killed
on the flight to the White House,
in Montreal, when all four engines failed at once.

P.M. (*again the clutching gesture between neck and collar*):
A villainous trick of fate, your crash—
no question, be careful, do not fly around so much.

SIKORSKI: But you said I should fly to my regiments in Persia.

P.M.: Yes, but make sure you have at least one important
Englishman on board—*not*
(*laughs*) to keep an eye on you, but so that
our Intelligence will be more careful.

SIKORSKI: Prime Minister, it was your own machine in Montreal!
British Intelligence would have done its best.
(*Making an effort to smile.*)
An engine is, in the end, no more reliable than a human
heart.
Let us not talk about me, but about Poland!

He has pulled a foolscap sheet of paper from his pocket, and holds it out to the PRIME MINISTER, *with a childlike trust in the value of contracts.*

Confirm that the Russo-Polish frontiers will not be discussed
before the victory over Hitler.
Your signature—is our last bulwark against the Kremlin.

P.M. (*heated, decisive*): I am sorry, General, I repeat:
no Englishman, no American, no Pole,
no single one of any of us
has so much as set foot on the Continent.
Why should Stalin let us tie his hands
regarding European frontier questions?
—since, from his point of view, we are not even
fighting a European war at all.

[SIKORSKI *is annihilated, since he sees the absolute cogency of* CHURCHILL's *argument. A last attempt.*

SIKORSKI: And were I to follow *your* wishes,
to forgo the investigation of the graves of Katyn? . . .

P.M. (*icy*): *My* wish?—Reason alone, General,
commands you to do it,

unless you wish to do Stalin the favor
of no longer obliging him to deal with you.]
Tear up that paper there—or else . . .

Silence. The Pole controls himself—a superhuman effort. Suddenly, as if he would otherwise say something irrevocable, he turns abruptly away, tears the paper slowly in two, and goes to the railing, like a man who is in no hurry since there is nothing more for him to lose. The PRIME MINISTER *takes a step after him. The Pole is no longer an opponent, but a man who awakens compassion.*

P.M.: No—don't tear it.
Give it to *me,* Sikorski.

SIKORSKI *turns, looks at* CHURCHILL, *holds out the two halves of the paper in both hands, as if he were surrendering. He smiles wryly, then, brusquely:*

SIKORSKI: All that is left—
two scraps—like Poland.
P.M. (*moved, approaches him*):
We will put them together somehow . . .
and keep them.
SIKORSKI (*without enmity*): In the British archives—
they may as well be scattered in the North Sea.
P.M.: Excellency—your struggle is not in any way diminished
because you must give in to *force majeure.*

SIKORSKI *looks past him, as he holds out the torn paper.* CHURCHILL, *deeply moved, takes it from his hands, folds and puts it into his pocket.*

SIKORSKI *speaks harshly, with a touch of quixotry, dragging out each word:*

SIKORSKI: That I have been defeated—may be true,
but, since it is not *right,* I shall fight on.

The Pole now understands that the Englishman, the poet who could not restrain his tears at the sound of bagpipes or at the christening of his grandchild ("poor infant, to be born into such a world as this"), also possesses the hardness of granite. La Rochefoucauld points out that passions often engender and nourish directly opposing passions—so weakness can produce obstinacy;

fear, cunning; parsimony, waste. CHURCHILL's *present striking gentleness and patience, with one of the few men in his own camp whom he cannot talk around, are perhaps conditioned by circumstances which will soon give Marshal Stalin occasion to remark to an American diplomat, in confidence and a spirit of amiable blackmail, that the British should not concern themselves with the Poles, as he was quite willing "to do everything to smooth Churchill's path out of an uncomfortable situation, since it would look very bad for the British, were all the details to emerge . . ."*

It is not the coolness of the approaching night that makes the Pole shiver, but the final unavoidable recognition that the British Prime Minister can no more help Poland than the Poles can themselves. The cavalryman finally realizes that he and his people are condemned always to fight on horses, not in tanks. The only thing which still holds him upright is the knowledge that he will be a victim of this struggle, which was decided before it began. All charm has deserted this Supreme Commander of a massacred officer caste. It is no longer the tragic knightly figure who stands before CHURCHILL, *who was to comment, seven years later: "In the dismal wars of modern democracy there is no place for chivalry."*

CHURCHILL's *face is like a rain-swept rock. Pause. Then:*

SIKORSKI (*as if* CHURCHILL *still had a choice in the matter*):
    You are elevating Russia to a power so great—
    and this time, Britain too will have to pay.

P.M. (*now it is he who raises his arms, but with great calm*):
    Sikorski—what can we know of the tides of history?
    Even the grandeur that was Rome lasted three centuries only.
    [The breath of history—leveling as a monsoon . . .
    Your native soil of Poland will become dust,
      driven before the squalls that blow from the eastern
        steppes—
    unless she shelters beneath the Kremlin's walls.

SIKORSKI: Never, while I am her leader.

P.M. (*leaning against the stanchion, fighting down the "black dog," as he called the chronic melancholia of the Marlboroughs*):
    Loyalty, tears, deeds—
    before the demons in the arena of power,
    these all collapse, like justice—in a gale of laughter.]

Excellency—I have only ever dreamed of *facts*—
my visions were all quite without imagination—
and this too is exact, no more:
If you do not acquiesce, then Poland will
be no more—no more than a bloody mire
on the tracks of the tanks of the armies of Russia.

SIKORSKI *tries to catch* CHURCHILL's *eye, but without success: the Englishman looks away.* SIKORSKI *salutes, goes out. Only then does* CHURCHILL *look up, after him. The fighters roar very low over the water, now almost as dark as the sky.*

CURTAIN

THE BED

In affairs he had that ruthless side without
which great matters cannot be handled . . .
he repeated to me Mr. Gladstone's saying:
"The first essential for a Prime Minister
is to be a good butcher," and he added,
"There are several who must be pole-axed
now."
    They were. Loyal as he was to his
colleagues, he never shrank, when the
time came and public need required it, from
putting them aside once and for all . . .
But how else can states be governed?
                —Churchill on Asquith

The world felt . . . that here was someone
who stood outside its jurisdiction.
                      —Churchill

*That the two most important areas where man expends his vital
energies, the bed and the battlefield, are impossible to represent
on the stage is a piece of good fortune from an aesthetic point
of view. But it is not merely a question of externals. One should
rather see, in this limitation, how decisively the experiences which
determine life escape the artist—and the historian. Perhaps some
doctors know—things which are as hardly susceptible of description or demonstration as a human soul, a tree, or the inner pre-
dilections of the man of action which once more write their
message on the wall, warning man against man.*

*What can be documented, the debris of certain facts—however
suitably they may be arranged for the theater—leads not only
historians to what Burckhardt called "a diligence which destroys
the instinct of religion." Ranke, obsessed as no one before with
facts, and still—at least at twenty-nine—convinced he could
"simply show how it happened," later, in spite of this confidence,
added the proviso: "Theology comes into it as well."*

We must be content to say "mystery."

*However, it is not when the past speaks that it allows room for
hope, but when it is silent. It is not what man can do—but the
fact that there are certain things he cannot do that makes him
tolerable.*

*Mystery—in the unhappiest sense of the word—compels us now
to the consideration of the dark events put forward in this act.
For it is a question of a secret service "operation," of which there
is probably no trace to be found in any history book, because it
demonstrates to our era, more alarmingly than any other event,
that a compulsion to evil is an essential element of the good, if it
wishes to be strong.*

*Attlee would have been as incapable of ridding the world of
Hitler as the German General von Beck was. Churchill was able
to do it, not only because as Moran puts it, his "genius was like
a bull elephant, trampling down everything that stood in its path,"
but because he was prepared to trample down certain things which
were not in his path. The qualities are mutually conditional: the
qualities of a Noah (the Hebrew means "man of rest"), which
CHURCHILL possessed in 1940, performing the salvage work of a
warrior and statesman on an apparently sinking vessel, and the
ambition of an Alcibiades, with which, at thirty-eight, First Sea
Lord and leader of the greatest armada in history, he drew England
into war in 1914.*

123

To do evil, that good may come about—it would be banal to point out that this is itself a platitude. Further, it is a platitude distorted and colored by professional attitudes to the same extent as the truism which states that political history, like love stories, keeps back the things that are really worth writing about. Fontane said one should never print love letters, since "no one ever gets to see the best ones." But how colossal is the professional researcher's optimistic faith in documents, even—to take one example—even after the defeats they have had to accept, since 1933, in investigating the Reichstag fire. Perhaps the available, but uncommunicative, television films of the assassination of President Kennedy, and indeed of the man who may possibly have shot at him, might—temporarily—bring about a victory of skepticism over a slavish belief in "sources." What is the value of witnesses, compared to the coincidence that not only Oswald, the supposed killer of Kennedy, but also Booth, the supposed killer of Lincoln, were themselves both shot—before being brought to trial?

Jaspers emphasizes that "the calamity of human existence begins when that which is scientifically known is taken for existence itself; when everything that is not scientifically knowable, is held not to exist." Or not to have happened: even official sources admit that the majority of the papers of the "Old Firm" were destroyed after the war.

Do the documents merit closer attention than the gaps? The relation of the document, if one may believe it, to the fact is that of the fragment to the whole vase. It is the man who, from the start, describes his history of Germany as a "story" who awakens one's confidence. Even Ranke spoke of the "legend of world history." Lytton Strachey wrote that dreams were the real stuff of historical science. If one looks through the pile of memoirs of the three leading Englishmen, the Prime Minister, the Foreign Secretary, and the Chief of the Imperial General Staff, and all other leading figures, for mentions of Sir Percy Sillitoe, and Generals Menzies and Gubbins, one is forced to the conclusion that these three terrible lords of the underworld of His Majesty's Servants never existed.

Bismarck's ironic disinclination to believe anything that could be read came from personal experience: "When one thinks how successfully one can lie about political events which lie only three years in the past . . ." He warned "never to confide in paper." Had Hitler not driven out his intelligentsia—in other words, had

*he possessed the atomic bomb—there would be no book in exist-
ence in which Auschwitz would be mentioned even as a footnote.*
CHURCHILL *said in 1943 that "it was foolish to keep a day-to-day
diary because it would simply reflect the change of opinion or
decision of the writer which, when and if published, makes one
appear indecisive and foolish. . . . For his part . . . he would much
prefer to wait till after the war is over . . . so that, if necessary,
he could correct or bury his mistakes."*

*Even his enormous memory breaks down completely, when it
comes to the work of a man like William Stephenson. This quiet
Canadian, a businessman and a millionaire, whom* CHURCHILL
*received in the Admiralty (he had not found time to move to
Downing Street, but found time for Stephenson) to send him to
New York "for the coordination of the work of the British and
American intelligence services," was the first foreigner to receive,
in 1945, from the President, the highest civilian award of America. The head of the FBI wrote to him: "Your contribution to the
victory of the Allies will be considered as of the highest signifi-
cance, when one is able to speak of these things," and* CHURCHILL
*recommended him for a knighthood with the words, "This man
means a great deal to me."*

*He could not, however, mention him in the twelve volumes of
his history of the war, since the time never comes when "one is
able to speak of these things." In any event, not when one is one's
self responsible for them. In contrast, in the First World War,
when* CHURCHILL *was simply head of a department or even forced
into private life, he was capable of confessing openly enough
whom and what he admired. None more than Balfour: "Never has
England had a more convincing or more energetic Ambassador
Extraordinary." At his death,* CHURCHILL *wrote of this man, who
"stood out so far from the ordinary," and of the tragedy "which
robbed the world of all the wisdom and the treasures gathered in
the life and experience of a great man." For three decades*
CHURCHILL *regarded and learned from this statesman: "Nothing
is more instructive than to follow the dispassionate, cool, polite,
and at the same time, ruthless manner in which Balfour changed
from one cabinet to another, from the Prime Minister who had
been his hero, to the one who had been his severest critic; like a
strong, graceful cat crossing a filthy street, carefully, without getting dirty . . . he [never] let . . . personal friendship, however
sealed and cemented, hamper his solutions of the problems of*

state . . . he would not have been required to read the works of Machiavelli. Had he lived in the French Revolution he would, when it was found absolutely necessary, have consigned . . . even an erring colleague to the guillotine, with much complacency."

As the chronicler of the struggle to bring down Hitler, CHURCH-ILL *is no longer so candid. It is unthinkable that he should have admitted, as he did of the First World War: "In the higher reaches of the Intelligence Service, the events in many cases resembled closely the fantastic inventions of romance and sensational fiction. Confusion within confusion, betrayal and counter-betrayal, genuine agents, false agents, agents working for both sides, gold and steel, bombs, daggers, and the firing squad: everything was often so inextricably entangled that it was hardly believable and yet it was true. The head and the high functionaries of the Intelligence Service romped about this underground labyrinth and, amid the hub-bub of war, went about their business with cold, quiet intensity."*

But even if, in CHURCHILL's *view, British Intelligence at this period "achieved greater triumphs than that of any other power, hostile, allied or neutral," the former Prime Minister, apropos of the Second World War, only mentions pieces of information which often did not even come in on time. In the case of the more interesting reports, he ordered Major Sir Desmond Morton to bring him the actual reports, not simply the evaluations made of them.*

On the occasions when the military men were assisted by the more innocent activities of the "Old Firm" or Cover Plan Branch —and the soldiers did not get to know of the less innocent—they are happy to mention them in their memoirs. Rommel, a cunning man himself, was on at least two occasions decisively outwitted in the desert.

Lieutenant General Sir Brian Horrocks *tells, and* CHURCHILL *confirms, that the talkative German General von Thoma, when taken prisoner, bemoaned the success of the subterfuge: "To ease Rommel's decision . . . Montgomery's Chief of Staff, Guingand, completely altered the aforementioned charts, which showed the condition of the roads behind the British lines. The trucks were driven into a German minefield. A few mines were exploded, so that the truck was damaged, then the patrol retired and watched . . . a German reconnaissance patrol searched the truck and found the maps. They were used as a basis of a plan of attack . . . and had a significant bearing on the course of the Battle of Alam*

Halfa." Rommel's tanks were caught in quicksands, and the Germans lost the initiative in the desert for good.

Captain Roskill relates how the body of a gardener, in naval officer's uniform and carrying important papers was "released" from a submarine off the Spanish-Portuguese coast, and fell, as expected, into the hands of German agents, diverting attention from the Sicilian invasion. (That an Intelligence Service should make use of dead bodies is unusual: for the most part they are occupied in providing them.)

But this is not science, this is theater, and the only thing that gives one courage is that between the reality of which the stage by its very nature can only reproduce a modest reflection, between history and ourselves, we can place the actor.

CHURCHILL asks, more than any other single figure in the history of our time, for this sort of stylization. And not merely because of his delight in picturesque disguises, which could lead him to make plans, to the horror of his bodyguards, to sally forth "disguised as an Egyptian demi-mondaine or an Armenian with the toothache." "To perform on the stage of history" was CHURCHILL's very reason for living. He was fond of talking of "the theater of mankind"; and Heinrich Mann, in 1943, the period of the play's action, saw in CHURCHILL "a hero out of Corneille, wearing the mask of our time." The bedroom, therefore, like the ship in Act One, should emphasize rather than conceal the fact that we are in a theater.

In 1939, an hour after England had declared war, when Chamberlain telephoned him to ask him to return to the Admiralty, CHURCHILL wept, overcome at having found his mission once again. (Cassandra herself would have been considered an idiot, had her prophecies not come true.)

"What are you going to do?" asked his daughter.

"I'm going to bed," he answered, since it was midday, and it was as important for him—as he repeatedly described, with the tender concern which he always showed for his own person—to sleep well, wherever and whenever necessary, as to be well fed. Only later did he hurry to the Admiralty—"The 'Bremen' is on the high seas, and we are going to get her."

The bed played an immeasurable part in the life of the man who has left, both as man of action and author, the most distinct mark on our times. Even in the Houses of Parliament he had a *bed, and not just any bed, but a thing like a royal catafalque. In the Savoy Hotel there was one too, since, when he was leader of the Opposition, he ate there every week. The bed which accompanied him electioneering was so enormous that, in order to get it onto a train, they had to remove the sides of the freight truck. If it happened that he was obliged to use an aircraft without a bed, then he pulled a black "velvet cloth or handkerchief out of his pocket, and covered his eyes. The effect was amazing. He fell asleep at once and only awoke when the airplane was running along the landing strip at Heliopolis."*

To the paradox, that historical happenings often have the opposite effect to that which they were intended to produce, one may here add a comic rider: that the man who is among the half-dozen in our century who have set the largest numbers of men in motion, set loose these tempests in time and space while sitting in bed, motionless as a Buddha.

To the realm of the bed also belongs the confession, at which one shudders, that he could only remember one night when sleep had deserted him. His doctor says CHURCHILL *exaggerates here— let us hope so. For there were nights, nevertheless, when at his command the invasion fleet steered toward Hitler's batteries on the French coast, when the fleet of France, the former ally, had to be destroyed, nights too, when tens of thousands of civilians were transformed into torches of fire. "In my long life," he dictated, never weary of the spectacle of himself, "I have experienced many ups and downs. During the whole of the war, even in the most difficult days, I never suffered from sleeplessness. I always managed to sleep deeply and awake refreshed, without any other feelings than a sort of joyful anticipation of getting to grips with what the morning's post had brought. That night, however, of February 20, 1938, for the only time, sleep deserted me."* CHURCHILL *had been informed late that evening that Eden had resigned as Foreign Minister because of the softness of Chamberlain's cabinet toward Hitler. "From midnight till dawn I consumed myself with torment and worry. . . . I saw through the window the day slowly rising, and in my mind's eye stood the figure of Death."*

It was in bed, too, that he received what was probably his most fearful telephone call: "The First Sea Lord. His voice sounded strange. I heard something like choking and a sob, and to begin with I could hardly understand. 'Prime Minister, I have to report that the "Prince of Wales" and the "Repulse" have been sunk by the Japanese—it is believed, by aerial attack . . . .' I put the receiver down, grateful that no one was with me. In the whole war, no blow came more unexpectedly. . . . But it was only when I turned over in bed, that the full appalling import of the news struck me. In neither the Indian nor the Pacific Ocean was there a British or an American battleship."

Even twelve years later, after the stroke which "nearly cost him his life," says Lord Moran, "Winston told me he had had a bad dream. I asked him what it was. But he could not bring himself to speak of it. For a long time he said nothing, then he turned to me: 'Do you know anything about dreams? You remember when the "Prince of Wales" and the "Repulse" were sunk?' He could not speak further, and seemed so agitated that I feared another stroke." (Roskill states that all advisers had warned repeatedly against sending the two battleships to the Pacific.) A month after the sinking, Moran noted: "I sometimes wonder whether the P.M. realizes how hard the decisions weigh which he has to take . . . it is as if Winston had a family of twelve children and not enough to eat for all of them. Some of them must go hungry. And he must decide which."

Every picture of CHURCHILL *that one comes across deepens the mystery of this figure.*

Thomas Mann realized that the demonic is something one can only intimate, not describe; CHURCHILL's *Chief of Staff had realized, during the war, the impossibility of "portraying Winston truly," and he pitied the historians of the future. In 1943 he painted the following picture, in Cairo, which doubtless does not belong in any history book, but which nevertheless is more evocative than countless documents.*

" . . . ordered for a tête-à-tête with the P.M. We lunched in the garden: he was looking very tired, and said he felt very flat, tired, and pains across his loins. However, he killed flies with his fly swatter throughout the lunch and counted the corpses. . . . Half-way through lunch he asked me whether I did not think I had better be made a Field Marshal . . . ! I shall always remember that lunch as a bad nightmare. He was dressed in his gray zip-suit . . . and his best Mexican hat . . . we . . . were served . . . by two Egyptian liveried waiters. . . . After two spoonfuls of soup he started discussing the question of the command of the Mediterranean . . . 'It is all quite simple, there are . . .' Then down came

the fly swatter with a crash, and a fly corpse was collected and placed in a fly mortuary near the corner of the table. He then had two more spoonfuls of soup, and said: 'This is the most delicious soup,' followed by another spoonful. He then started again: 'As I was saying, it is all quite simple, there are just three areas . . .' Crash, down came the fly swatter and another corpse was conveyed to the mortuary!

"This procedure went on through most of the lunch but we never got beyond the 'three areas' before having to convey another fly to the mortuary. The interesting part was that there were not 'three areas' in this problem of command, yet I knew well that in his present condition it was impossible to make him grasp this fact. I let him go on killing flies . . ."

That is Theater of the Absurd, while those plays which are at present so called are mostly not absurd at all, but pointless, more often than not wretched copies of Maeterlinck's The Blind *or* The Intruder. *The existence and the decease of man in history is absurd. And so is his hope, in spite of history.*

If a performer brings out the comic aspects of these details, he must not thereby conceal the awe-inspiring quality displayed by such a man in his every remark even in moments of cheerfulness. The atmospheric pressure must be felt all the time, which CHURCHILL's *presence produced, even in a small "intimate" circle: "No one dared to pursue a conversation which did not appear to have his approval, no one dared say anything. Many guests would have found it easier to talk to royalty," writes Virginia Cowles, who frequently lunched in Downing Street with four or five other guests. The guests were also silent, naturally, when he recited poems or sang soldiers' songs, and they looked on "without, astonishingly, a trace of embarrassment," as the old man wept silently into his dessert.*

Here we see him as BROOKE *was accustomed to see him in the mornings, "sitting in bed, a pile of cushions at his back, his magnificent head disheveled, a cigar in his mouth. Beside him, the empty breakfast tray. The bed strewn with papers and despatches. The red-and-gold dragon dressing gown in itself was worth going miles to see, and only Winston could have thought of wearing it. He looked rather like some Chinese Mandarin . . . This bell was continually being rung for secretaries, typists, stenographers, or his faithful valet, Sawyers."*

*Beside the bed is a large Victorian folding table on which stand
three telephones of various colors. At the window is* LORD CHER-
WELL: *dark suit, jacket open, finger tips in his waistcoat pocket.*

CHURCHILL, *his elbows cushioned on two large sponges, to
avoid rubbing them raw, lights the only cigar smoked in this play:
he takes off the band, pierces the formidable object with a special
match, warms the end of the cigar, wraps a strip of brown gummed
paper around it—("The band, Norman," he explained to a servant,
"prevents the juice from running down.")—and smokes away—*

*The C.I.G.S. is silent for a quarter of a minute after the rise of
the curtain, while* HELEN *is taking out the breakfast tray along
with all the newspapers which have already been read, some of
which are on the carpet; then* BROOKE *takes advantage of a moment when the* PRIME MINISTER *cannot, for once, interrupt him,
to voice a contradiction, quickly, vehemently, and like an engine
revving up:*

BROOKE: No, Sir!—not North Sumatra.
  [What is the point of bombing Singapore?
  And other operations in Malaya
  are not to be started from the North Point.]
  We need every man we've got in the Mediterranean.
  What can we achieve in the jungle?
P.M.: Jungle? Who said anything about a jungle campaign?
  If you want to kill a shark
  you don't go into the water after it.
  [Do you think I've forgotten Wavell's Burma campaign?
  Only a fool learns from experience;
  a wise man from the experience of others.
  Never again in the jungle.]
  Just a bridgehead at the North Point.
  (*To* CHERWELL:)
  Don't go, Prof.: we must talk about the rockets—
  (*To* BROOKE, *with intensity:*)
  At last a first step toward
  the resurrection of the empire in Asia.
BROOKE (*furious*):
  And the landing craft?—We haven't any for Asia.
[P.M. (*coming around*): Now is not the time
  for using the usual storming and landing craft.
  Brookie—can we not use these kayaks that the Turks have,

between ship and shore?
BROOKE: If we had any!
I repeat:]
We need every ship we've got in the Mediterranean.
P.M. (*seething inside, till the volcano erupts*):
When—tell me, C.I.G.S., when is Salerno, then?
Where were you last night at one o'clock?
No one could reach you on the telephone
—it was . . . reported to me from Alexander's headquarters
that the *six* divisions for Naples could not land
in Salerno before the first of December.
Out of the question.
That is the sheerest defeatism.
What are they supposed to be doing all that time?
Sicily is a springboard, not a sofa!
BROOKE: Prime Minister, your information did not come
through the proper channels; how did you come by it?
It is not true.
P.M.: What? I consult whom I please. Untrue?
I consult whom I please—whom I please,
that is whom I consult.
BROOKE: Of course. Only it is not December;
according to my plan, we shall be in Salerno
on the ninth of September.
P.M.: In any case, C.I.G.S., I shall not permit
us to crawl up the leg, like a harvest bug,
from the ankle upward!
Let us rather strike at the knee, and at once.
BROOKE: Agreed, Sir: Salerno is the knee.
P.M.: Rome is the knee, where men go on their knees.
Ostia—the *only* beach for landing craft.
BROOKE: Impossible, Sir: far too far.
[P.M.: How did MacArthur land in New Guinea?
Stroke of genius: knights' moves only,
and every jump right on top of the Japs.
Amazing!
BROOKE: To be sure—MacArthur got what he needed.
For every aircraft carrier we have to fight
harder with Washington than with Hitler.
The Sicilian landing fields are too far for our fighter escorts.]
P.M. (*irritated*): —You are demanding too much safety:

if you knock a nail in up to the head,
you can't hang your hat on it.
Safety lies in surprise.
Prof., has anything occurred to Intelligence?

CHERWELL: Prime Minister, two thousand five hundred and ninety
    ships
are steering toward Sicily,
the effect lies in their strength, not in surprise.
The German air reconnaissance must be made to think
that Malta is the one magnetic point
to which all convoys are being attracted.

P.M. (*anxiously*):Precisely—the assembly of the fleets at Malta;
the fact however, that they are heading for *Sicily,*
and not for Corsica or Sardinia,
that must be camouflaged with some device.

CHERWELL: "C" wants to get hold of some gardener
who is going to die in a day or two:
we shall promote the body to the rank of Major
and eject him from a submarine off the Spanish coast.
[The Iberian peninsula is more or less
rented by Canaris's bully-boys.]
Our deceased friend will be washed into the Germans' laps—
and discreetly deliver the letters which we
shall have placed in his breast pocket.

[P.M.: Codeword?
CHERWELL: Operation Mincemeat.

BROOKE *has pressed a bell,* HELEN *enters, he gives her a note,
without speaking.* BROOKE *sits, quickly writing another note; inter-
jects:*

BROOKE: Highly optimistic.]
P.M.: Have you tested the maximum length of time
the body may remain in the water
without the letters becoming illegible?

CHERWELL: The "floating body" in Cadiz, last November,
had made the fishes happy for days—
and his letters were still readable.

P.M. (*sitting up, anxiously*): Wait!—Prof., even I know this:
any doctor will see
that the body was not drowned, if the lungs . . .

CHERWELL (*piqued*): Please, Winston—we shall imply that he
    crashed. That he died on the impact of the courier aircraft.
    When we've dressed the body up,
    he must fall out of an aircraft into the water.
    Then we put him in cold storage
    till he goes on board the submarine.

P.M.: Cold storage? How comforting—what's in his letters?

CHERWELL: The Admiralty will be writing to Cunningham in
        Algiers,
    that, according to the agreement with the army,
    the actual landing grounds
    are only to be shelled and bombed in moderation
    so as not to indicate them to the Germans—
    on the other hand, they write, Sicily,
    and Syracuse in particular,
    are to be subjected to heavy attack.

P.M.: Fine. Syracuse. The first port we actually take. Good.

CHERWELL: When the Germans read the letters
    they will take *Corsica* for the invasion point
    and perhaps move more troops there from Sicily.

BROOKE: Pray Heaven we do not underestimate the Boche's
        cunning.

[P.M.: C.I.G.S., Hitler's generals are doing
    almost as much as our own to help us win the war.
    That von Thoma—astonishing.
    (*Roaring.*)
    Helen!

CHERWELL: The oldest old hat in the Intelligence repertoire
    is just the right size for a German blockhead:
    they chatter away in the POW camps
    as if they were in their hunting lodges—
    tacticians of the bridge table.

HELEN (*entering with notebook*): Sir?

P.M. (*his face becoming round as the moon with amusement*):
    There you are—just a note for the next cable to Washington.
    In the course of certain remarks made by the
    German General von Thoma, our prisoner of war,
    and monitored by us, he has not only stated
    that he has already seen Hitler's rockets
    in the air but implemented this with the

remark: "Our only hope is that they . . ."
how did it go, Prof.?

CHERWELL (*continuing the dictation*):
". . . that they come, where we can use the army upon
them."

HELEN *waits till the conversation shows she is no longer needed.*

P.M. (*nods to* BROOKE, *thinking of the undertaking which causes
him so much anxiety, pensive. He whistles through his teeth*):
". . . where we can use the army upon them."
Brooke, how can we make Roosevelt understand
that we shall *not* be in Berlin sooner,
because we shall be in Calais sooner?
The President sees the invasion as the first straight to the jaw.
I see it as the last.

BROOKE: You gave too much away, alas, Sir, not long ago
when Roosevelt sent Stimson to snuffle around.
The White House is now afraid you want to avoid
the Channel crossing next year as well.

P.M. (*angry*): Do they blame me for that?
The landing will bloody the Straits of Dover
like the gully of a slaughterhouse—
Brookie, I do not want you and me
to go down in history like the butchers
of the First War. *Sixty thousand* English dead,
wounded taken prisoner, in a single day,
I will not have such an obscenity laid at my door.
Why do we have the Red Army and the bombers,
if not for that?

BROOKE: It is no use, Stimson has rung the alarm:
the White House regards me as a defeatist.

P.M.: They do you honor.
Stimson, Stimson—don't tell me about that "icicle."
He recited his motto to me the other day:
(*He recites, in an idiotic singsong, in cheerful imitation.*)
"The man who tries to work for the good, believing
in its eventual victory, while he may suffer
setback, and even disaster, will never know
defeat. The only deadly sin I know, is cynicism."

*Actually, the U.S. Secretary of Defense held so firmly to this motto,
that two years later, at the age of seventy-eight, he was the main*

and keenest advocate of the dropping of the two atomic bombs. He was arguably the most coldly calculating of all the war criminals not on the German side, since he concealed from Oppenheimer and other of his henchmen the fact that Japan had already taken the first steps toward surrender negotiations.

CHERWELL (*has to moderate his amusement by taking a pill*):
Winston—where should we all be without these industrious cretins?

BROOKE: Roosevelt says old dogs hunt best.

P.M. (*tired*):
Nearly eighty years old and still optimistic—disgusting.
The fact that we shall *have* to risk
an apocalyptic rebuff in the Channel
or the Kremlin will otherwise bow out of the war,
is something that vulgar little solicitor
might have the grace to think about as tragic.

CHERWELL (*as if the* PRIME MINISTER'*s demands were too absurd*):
Tragic—the word does not yet exist in America.
They call it migraine.

P.M. (*sighing like a grampus*):
Aaaaah—we shall pay for it in France next year
if we do not test the floating harbors now in Sicily.

CHERWELL: We can't go hauling harbors through the Mediterranean.

BROOKE: That is why Syracuse must fall in twenty-four hours.
We need seven hundred tons of supplies per division per day.

P.M.: Reckless—to assume the harbors will fall to us so fast.
In France it is out of the question.
The invasion there will drown if we do not
bring two harbors with us.

BROOKE (*impatient*): Your harbors will be ready.

P.M. (*puts his cigar down, to demonstrate how the harbors—like the tank, his idea, if not his actual invention—should rise and fall with the tides*):
The piers *must* float up and down with the tide,
move up and down with the tide.
The anchor problem must be mastered.
The ships must have a side-flap cut in them
and a drawbridge long enough to overreach the moorings of the piers.

Don't argue the matter! The difficulties will argue for themselves.

BROOKE: The possibility of surprise is not to be excluded.
The maximum difference between ebb and flow
in the Channel is more than eighteen feet.
And the Channel weather is, after all,
not the most easily predictable.

CHERWELL: I prefer concrete construction to pontoons
for the breakwaters—you know where you are with it.]

BROOKE (*with extreme impatience*):
Now I really must get back to my desk, Sir.

P.M.: Yes—no: hear what the Prof. has to say about Hitler's
rockets—

CHERWELL: Sir Alan has been informed.

P.M.: Thank you, then we have finished, C.I.G.S.
—what's that you have?—wait a moment.

BROOKE, *already at the door, is called back as* HELEN *enters and
silently passes a cable to the* PRIME MINISTER.

From the President: he is most anxious
Rome be declared an open city.

CHERWELL *laughs, as at an indiscretion.* CHURCHILL *drains his
glass, holds it out to the Second Officer, looking at* CHERWELL
and BROOKE. HELEN *pours whisky and soda.*

[CHERWELL (*angrily*): Put him off, put him off:
The whole question of open cities is one that only frightens
clergymen.]

P.M. (*amused*): It all comes of writing letters to the Holy Father.
Me he cannot abide:
I find it infinitely more agreeable.
Helen, give the C.I.G.S. a drink.

HELEN (*to the teetotaler* CHERWELL, *as she pours* BROOKE *a drink*):
Ice water, Sir?

CHERWELL *shakes his head, and smiles. The* PRIME MINISTER
raises his glass to BROOKE, *hands the cable to* HELEN.

P.M. . . . such ideas, hm!
Take that water bottle out of my sight,
it depresses me to look at it, too depressing.

HELEN *leaves with cable and carafe. The* PRIME MINISTER *calls after her.*

> Rome: last point on today's agenda.
> Where have the photographs of Gomorrah got to?

HELEN (*coming back*): They're on their way, Sir.
> (*She goes out.*)

P.M. (*to* BROOKE, *who is drinking his whisky*):
> *Ideas!* The Americans were lately of the opinion
> that we should depose the monarchy in Italy—
> as if the little King were not
> the ideal bootjack for the Allies.
> [Helen—basket!

As frequently happened, the wastepaper basket is once more on fire. The PRIME MINISTER *has raised his voice slightly on account of this by no means minor conflagration caused by his misplacing his half-smoked cigar in the wrong receptacle, since by the bedstead, at bed height, both wastepaper basket and ashtray are on metal stands.*

> LORD CHERWELL *automatically hands the soda-water syphon to* HELEN, *who has hurried in. She extinguishes.*

> CHURCHILL *has not paused in his speech.*]

> Rome must be bombed one day before
> and one day after the Salerno landing.
> If the Trastevere mob can be drummed up against Mussolini,
> they will throw the bull, an ox by now more like,
> from the balcony of the Palazzo Venezia.

BROOKE: But if Hitler gets ahead of us and declares
> Rome an open city himself,
> he will have won a moral victory.

CHERWELL: Let him have it: he could do with one.

P.M. *Rome!* How Macaulay adored it,
> that splendid literary fraud.
> ["The Church saw the commencement of all governments
> and all the ecclesiastical establishments of the world—and we
> feel no assurance that she is not destined to see the end of
> them all.] No other institution is left standing which carries
> the mind back to the times when the smoke of sacrifice rose
> from the Pantheon, and when tame leopards and tigers
> bounded in the Flavian amphitheater. The proudest royal
> houses are but of yesterday, when compared with the line of

the Supreme Pontiff. The Church may still exist in un-
diminished vigor when some traveler from New Zealand shall,
in the midst of a vast solitude, take his stand on a broken
arch of London Bridge to sketch the ruins of St. Paul's."
What an obituary.

CHERWELL *has had frequent experience of the* PRIME MINISTER's
*impotence before the baroque utterances of the favorite author he
most dislikes.* CHURCHILL's *extremely delicate white hands have
conducted the gilded nonsense, as if he were throwing out paper
streamers—and the Prof. knows that only a joke can get him away
from literature and back to business. The frigid cynic, therefore,
now speaks pointedly fast, since he has had it stored up for some
time.*

CHERWELL: Since Macaulay assures us
    that Rome will survive us nevertheless,
    then we should leave the Germans time
    to organize its defenses, which will justify
    a colossal bombardment.
    [In Milan a single raid worked miracles
    of demoralization—
    the industrial proletariat are simply not going back to work.
BROOKE: Not bad—if Kesselring
    brings up as few as a thousand men,
    we are justified in attacking.]
P.M. The Hitlerite hordes will then be brought
    into such universal disrepute,
    that not even the Pope will be able to bless them any more,
    as he does in his weekly mass audiences.
    We shall not, however, give that explanation to the President.

HELEN *comes in, in a great hurry, speechless.*

Helen—what have you got now?
(*Gives her the Rome cable.*)
Here.
The Foreign Secretary is to think up some answer
or other—well?

HELEN *takes the cable, suddenly hesitates to give him the new
one she has brought in,* [*says in extenuation:*

HELEN: A long cable from Marshal Stalin
is just being decoded—
P.M.: Hurry up with it.]
HELEN (*mastering herself*): Sir, read this one.

She steps back. The PRIME MINISTER *has looked up, startled, as he takes the cable from her.*
He reads it: then his hand, with the telegram in it, falls on the eiderdown. CHERWELL *picks up the cable.*

P.M. (*to* BROOKE, *while* CHERWELL *reads the cable*):
Worse than a disaster at the front.
CHERWELL (*handing* BROOKE *the cable*):
Stalin has broken off relations with Poland.
P.M.: I begged Stalin, I implored him,
not to deal Hitler such an ace.
CHERWELL (*the only time in the play that he shows any deep emotion. He forces the words out*):
Now, finally, overboard with that Pole.
P.M. (*choking with rage*): Sikorski . . . Sikorski . . . Sik . . .

Since, four years later—at seventy-two—he was still able to turn somersaults in the swimming pool, he can now, despite his two hundred and some pounds, get out of bed with a single spring. He shouts at HELEN:

Maisky—go on, go on: get him here, at once.
Tell Sawyers to run my bath: at the double.
What are you waiting for?
HELEN: You can't, Sir: you cannot see the Russian Ambassador
now.
You are lunching at the Palace in an hour's time.
P.M. (*still excited, then quieter*):
Today!—how on earth? oh, of course, Tuesday.
Then get him on the telephone.
HELEN: Right away.

She goes out. Pause. All at sea.

[CHERWELL: When three Poles meet,
they found three newspapers.

The PRIME MINISTER *rubs his chin, stumps up and down in all directions.*

P.M.: Seventeen. Seventeen Polish newspapers we have in England.
Not *one* of them gives credit as it should
to the sacrifices of the Russians
for the liberation of Poland.
Nothing but agitation—even *before* Katyn.]

BROOKE: I had luncheon with Sikorski the other day:
Katyn or no, he still wants peace with Stalin:
but first of all he had to—

P.M. (*as if he was going to massacre* BROOKE—*"He held his fist
under my nose."*):
Had to? *What* had he to do, pray?
Go behind my back to the White House,
three times, *three times,* to talk the President
into *forbidding* the British government
to guarantee the Kremlin the re-annexation
of the Czarist-Russian territories?
[Sikorski managed to persuade Roosevelt
publicly to threaten to dissociate himself
from all such agreements with Russia—
Roosevelt sent his ambassador to Chequers
when Molotov was actually in London waiting for my signature . . .
which I then had to refuse to give him.]

CHERWELL (*as the* PRIME MINISTER *cannot speak for emotion*):
As long as this Pole is with us, Sir Alan,
Great Britain can have *no* guarantee
that the Kremlin is not going to back out of the war,
and make its own arrangements with Hitler once again.

BROOKE (*at a loss*): Why does Roosevelt give in to Sikorski?

P.M. (*impatiently, roughly*): Because Sikorski decides the votes
of eight million Poles in America, of course.
Until next autumn, F.D.R. *must* take heed of him.
[The Pope has recognized Sikorski's government:
the only government-in-exile he has recognized.]

HELEN (*re-entering*): The Russian Ambassador is out, Sir.

P.M.: Is he coming here?

HELEN: No, he is just out. The Embassy
will call us the moment he gets back.

BROOKE (*laughs contemptuously*):
The Kremlin as protector of Poland!

Is Sikorski supposed to tie the bone to the dog,
to protect the bone?

The PRIME MINISTER *makes a gesture of his hand to* CHERWELL
*as if to say that what is too absurd to be spoken, should be sung, and
that it is as great a waste of time talking to the soldier* BROOKE
as to the soldier SIKORSKI.

CHERWELL (*to* BROOKE): Brooke, Sikorski hasn't got the bone,
nor will he ever have it without the Red Army.
His conduct is *improper*.
[BROOKE: Improper!
CHERWELL: Yes, He expects, quite rightly,
territorial accretions for Poland.
He also expects, however, that the Russians
invest gratis, a whole generation,
to rid Warsaw of the Teutonic hordes for him.
BROOKE: Gratis? Russia will be getting Bessarabia and the Baltic.
P.M.: That's no profit. It was Russian in the first place.
Always has been.]
CHERWELL: Not even Königsberg—
is he prepared to allow the Kremlin.
P.M. (*shouting*): Helen!
(*Muttering.*)
This business must be settled—once and for all—
(*To* HELEN, *who has entered with her pad:*)
Just a note, for a cable to Stalin:
"It appears to me, the Russians have an historically well-
founded claim to Königsberg. His Majesty's Government re-
gards this war against German aggression as a Thirty Years'
War begun in 1914 and will remind the Poles that this part
of the world is soaked with Russian blood. It was *here*—italics
—that the Russian armies forced the Germans in August,
1914, to withdraw two army corps from their march on Paris,
thereby making possible the victory of the Marne, which was
by no means canceled out by the catastrophe of Tannenberg."
That is all. Thank you.
CHERWELL (*at once*): Is Stalin supposed to *believe* that, Winston?
P.M. (*quietly*): I beg your pardon, Prof.
You *know* it is the truth.
CHERWELL: I know, but does Stalin?
If you persist in holding on to this man,

whose life is devoted to keeping the Russians
from Königsberg, Vilna, and Lvov?

CHURCHILL *has thought this for some time. He is silent, frighteningly so.*

BROOKE *(on the point of leaving, feeling he is in the way)*:
Prime Minister—we shall see each other in the Cabinet.

He nods to CHERWELL, *who raises his hand, holding his handkerchief, with which he frequently dabs at his lips. The* PRIME MINISTER *has nodded amiably to* BROOKE, *but as usual when he is thinking he takes no cognizance of his surroundings—persons or things—except insofar as they impinge directly on what he is thinking, and he completely fails to notice* BROOKE's *departure.*

(Air Chief Marshal Harris later wrote that during the many film shows at Chequers the PRIME MINISTER *would constantly make loud interruptions, and would even dictate letters.)*

HELEN *(who has come in)*: Sir, Sawyers is running the bath.
P.M.: Where's that telephone call from the Russians?
HELEN: The Ambassador is not there—
P.M. *(making as if to get back into bed)*:
When am I going to see that cable from the Kremlin?
HELEN *(nodding)*: Sir, your bath is ready,
you really must get up now.
(She looks at the clock.)
P.M. *(getting back into bed)*: I am up.

HELEN *waits with visible impatience.*

Prof., did Eden tell you
about how he tried the other day
to make the Poles a present of a cruiser?
CHERWELL: I take it they asked for a Dreadnought.
P.M. *(with glowering amusement)*:
Anthony informed Sikorski the navy would give Poland
a good strong ship. Result: Sikorski insisted
on calling the cruiser the "Lvov."
Eden begged him—
in the eyes of the Kremlin, Lvov is a Russian city.
Couldn't they call the cruiser "Warsaw," or "Gdynia"?
CHERWELL: And?
P.M.: Sikorski *insisted* on "Lvov"—

And that is how the Poles lost their navy.

CHERWELL: That is what is known as practical politics
—among drunkards and Germans.

P.M.: And Poles it would appear. [Where has Brooke got to?
—what did I want to say to him?
I can't remember. Ah, yes, it struck me,
he's looking exhausted.
(*To* HELEN:)
Find out, under some pretext or other,
from his A.D.C., what time Brooke
is to inspect the amphibious tanks this afternoon.
I'll fly after him: order an aircraft for Norfolk,
so that I get there about an hour after the
C.I.G.S. No one is to expect me.
Now fetch those Gomorrah pictures.

HELEN (*going*):
They've just been brought over.
Sir, you really must get up now.

P.M. (*nods amiably, without listening*):
It's spoiled my appetite to hear
the tanks still won't hold up in the slightest swell.
We can't call off a whole invasion
all on account of a rough sea—

HELEN (*entering*):
The photographs, Sir.

CHERWELL: Wait till after Sicily—have faith in the landing craft.
What interests *me,* is how far they are with the flame-throwers
we're going to mount in front of the Churchills—
and the chaindrums which the Shermans
are supposed to flail in front of them.]

HELEN (*announcing*):
Group Captain Clark.

P.M. (*nods* [*but continues talking to* CHERWELL):
All very well, the drums will explode the antitank mines,
but surely it will mean a great loss of speed for the tanks
themselves?]

CLARK *enters, salutes, waits in the doorway.*

At least you bring me good news.
The Germans can now thaw out in Hamburg
from the cold of a couple of Russian winters.

CLARK *has eyes like oysters—even the pupils are glaucous and watery. Thomas Mann speaks of a sculptor he knew, whose success in obtaining the most expressive results in his portrait busts of prominent contemporaries Mann attributed to his having been first and foremost an animal sculptor.* CLARK'*s face would have suggested, superficially, a frog.*

More even than the eyes, the immense mouth, the overlarge upper part of his body, bent forward in an attitude of perpetual expectation, and the never-quite-straightened knee of the General Staff Officer and the bug-hunter, all bear out the impression that in all of us some remnant of our animal forbears remains, usually more sympathetic than the later human species.

CLARK, *a textile manufacturer of material for uniforms recalled to the colors he weaves, has, as the bringer of the Gomorrah photographs, taken to heart the Chinese saying that he who has not a friendly face, should not open a shop. The brusque rough-diamond tone which he uses from time to time he has learned from listening to Harris: in the belief that this sort of thing is welcome here, and in his uneasiness in the* PRIME MINISTER'*s presence, he rather overdoes it.*

CLARK: Prime Minister, the landings in France need not take place.
By the first of April, 1944, you will be
the victor over Germany . . .
through the total "Hamburgization" of Berlin—ha!
P.M. (*happy, confident*):
If you can do that, hundreds of thousands of
mothers, wives, sweethearts in this island will bless the name of
Harris. . . .
You've brought a whole caseful of . . .

CLARK *opens his slim, black briefcase and takes out a handful of large photographs.*

CHERWELL: Group Captain, you are aware that I,
as . . . ah, torchbearer of saturation bombing,
am among your most devoted admirers.
But I know Berlin—I was a student there—
the town is too little built-up.
You will be as little able there
to organize a firestorm
as the Huns were in London.

CLARK (*annoyed at* CHERWELL'*s justified claim to be the originator
of area bombing and at his quite unjustifiable comparison of
Bomber Command's capabilities with those of the enemy.
Curt*):
What a comparison, Lord Cherwell!
Prime Minister, perhaps a strong word from you to the Ameri-
cans—
they still refuse to plaster residential areas . . .
They consider it—ha!—ineffective.

P.M. (*studying some of the photographs through an old-fashioned
stereoscope, as described by Harris in his memoirs, purring,
not listening to* CLARK):
Amazing . . . Prof., I must send Stalin one of these things,
it shows up so much more!
What have you got there? More pictures?
(*Points to the briefcase.*)

CLARK: No, Sir. Butterflies.

P.M.: Butterflies?

And while CHERWELL *looks at the photographs of Gomorrah,*
CHURCHILL *transfers his attention to the fine wood box which*
CLARK *is holding out toward him: a black lacquered coffin for
butterflies, upholstered in white velvet with a glass top, about the
size of a Victorian lunchbox.* CHURCHILL *never bothered to modify
his swift changes of thought for the benefit of visitors; everyone
who has written about him agrees about his total lack of interest
in people whom he could not or would not involve in the sphere
of his own ideas and projects. His doctor, an intimate acquaintance, bears witness, without offense, to this as often as the
C.I.G.S. "War has always fascinated him: he knows the most
surprising details of battles . . . but he never interests himself for
a moment about what was going on in the minds of the soldier,
never tries for a moment to share his fears. In the P.M.'s opinion,
if a soldier fails in his duty, he must be shot. It is as simple as that
. . . what a man does, not what he is, is what counts with him."*
*It is impossible to clarify in words what this scene demonstrates
indirectly, namely the truism that the great men of action today
are as far removed from their action as one age from another.*
*During this conversation, tens of thousands of civilians are
suffocating in the cellars of the working-class districts of Hamburg, or battling with falling masonry like trapped miners. In*

British merchant ships, the crews—with a casualty rate of one in five—are fearing a fresh attack of Hitler's U-boats, whose crews hate and fear their enemy less than their own handiwork, much as Air Marshal Harris's bomber pilots do theirs. Hitler's U-boats are the arm which was most nearly wiped out in the European war, just as the Bomber Commands were the most heavily punished arm of the Western powers: out of 37,000 sailors, 32,000 were drowned, and 56,000 British and American air-crew personnel were burned to death in their aircraft, unless they had the good fortune to be killed outright. These figures are as important as they are hard to credit. History and the writing of history bear the same relation to one another as the iceberg to that part of it that shows above the water.

The magnificent corpses of the butterflies have been arranged in close formation—a memento of the collector's days of active service.

CLARK (almost with tenderness, holding the coffin):
    I collected it from the jewelers;
    In the middle—the big four-engined stuff,
    Lancasters, and around them, fighter escort . . .
    The moths in Southern England
    have almost subtropical colors.
P.M. (anxiously):
    Clark, you don't climb trees yourself . . .
    I won't allow it . . .
    to catch these things? [How many have you got?
CLARK: Nine thousand, three hundred—and eighty odd.]
    Haha, don't worry, Sir.
    Butterflies die on the ground, not in trees,
    for the most part, like airmen.
    [Air Marshal Saundby first got me interested in them.
    A hobby for me—though it is a science for him, haha.]
    What else can one do at night?
    (Seriously.)
    Before we can get to sleep, we like to count
    the aircraft . . . which will not be coming back.
P.M.: [Nine thousand—]
    What colors: in the whole of this war
    I have only been able to paint one picture!
    Prof., look at those blues—Helen?

She is not there.

CHERWELL (*looking through the stereoscope at an obviously im-
      pressive slide, hardly taking it from his eyes, mutters, without
      sarcasm*):
      Nice, very nice. If there were only . . .
      something in color to be seen here.
      Winston, Gomorrah is a definite success.
P.M. (*with the butterflies*):
      Will you have to go back over Hamburg?
CLARK: Tonight with three hundred and fifty aircraft.
[CHERWELL: Losses?
CLARK: Less than ever before, fifty-seven,
      i.e., two point four instead of six per cent—
      we have your Christmas tree decorations to thank for that,
            Lord Cherwell.
      With "Window" in operation, they have no idea where to look
            for us.
      If it hadn't been for some icing up last night,
      we'd have lost fewer still.]
P.M.: It will mean we have the Bishop of Chichester
      at our throats again—
      let alone Master Stafford Cripps.
      They think we're homicidal maniacs
      because they haven't the imagination
      to see the landing in France . . .
      to see the beach there as a chopping board.
CLARK: Why don't you lock the bastards up, Sir?
      [Even the Labour Party has empowered you
      to arrest the intellectuals and unreliables.]
P.M. (*shaking his head angrily*): Arrest intellectuals?
      I'm not a German.
CHERWELL: Hitler doesn't arrest them,
      he beheads them.
P.M.: I'll tell the Bishop military secrets,
      then he'll have to keep his trap shut.

CHERWELL *laughs.*

[CLARK: The nonsense talked by the member for Ipswich
      is also undermining the morale of our crews.
P.M. (*breathing fire*):

Stokes I shall not receive—as a Catholic
he is simply playing the organ for Rome.
I shall speak with him, when and not before
Pius protests against the extermination of the Jews.
We have asked the Cardinal Secretary of State,
several times already, through Osborn,
that the Eternal Speechifier shall actually *say* something
but he only makes himself clear,
when he is objecting to air raids.]
CLARK: Sir, may I warn you against these defeatists?
We once allowed a lecture in Bomber Command;
Cripps spoke on the subject:
"God is my co-pilot"—result:
complete moral confusion, and
cowardice increased.
P.M. (*angrily*): Well, if Harris must ask Stafford . . .
he is far too clever for this world.
[CHERWELL: There's no point, Winston, in discussing things.
Knock Hitler's rockets out of his hand,
and give *that* in detail to the papers:
the surest possible diversion from Gomorrah.
P.M. (*impatient*): But why deny that we are doing it?
You need half a dozen lies to cover up one.]

He has rung the bell. HELEN *comes in.*

—Make a note, to ask the Bishop of Chichester
down to Chequers some time!
(*Fingers her navy-blue jacket, indicates the butterflies.*)
Just compare the blue of those wings
and this wretched stuff—all the difference
between God's heaven and a black eye.
HELEN: It's fantastic. How do you catch them, Sir?
CLARK: As easy as pie: stretch a cloth at the edge of a wood,
shine an acetylene lamp on it—
and pick 'em up like autumn leaves.
HELEN: But they would still be alive.
CLARK: Easy as pie. Put them in the killing-bottle . . .
pfft!—dead as dormice. Prussic acid.
[Air Marshal Saundby finds it all very unscientific.]

The PRIME MINISTER's *face indicates that he can imagine hobbies
which call for neither cyanide nor prussic acid nor pins.*

HELEN (*repelled, but fascinated*):
    —that the wings should keep so well.
    (*She hands the box back, he puts it in his case.*)
P.M. (*already bored. Suddenly sharpness*):
    Helen go—and behave like a blockbuster
    out there.
    If the Russian Ambassador isn't finally . . . dammit
    get him here, I don't care where he is . . .
HELEN: I will see about it: now, Sir, please get up.
P.M. (*like a naughty boy*):
    No.
    (*As* HELEN *does not go:*)
    No!—What else?
HELEN (*hesitating*):
    Sir, Lord Moran left a message that
    his bulletin about your complete recovery
    has not dispelled the rumors
    that you are . . . still very ill.
    Would it not . . .
P.M. (*irritated, depressed*):
    [Very? What is that supposed to mean: very?]
    Don't you get in league with that bloody old man!
    Very well then: announce to the press:
    (*surly*)
    "This morning, among other things, I received
    a further report of my death the previous night.
    This report is considerably exaggerated."
    Enough?
CHERWELL: Indeed not—it does not deny
    that you are actually ill.
[CLARK (*a great attempt at joviality*):
    Prime Minister—show yourself once more to the Londoners.
    It is really quite splendid the way they stand for hours,
    just on the rumor you might be coming.
P.M.: And how they would come running,
    if I were going to be hanged.]
CHERWELL: Winston, don't take it too lightly—
    your second bout of pneumonia caused great disquiet.
    You ought to . . .
P.M. (*tired, serious*):
    What is there I ought *not* to do?

HELEN: Prime Minister—that American woman from *The New York Times*
   you threw out a short time ago,
   couldn't you let her have a few lines?
P.M.: That shameless hussy—
   she described me as an old man.
HELEN: Yes, but one who had kept his youth.
   She wanted to know the secret—
   you needn't mention your illness at all.
CHERWELL (*calculating*):
   I think it would be extremely advantageous to answer.
P.M.: If you think so—the formula;
   One: never take any exercise,
   Two: never smoke when you're asleep,
   Three: drink in moderation, but hourly,
   Four: ...
HELEN (*who has taken this down*):
   Thank you, Sir, no four:
   there are the women's guilds over there to think of.

HELEN *goes out.*
   The PRIME MINISTER *addresses* CLARK *by his rank, since he has already forgotten his name.*

P.M. (*as* HELEN *goes out*):
   Group-Captain, you must not rest upon
   your Hamburg laurels! You must go at once
   to Peenemünde.
   Cause for alarm: the Huns have rockets
   in the air already.
CLARK (*stands up in alarm*): *In the air?*
CHERWELL (*again resentful, as he was earlier*):
   Yes. We've known it since yesterday evening.
   Von Thoma, the German general we caught
   the other day, was bitterly complaining:
   "Where have the Führer's rockets got to, then?
   I've actually seen them being launched."
CLARK (*shaking his head in disbelief*): A German general?
   Did we bribe him?
CHERWELL: No—he is too priceless, in every sense.
P.M.: Really too depressing.
   We have five thousand spies eating their heads off,

then some Prussian buffoon talks *his* head off
into a microphone, in the prison camp.
[If history were made like that,
what would our victories be worth?
It's an insult to me, to you, to Harris,
to every single pilot and spy.

CHERWELL (*laughs, his jaws clenched*):
Oh, come, does a trick like the Trojan horse
take the credit from the victors?

P.M. (*violently, apparently outraged*):
The horse?—that horse was . . .
the lowest literary fraud of all time!
Troy can be compared only with Verdun;
the perfidy to ascribe to the defenders
that they were taken in by that nag—
Tcha, Prof., the usual victor's lies
to vilify a great opponent.

CHERWELL (*since the* PRIME MINISTER *obviously expects him to play up*):
Clark—give me a hand, if the horse
is only the invention of the historians—
how did Agamemnon get into the citadel?

CLARK (*with an effort to mitigate the character of* miles gloriosus *by laughter*):
Like us, by fire—and only by fire.
Cities and women—take 'em both by fire.

P.M. (*whose face betrays some disagreement with* CLARK's *taste, speaks, relaxed and amused, with the assurance of an eyewitness*):
Not fire—it was *Aeneas*—
he opened the gates for the Greeks by night—
in exchange for a safe conduct for himself and his family.

CHERWELL (*odiously*):
How apropos that it should have been that tedious old wife
he had to drop on the way.

P.M.: And the fact that he is the only leading character
who later was spoken of as the bravest, second only to Hector,
is a clear indication that Aeneas didn't fight at all.
(*Very serious.*)
The man who survives a tragedy is not the hero of it.

(*To* CHERWELL:)
Prof., it was a Pole who said that.

CLARK (*since the other two are silent a long time*):
Prime Minister, if your opinion of history is such,
why do you make it?

P.M.: Because I want to write some more of it.
Aeneas was able to tell his own story,
and so is not the traitor but the hero.
That is the only reason for that monstrous horse.

CHERWELL (*making an effort to help his friend combat the "black
dog"*):
Hm—n—no, no: in that case, why did the victors
not disclose Aeneas' inglorious activities?

P.M.: My dear Prof., if one has been blockading a fortress
for ten years is one going to admit
one only got into it by treachery?
Of course, both sides always make use of traitors
but only the defeated speak of them—as scapegoats:
Look at the Persians after Salamis.
Do you imagine Monty, in his memoirs,
will tell us about our friend in the Admiralty in Rome
who told us about every German convoy to Africa
—and much besides?
All the same, Monty's cunning is his strength.
That Monty, before Alam Halfa,
supplied Rommel with a false set of maps
and led Hitler's tanks into the quicksands,
that we shall read about,
that is entertaining and praiseworthy.
When Ludendorff prepared his Cannae at Tannenberg,
he had the Russian radio code.
Generals are allowed to boast about their artful dodges;
not statesmen, though—it makes me jealous.
Or should I blow my own trumpet a bit, Prof.,
for having told our Ambassadors in Washington and Berne,
after our calamities at Dunkirk—
for having told them, to tell their closest friends . . .

CHERWELL (*smiling; he knows the story*):
. . . in strictest confidence,
so it would filter through to Berlin . . .

P.M. (*not to* CLARK):
> . . . tell them that Britain would be forced
> to lay down her arms within a matter of weeks?

CLARK: But, Sir, you cannot for a minute
> have considered doing that.

P.M.: That is precisely the point. Hitler fell into the trap—
> he thought that we would fall as easily,
> as naturally as the cowpat from the cow.
> He could save himself the trouble of an invasion.
> By the time he realized in September
> that we would never surrender,
> we had got ready to stamp the buggers out.

HELEN (*entering with a piece of paper in her hand*):
> Sir—the Russian declaration of the breaking
> off of relations with Poland.

P.M. (*takes it from her, puts it down angrily, unloads his anger by shouting*):
> Once and for all,
> I want that bloody *cable* . . .

HELEN (*firmly*): Three minutes, Sir.]

CHERWELL *has taken* CLARK *by the arm and led him forward. The* PRIME MINISTER *loses himself straight away in the paper.* CLARK *has lit a cigarette and says, with hushed admiration*:

CLARK: Might not the German general be tricking us about the rockets?

CHERWELL (*firmly, crossly, balancing on tiptoes*):
> I was, as you know, doubtful whether the things—
> could fly at all, let alone so soon. So! we must hurry.

HELEN *tries, with gestures, to enlist* CHERWELL's *help with regard to the time.* CHERWELL *smiles, looks at his watch, then toward the bed. He shrugs.*

CLARK (*snapping, without a pause in the conversation*):
> We'll get rid of them—
> but at a single blow,
> too expensive otherwise.

CHERWELL: It couldn't be.

CLARK: Peenemünde is a long way—
> we run into all Hitler's night fighters
> from the Zuider Zee to Berlin.

CHERWELL: Fly over Sweden.

CLARK: We'll wait and see . . .

P.M.: And the dams? When are you . . .

CLARK: The next full moon, Prime Minister.

The P.M. *calmly and disgustedly produces his most terrible threat, whose practical implementation had later to be thwarted with considerable trouble by* CHERWELL *and Eisenhower.*

P.M.: For every rocket that falls on London,
    I shall repay the Germans in poison gas.
    Good-by, Group Captain, if Harris is all right
    by Sunday evening, tell him to come to dinner, with his wife,
    there will be plovers' eggs—you have given me new hope.
    Gomorrah—if that could be the prologue to Berlin . . .
    (*Points to the telephone.*)
    Helen, get my wife.

CLARK (*with obstinate sureness*):
    Yes, Sir—it's guaranteed—by the first of April
    you will be victorious. Tell Marshal Stalin
    our bombers *are* the Second Front!

He salutes and leaves—to prepare, with HARRIS, *the worst slaughter of airmen in the entire war, the Battle of Berlin, later called off as being too wasteful.*

CHERWELL: Slightly off his head—the good fellow.
    Really—such airs—"his" bombers.

P.M. (*relaxed*):
    Ah well—the higher the monkey climbs
    the more you can see of his bottom. Still, he works hard.

He has taken the telephone from HELEN *and passed* CHERWELL *the note from the blanket.*

    Yes, Clemmie . . . yes catastrophic:
    Stalin has finally called it off with the Poles.
    About Sunday, I fear I've been a bit previous—
    I promised Brooke and Harris and the Prof.
    plovers' eggs—have we any?
    Well, we must somehow make them stretch . . .
    (*pause*)—and as if *that* wasn't enough—the Kremlin
    is whistling both Ambassadors back home.
    Yes—Washington as well. What?

But I *am* up . . . what?
No, tell me, please, who?—No, no—
how could it possibly—the brute!
I'll kill him—I want him—he—no!
I don't want him to explain anything.
Bloody fool.

He throws the receiver down without hanging up, which CHER-
WELL *does, alarmed. The* PRIME MINISTER's *face is contorted—
the anger luckily is resolved in tears.*

Prof.—the black swan—the pen—mangled,
a fox in the cage, the man didn't make sure—
the swan. The brute!
CHERWELL: Who, the fox?
P.M.: Tscha, the fox, the fox—the gardener!
Can the fox help its appetite for meat?
The poor, poor thing. What a world!
No one who knows it would willingly have come into it.
CHERWELL: I said a year ago—
P.M.: I don't want to see him ever again—the idiot.
CHERWELL: I told him,
without a concrete foundation
the fence can be undermined
by any beast of prey.
P.M.: At last, Sergeant: *when*
are you going to bring me some good news?

HELEN *enters, behind her a* MESSENGER *with a pronounced limp,
a Passchendaele veteran with an Old Bill mustache whose salute is
the more punctilious for being performed with considerable difficulty. Bemedaled jacket. The black and red briefcase is hand-
cuffed to his left wrist.* HELEN *takes the key ring, which hangs on
a long chain on the bedpost, and opens the case. She lays the
decoded cable on the eiderdown, giving a copy to* CHERWELL.
CHURCHILL *reacts purely automatically to the* MESSENGER's *salute,
pointing to the cigar box, nodding equally automatically to the*
MESSENGER's *reply, of which he does not hear a word, being
already eagerly immersed in the cable.*

MESSENGER (*inclining respectfully to* CHERWELL, *who raises his
hand*):
Good morning—your Lordship.

(He hesitates—a ritual—before taking a cigar.)
Thank you, Prime Minister—well, from what you read
Hamburg was good news all right; a right smack.

P.M. *nods without seeing or hearing him, and says, while the*
MESSENGER *withdraws silently:*

P.M.: Helen; Sawyers. I'm getting up,
 get him to run me a bath—I'd rather
 spend the whole day in bed.
 What a day—the poor creature.
 (Spectacles in hand.)
 Prof., will you talk to Maisky.
 (Not pausing, as HELEN *is about to leave, roughly:)*
 Helen, where is that call from the Russians?
HELEN *(very firmly)*:
 Sir—the Ambassador is not at home.
 Sawyers has already run the bath.
P.M. *(amiable)*:
 Wait—make a note.
 Will you, after I have got up,
 give Lord Cherwell all the cables
 the Kremlin has sent since the discovery of the corpses at
 Katyn.
CHERWELL: And copies of all Stalin's telegrams
 to the President, please.
P.M. *(while* HELEN *nods to* CHERWELL *)*:
 Can one give any answer to them?
CHERWELL: You *must!*

The PRIME MINISTER *has sat upright in bed, his face seems to
have no surplus flesh but to be all muscle, hardness, the quite un-
private face of the leader, above personality, that of the man who
found, in 1911, his rule of life in the words:* "Understand therefore this day, that the Lord thy God is He which goeth over before
thee; as a consuming fire. He shall destroy them and bring them
down before thy face; so shalt thou drive them out and destroy
them, as the Lord has said unto thee."

CHERWELL *(underlining with a red pencil certain sentences, which
 he dictates quietly to* HELEN *)*:
 [". . . that the Soviet government are
 unable to acquiesce in such a disregard

of their own best interests . . .
that your grave decision to postpone
an invasion in Western Europe for this year
as well, was taken without consultation with the
Soviet Union . . . not here a question of the Soviet Union's
    disappointment,
but of the saving of millions
of human lives in the German-occupied territories of
Western Europe and Russia, and of diminishing the
enormous sacrifices of the Soviet Union, in
comparison with which, the sacrifices . . .
(*Here* CHERWELL *raises his voice and speaks this in the* PRIME
MINISTER's *direction:*)
. . . of the British and American troops are *insignificant.*"]
P.M. (*nodding*):
Nearly as bad as Stalin's tone of voice
is the fact that he's *right*.

CHERWELL *nods. Pause.*

[I shall have to send a convoy even
if the "Scharnhorst" sinks 80 per cent of it.
CHERWELL: We have no ships for one
before the Sicilian landings.

He looks at CHURCHILL, *then sends* HELEN *out, holding the door
open for her himself.*

Helen—would you?—the cables since March right away.
HELEN: Yes, Sir . . .]

CHERWELL, *power in his movements, shuts the door, takes the
cable and says, articulately, precisely, in a tone of insistence, almost of command:*

CHERWELL: Winston, you deceive yourself if you are limiting
Stalin's anger to, A, the convoys and
B, the invasion.
These sentences here are demands from Stalin
that you could fulfill. "At a time
when the peoples of the Soviet Union
are working with all their strength
for the destruction of the common enemy
the government of General Sikorski is striking

a treacherous blow at the Soviet Union,
and for the good of Hitler's tyranny . . .
It is hard to suppose that the British government
was uninformed of the comedy of the projected
investigations in Katyn . . . [it would, in
the spirit of our alliance, be only natural
to prevent an ally from striking
a blow of this sort at another ally . . ."]
and here he is quite open about it, Winston,
". . . and that Great Britain, the USSR, and the USA
should take steps toward the improvement of the
constitution of the present Polish government."

P.M. (*tonelessly*): Steps.

CHERWELL *throws the cable away. Two long strides. Then, finger-tips in the waistcoat pockets, springing up and down on his toes, he says—his eyes closed, as if he were assuring himself with a formula before beginning a physical experiment*:

CHERWELL: A patriot who has lost his country must lose his life.

The P.M., *his face contorted, looks up questioningly.*

Oh, a quotation merely, Napoleon . . . the diaries.
(*He gestures fleetingly to the bust of Napoleon.*)
Winston, have you told Stalin, in writing,
that Sikorski is the one Pole
we cannot do without?

P.M. (*shortly*):
Ten times over—in every letter.

CHERWELL (*as if he was now speaking of something cheerful*):
By the way, we should . . .
give Stalin's Ambassador a farewell treat.
Before the Kremlin whistles him back,
invite Maisky to visit Gibraltar for a . . .

P.M. (*surprised*):
Maisky will be flying home via Gib. anyway . . .

CHERWELL *looks into the distance, as if gazing at the Rock.*

CHERWELL: Of course—but you must give him a fixed date for it.
P.M.: Prof., make quite sure Menzies is on his toes.
Maisky must be looked after

    as if he were the hemophiliac czarevitch,
    as if he were our final gold reserves.

CHERWELL: Especially his aircraft.

P.M. (*interrupting*):
    The best watchdogs we have—
    give him them, in Gib.

CHERWELL: No question . . . since, on account of Operation Husky,
    Sikorski must end his tour of inspection of the Near East
    in Gibraltar on the same day:
    and he will also need looking after.

P.M. (*roused*):
    What—on the same day? Are you mad!
    [All we need is for Sikorski's childish attempt
    to kiss and make friends with Stalin,
    to encourage Maisky—he can be crude enough when he wants
        to—
    to let it out that East Poland is no longer
    a subject of discussion between us and Russia.]
    On no account must they be allowed to meet.

CHERWELL (*patiently*):
    They need not do so: we shall ensure
    that they pass each other smoothly,
    like two buckets in a well. As the Poles
    will be the Governor's guests at The Convent,
    the Russian, who will be arriving before daybreak,
    will, I am afraid, have to fly on after breakfast,
    before the Poles are awake.

The PRIME MINISTER *looks quickly at* CHERWELL, *only to stare past him, during what follows, as scrupulously as* CHERWELL *stares past him: They speak now quickly and quietly, as if they were forced to work their way past a sleeping tiger. Both are so agitated and upset that they are at pains to remove all expression from their voices, so as not to offer the other a "dramatization" of their engagement and concern. Here both of them must do something they never otherwise do: employ hand gestures to camouflage their facial expressions.*

CHERWELL: Still, it is alas unavoidable
    that, for an hour or two at least,
    Maisky's aircraft is parked next to the Polish machine.

P.M. (*as if prompting*): Why?

CHERWELL (*as if he had not heard*):
  It does not bear thinking of that the Russians
  should get at the Polish aircraft.
  Or the Poles at the Russian, come to that.
P.M.: Or the Germans. Why do you not mention the Germans?
  Have we, or have we not, already
  had Canaris' saboteurs in Gib.?
  Putting sugar in the petrol tank?
  [If the Germans were to get at the aircraft—
CHERWELL: Exactly—even newspaper readers will be afraid
  when they read that Maisky is visiting Gib., that . . .
P.M. (*nods, disgustedly, depressed*):
  Yes, yes—that the Germans will try to pull off
  some squalid nonsense.]
CHERWELL (*nods and brings the argument to a swift, strong conclusion*):
  Were anything to happen to the Poles,
  the world would automatically suspect—God forbid—
  Maisky's entourage.
P.M. (*hard*):
  On no account—on no account whatsoever
  must there be a repetition of last winter's events
  with Sikorski's machine—
CHERWELL (*pouring oil, defensively*):
  Oh, Montreal? Out of the question; now *that* was sabotage,
  or so the President thinks. No,
  this time . . . nothing *can* go wrong.
  C. will be putting some star performers from Security Middle
    East
  onto Sikorski in the aircraft itself.
P.M.: In the aircraft?
CHERWELL: Yes.
  (*Pause.*)
  [As they have to come to London anyway,
  they can best look after Sikorski
  by flying in the aircraft with him from Cairo.
P.M.: Ah—yes. We *cannot* have another Pole
  brandishing a smoking time fuse under our noses
  which he claims to have found in his pajamas.
CHERWELL: Ah—you mean the Colonel. Sikorski had
  a court jester in tow there.

He was killed in a car crash in Edinburgh.]
These Poles are without shame.
Sikorski's men are telling him openly, all the time,
to be like de Gaulle (who, since his accident
in April, will not fly except with Frenchmen),
and fly with only Poles, not British air crews.

P.M.: British—I thought you were giving him a Czech pilot?

CHERWELL: Exactly—and that is precisely why it would be
inevitable that things should be said
if anything were to happen . . . since it is well known
that Benes' supporters detest Sikorski's party.

P.M. (*calmer*): Of course.

CHERWELL (*looks at his watch, a nervous reflex action*):
Nothing must be allowed to happen, if only
because there is no possibility of salvage operations in
Gibraltar . . .

The P.M. *looks up uncomprehending.* CHERWELL *in explanation:*

All our heavy-diving teams, alas, have had to be transferred
from there, in readiness for Husky.
(*Pause, softly:*)
Winston, you should get up now.

P.M. (*sinks back in bed, motionless—then, sitting up, he forces
himself to speak, as if he could not tolerate the silence*):
Smuts—there is no wiser man—
reproached me lately with failing too often
to act like Gandhi, from religious motives.

CHERWELL (*jealous of the* PRIME MINISTER'*s having another man
near to him to whom he listens*):
That was not so very wise of the wise old Smuts.
When a man says
that he is bringing conscience to diplomacy,
it only means he is hiding the fact
that he is bringing diplomacy to his conscience.
Hypocrisy!

P.M.: Hypocrisy is a concession to virtue all the same.

CHERWELL (*irritated*):
Are you prepared to order eighteen-year-olds to shoot,
and expect to keep your own hands free from—

P.M.: And yet, Prof., in these days
I think often of our Lord.

[Why did He collapse before His crucifixion?
CHERWELL: Because He was only a man, of course.
P.M.: No—it was because He foresaw
it would not be the enemies of His teaching
but His prophets and His disciples who
would unleash the terrors of the earth:
Puritans, Crusaders, Idealists, Inquisitors—
and Statesmen.
CHERWELL (*calmly*): Why should He have been spared the things
that are spared no man who teaches, who acts,
and thereby sows the seeds of future atrocities?
Him most of all, whom the rabble has since called God—
since every man has *His* price;
that could even be why.
P.M. (*tearing free*): You mean well with me, Prof.]
He would have left the whole flock in the lurch
to run after the one lost sheep.
CHERWELL: With what justification?
Anyway, you've done that—for too long already.

The PRIME MINISTER *is once more master of his actions, even if they are at the moment only enough to get him out of bed and over to the bathroom door, which has hitherto been shut. As he goes, he says:*

P.M.: Wait till I have talked to Maisky.

CHERWELL *alone. The bathroom door stays ajar. The Prof. takes a few steps, glances at his hunter, takes pills, then opens the other door.*

CHERWELL: Helen.
(*Speaking into the next room.*)
Have you the file with the correspondence—

HELEN *enters with a thick folder under her arm and says cheerfully:*

HELEN: Thank you, my Lord, for getting him out of bed.
CHERWELL: Have you telephoned the Palace for a reprieve?
HELEN (*quietly, with a glance toward the bathroom*):
No, Sir, there's time, we didn't tell him
His Majesty is not expecting him till two.

(*Without pausing, while* CHERWELL *again takes out his watch
and murmurs agreement:*)
I've looked through these already
to underline the Polish references;
impossible—since April it's nothing *but* Poland.
CHERWELL: Of course—and the invasion.
Let us dig out a few sentences
so that the P.M. doesn't have to work his way
through the whole rubbish heap before giving his answer—

HELEN *has sat down, and takes down what he points out to her.
He turns the pages. More writing. Then he dictates, in his hesitant
Establishment style, accompanied by many clearings of the throat.*

Stalin, April 25th: "I have been forced to consider public
opinion in the Soviet Union, which has been deeply outraged
by the ingratitude and treachery of the Polish government
. . ."
(*More turning of the pages.*)
Then, May 4th: "that there are no grounds for the supposi-
tion that Sikorski will keep faith in his relations with the Soviet Union does not preclude the taking of steps for the
improvement of the constitution of the present Polish government for the purpose of strengthening the united Allied front
against Hitler."

Telephone.

Is that the Russian Ambassador at last?

CHERWELL *signs* HELEN *to go on writing and lifts the receiver.*

Cherwell. Yes.
Good morning, Excellency—one moment.

CHERWELL *has taken the telephone on its long flex to the bathroom door, which stands ajar.*

Maisky—shall he ring back later?
P.M. (*roaring like a great wave breaking on the shore*): Coming.

HELEN *takes to her heels, as she is well aware that the* PRIME
MINISTER *is not above passing even the respectable Swiss house-
maids in a state of complete nudity with a friendly "Good morning."*

CHERWELL (*into the telephone*):
He's coming right away—oh—hm, yes,

we're only puzzled, Excellency,
that your—ah, pastors and masters should be recalling you—
and Litvinov from Washington as well.
. . . hm, yes. Here is the Prime Minister himself.

The PRIME MINISTER *has entered from the bath, dripping and naked as Neptune rising from the waves. The broad black bath towel draped over the sea-god's nakedness should not contribute to the petty naturalism of the* CHURCHILL *monuments, with bow ties and replaceable bronze cigars which are currently being erected even in parts of the world where the figure gets icicles on its nose in the winter months.*

This is the moment in the play where the author can do nothing more, the actor everything, to make the leap from comedy to myth. That the comic element in his barefooted irruption shall take to its heels before this impassioned fighter: that the harmless element of laughter shall, for the length of a heart beat, reveal the hidden depths below—this is something the actor can achieve, the author cannot describe. There must be magic in the performance —if the actor can call it up, he will have come level, after the event, with CHURCHILL's *achievement in creating a figure that people "imagine of their own accord," the condition which Burkhardt demanded for greatness to be possible.* CHURCHILL *spent nearly seventy years in riveting the imagination of his contemporaries, their power of imagining greatness, to his own person.*

"At last he saw him. He saw a broad striding figure, from whom the cloak's fall took away all the heaviness"—so Rilke described Rodin's vision of another "prodigal of Destiny," Balzac, who had, however, merely "the face of an element." CHURCHILL *is the element itself, the personification of the war-drive, the bloodstream of the century in which more human beings have been done to violent death than ever before in world history. The ancients imagined their disappearance into the Kingdom of the Dead as a journey by water, decorating their coffins accordingly with pictures of Poseidon and his Tritons—this Neptune, when, at thirty-eight, he stepped onto the bridge of the flagship of the greatest armada in history, became Lord of the Seas. Thirty-three years later he could tell the Marshal of the largest army in the world that in a single night he was able to send from his coasts against the enemy of mankind five thousand ships and eleven thousand aircraft. (*CHURCHILL *was also the founder of the air strength of his island.) At that moment, the most com-*

plete triumph of arms that his people and his allies were ever to achieve was already in his hands. Fourteen months before, however—at the point we are now at in space and time—it was a question of surviving the most perilous moment of the war since the Battle of Britain. The chronicler of the White House wrote: "Stalin recalled Litvinov from Washington and Maisky from London. There was now an atmosphere alarmingly reminiscent of that which had preceded the Molotov-Ribbentrop Pact of August, 1939, and the fears of a separate Russo-German Armistice were revived . . . It was fortunate that Hitler did not know how bad the relations were between the Allies at that moment, how close they were to the disruption which was his only hope of survival."

The P.M. *with the telephone. He mutters, listens perforce, easing himself into the conversation, but soon unburdens his "partner" of the need to speak or express his own opinions.*

P.M.: Excellency—yes! Maisky, I am appalled.
    How often have I *begged* your Chief to give me time
    to make the Poles see reason.
    Almost enough to console Hitler for the burning of Hamburg.
    —What? You will be getting the pictures:
    that is, if Marshal Stalin still allows you
    to receive photographs from me—a great pity,
    your recall, my dear Maisky.
    Another victory for Hitler—
    [the Kremlin's replacing, at this moment in the war,
    their cleverest diplomat with a *chargé d'affaires*
    at the court of St. James.]
    No, my dear friend, I do not flatter you.
    [But since my son
    brought you to Chartwell for the first time in 1938,
    so much has happened
    and we have become friends as well.
    Please—Marshal Stalin must be told
    how deeply disappointed I am.]
    Not on the telephone;
    come and see me, if you are still allowed to.
    (*A laugh on many different levels.*)
    Although we must put off the landings
    in France once again.
    (*Pause, listens, then, violent:*)

No—Marshal Stalin is showing our film *Desert Victory*
all over Russia: he seems though to have forgotten
that we have after all
given the Hun a second Stalingrad in Africa.

CHERWELL *has been pacing up and down, precisely, his own
pedometer. The* PRIME MINISTER *gestures him to pick up the
extension. He repeatedly scribbles something on a piece of paper
which he holds out to the* PRIME MINISTER, *who nods in grateful
acknowledgment, or shakes his head brusquely, at which* CHER-
WELL *burns the note in the candle flame and throws it into the
metal wastepaper basket. On one occasion, he holds the file with
the cables from the Kremlin up for the* PRIME MINISTER *to read.*

The bombers *are* the Second Front.
(*Reads from* CHERWELL'*s note.*)
In one week alone
we have presented Krupp with eight hundred tons,
Duisburg, one thousand four hundred and fifty tons—
Stettin, seven hundred and eighty,
Rostock, a hundred and seventy . . . what?
Please, with all due respect, there I must disagree:
If we lose sixty bombers, we are losing
over four hundred men of our elite
not infrequently in a single night.
(*He listens.*)
[Excellency, that is quite simply misunderstood.
To be sure, we are stopping the convoys till the winter,
we cannot get them through in the north with any safety,
and we need our freighters ourselves in the Mediterranean.]
(*Reading again.*)
—No—no—write this down:
We are sending four hundred and thirty-five aircraft
via Gibraltar—yes, they will be assembled there.
(*To* CHERWELL:)
Aren't the Americans sending any?
(*In the receiver.* CHERWELL *goes out quickly.*)
I'm getting the figures . . . I mentioned Gibraltar.
[Naturally I accept your recall
in the spirit in which it is given—
as an affront, an extreme threat:

which I, however, am meeting in
a spirit of high forgiveness.]
I've asked [Mason MacFarlane]
the Governor to give you a royal reception,
I do beg your pardon—put out the red carpet.
Yes, a red one.
(*Laughs.*)
I'll see you get my best pilot—what?
Only fly with Russians? Splendid. Of course;
I just thought we ought to
take care of you a little—you're as bad as
de Gaulle: he won't go anywhere without
French pilots.
Even if you only have breakfast in Gib.
don't miss seeing the new gun emplacement;
eight quick-firing guns—get Mason Mac to show you.
[If you had had them in Sebastopol,
Manstein would have tried in vain
to take it, from the sea, at any rate.]
(*Holds the mouthpiece and says quickly to* CHERWELL, *who
has re-entered, and is holding out a note:*)
Sikorski in Gib. When?
(*Back to the telephone, while* CHERWELL *writes:*)
Oh, just the figures: the Americans
are sending through the Mediterranean and the Red Sea
the same number of aircraft
as the North Sea convoy would have brought you.
Some people are never satisfied—
You're as bad as the Poles—what . . . the *Poles!*
(*Now he listens, so does* CHERWELL *on the extension.*)
Excellency, a hundred and fifty thousand Poles are fighting
on our side, and fighting bravely.
Nevertheless, this does not make me the lackey of Sikorski,
as Marshal Stalin appears to think.
Katyn was none of my discovering!
Russia and Poland have a relationship
like that between a dog and his fleas:
let them live, these irritating neighbors.
I must go, I have to lunch with the King.
(*Casually.*)
Wait, before I forget, my dear Maisky,

I shall have to give you a date
for your arrival in Gib.
as Operation Husky begins in early July.
The Mediterranean will be like a cauldron,
we can't have you running around loose
in the middle of the greatest invasion in history!
[What island—ha! I mayn't even tell the Cabinet,
however, you may assume Sicily,
though Crete or Corfu or Sardinia
have most attractive bathing beaches, they tell me.
At all events, your visit to the Rock
must be between the fourth and the fifth of July.]
After that date my security men
will not be able to guarantee your safety,
although—I am really very fond of you—
you will be getting my very best watchdogs.
Good-by.
(*He hangs up. Looks at* CHERWELL. *Nods.*)
I was thinking in the bath—on the ninth,
in the Mediterranean,
these most dangerous landing operations will be beginning.
If the enemy should get wind of it, all will be over . . .
(*with sudden fury, clearly occasioned by some other cause
than the one he now expresses*)
and C. can think of nothing better
than precisely at this moment to withdraw his best men from
    that sector . . .
to look after Sikorski—
CHERWELL (*reassures him, without raising his voice*) :
But they only have to bring him to London on the fourth;
by the fifth, they will be back where they are needed
to keep Husky's security under hatches.
(*To show that the problem can now be considered settled:*)
Maisky is, of course, to be received
with the usual ceremonial for an ambassador?
P.M.: No—more than the usual.
He is the Russian Ambassador, after all.
What is that splendid brass band of MacFarlane's there for?
CHERWELL: And Sikorski?
Reception with all honors due
to a Head of State?

P.M. (*agitated, suddenly extremely ill at ease*):
    What are you thinking of?
    It isn't a State visit! Have you gone mad?
    It's a—single station of a tour of inspection
    by a—a General.
CHERWELL: The end station—all the same.
P.M. (*still fiercely*): A perfectly ordinary stopover in Gib.
    for the overhauling of the aircraft—
    What were you thinking of, for God's sake?

CHERWELL, *going, reaches for the doorknob, misses it, misses it
again, says nothing but looks at the* PRIME MINISTER *and away
again.*

    What were you thinking of, Prof.?
CHERWELL (*icily amused, his camouflage for feelings which he
    would find embarrassing*):
    This time—I only thought, forgive me . . .
    perfectly absurd, of course . . .
    I simply thought—
    felt, *without* thinking, rather . . . that this once . . .

CURTAIN

THE GARDEN

On the occasion of the twenty-first
anniversary of the cessation of hostilities,
the Warsaw government published the
final figures of the losses of the Second
World War. More than six million Poles
lost their lives, of whom three million,
two hundred thousand were Jews.
Only one tenth of the victims, some
six hundred and forty thousand persons,
of whom a hundred and twenty thousand
were soldiers, were killed in the fighting.
With two hundred and twenty dead per
thousand inhabitants, the Polish losses
were heavier than any other. (*May, 1966*)

"*God* Almightie *first planted a* Garden. *And indeed, it is the Purest of Humane Pleasures. It is the Greatest Refreshment to the Spirits of Man: without which,* Buildings *and* Palaces *are but Grosse Handy-works.*" *With these words Francis Bacon begins his* "*Essay in Praise of Gardens,*" *and here everything should be done to make this rustic counterpart of the seascape of Act One come up to the demands of the seventeenth-century courtier. The decor is to be an ironic reproach.*

The two people present at the beginning of the act, like the leader and the priest and the subject of the quarrel, show how far Man has got from the "*garden,*" *and how it has affected him. It is well known that it was not his fault that he could not stay there— which does not stop Pascal from aphoristically regretting this banality:* "*All man's sufferings come from the fact that he cannot sit quietly in his room.*" *Room or garden—three centuries later, Maeterlinck, to whom repose was anathema, flatly contradicted Pascal:* "*The good and ill fortune of mankind today are decided in small rooms, at the table, by the fireside.*" *Sometimes even the power maniacs themselves felt this:* "*That is easily said while both of us are sitting here in our armchairs. But behind it is an incalculable amount of suffering and blood. And do you wish to be responsible for that, Herr Schuschnigg?*"—*Hitler's words, before he overran Austria.*

At the front they are only carrying out sentences passed long before in what Hartlaub, writing his diary in Hitler's Command Headquarters, described as "*the dead, windless center of the typhoon.*" *This perhaps justifies the depiction of a theater of war from where its directors and stage managers sit. In any case, all that it is possible to show in the actual theater is the* "*green table*" (*the only title which, without being pretentious, will fit any historical play*); *a conifer plantation in East Prussia, a beach in Casablanca, or this apple orchard at Chequers, where one would hardly guess that the fall of man has already taken place.*

Nevertheless, a nervous irritability betrays how the peace of the sunny apple orchard under the fatuous smile of the blue sky gets on the nerves of the wire pullers and their marionettes: as if they were all aware how comfortless the path of man is on this earth since he ceased to be its gardener.

This can be seen in the lack of pleasure, the purely professional interest which CHURCHILL *shows here in the captured German*

173

machine gun. In such a garden he would normally have busied himself with painting or building: in wartime his desire to compensate in manual work is pent-up. This is a mechanical rather than a manual activity, with none of that avid pleasure that was otherwise inherent in even his most practical doings. (Even at seventy-five, he told the Director of the Tate Gallery that if it weren't for painting he could not live: he could not bear the strain of things. He occasionally amused himself with a pinball machine—once he tore the whole apparatus apart, cursing and swearing, until he had managed to get all the balls in play at once. It irritated him that one could only play a limited number of balls at a time. A bystander commented: "It certainly took away any point the game might have had, but Churchill was quite contented, and for ten minutes it gave him great satisfaction.")

GEORGE KENNEDY ALLEN BELL, *Bishop of Chichester, Honorary Doctor of the University of Basel, is the British Fénelon—a comparison which does not however permit us to mention* BELL's *antagonist, the* PRIME MINISTER, *in the same sentence as Louis XIV, whom Churchill regarded as the curse and plague of Europe— never had a worse enemy of human freedom appeared in the finery of civilized society.*

Hitler exceeded the sovereign of Mélac—but, keeping hold of this comparison, nothing points up the difference between CHURCHILL *and Hitler more than the way in which they treated their respective Fénelons. While Hitler fed the unimportant to the guillotine and was so afraid of the men of influence like Martin Niemöller and the Bishop of Münster that he reserved their murders until after the final victory,* CHURCHILL *refused even to place the British opponents of area-bombing under arrest.*

This is to WINSTON CHURCHILL's *personal credit far more than simply to that of British law. It was not just that Labour members had recommended the imprisonment of printers of opposition leaflets; the feeling throughout the whole country at the time sanctioned an orgiastic recommendation by Parliament to the Secretary of State for Air of Cromwell's policy of "killing in the Name of the Lord." Even in England, hardly anyone would have tried to stop* CHURCHILL *from arresting such defenseless advocates of humanity as the Quaker couple, the Catchpools, and not a few others. This* CHURCHILL *never did. He left it to the press, always usable in a crisis, to suppress and ridicule the letters and mani-*

festoes of the Bombing Restriction Committee. The largest number of protests were the work of Vera Brittain and the Catholic tank-manufacturer and Labour M.P. Richard Stokes.

Even the way CHURCHILL *dealt with* BELL *is to his honor. He did, to be sure, invariably and disconcertingly cause* BELL *to be received by Eden: The meeting with the* PRIME MINISTER *probably only took place in our imagination. Further, he maintained a studied ignorance of the highly provocative speeches made by the* BISHOP *in the House of Lords. Moreover, although as the leading figure of the Geneva Ecumenical Council* BELL *was the most celebrated of the British bishops, he was never nominated for the Archbishopric of Canterbury. But* CHURCHILL *nevertheless suffered* BELL *to stir up subversive religious misgivings and, in not a few cases, inner revulsion among the air crews of Bomber Command. And what the* BISHOP *expected personally of the* PRIME MINISTER—*who at the time of Gomorrah was the almost uncritically accepted leader of the Western world—was all the more hazardous since it was a full year after the attacks on Hamburg before the Air Chief Marshal's superiors realized that the destruction of residential areas was strategically useless. Even then they were unable, despite their efforts, to halt the progress of* CHURCHILL *and of Bomber Command, whom victory had sent out of control.*

BISHOP BELL *is a lover of the word. In 1904, at the age of twenty-one, he won the Newdigate Prize with a poem on Delphi and he continued to write poetry into his old age. In 1960, two years after his death, his widow had a handful of his poems printed for his friends.*

The BISHOP *has a short, wide nose, like* CHURCHILL's, *and his wide, strong chin and broad-lipped mouth indicate a passionate, aggressive nature, an impression relieved by the humor, which his friend Karl Barth emphasized as his most typical characteristic, visible undisguised in the corners of the eyes and nose. This humor can, however, quickly become as uncomfortable as the subject matter from which he strikes sparks; he uses it then as a supplementary weapon.* BELL *must have needed all his humor between 1943 and 1945 to help him overcome the shrill insults of the white-haired lords in the House—and of the press.*

It is irony that leads BELL *to pander to his adversary's weakness for the baroque and the ornamental in whatever form, and, although he is compelled to appear without the retinue of which* CHURCHILL *was so fond, nevertheless he appears dressed with some ceremony. Instinct warns* BELL, *as a civilian, not to come onto a stage mainly full of highly-decorated uniforms. Now, if ever, the astute churchman has planned to exploit to the fullest effect his seventeenth-century vestments.*

The fact that it is Sunday is a relief to the BISHOP *as it provides a necessary means of disillusioning the* PRIME MINISTER *that it is for his benefit that the* BISHOP *has donned the black, white, and gray robes which he had not worn since the father of the present King visited the Cathedral and Bishop's Palace of Chichester.*

BELL *is a very experienced and a very English orator. Anger makes him quiet, the excitement is in what he says, not the way he says it. He also knows what a member once said to Joseph Chamberlain after his fluent maiden speech: "The House would feel a lot easier if you could manage to stutter a little here and there."*

In Reiner's biography of the most assured orator Germany ever had, he quotes an eyewitness: "Bismarck stumbled while speaking: he had a still, small voice, he interrupted himself, corrected himself, emphasized the wrong words, he was choked with the plentitude of his thoughts and his knowledge, he battled with words . . . he heaped up inversions on one another, anacolutha, every possible grammatical mistake, repeated himself, doubled back, lost the thread of the sentence . . . I have often thought his formidable clearing of the throat to be an oratorical trick."

BELL *does not do this but one can see he knows all about it.*

There is the same amount of space here as on the deck of the battleship.

At the back of the stage and to the left, a splendid French window connects the terrace with the inside of the house. At the left of the stage, a brick wall, starting right downstage, continues for a few yards upstage, far enough for these two walls to enclose a narrow terrace with three wide shallow steps leading from it, and a low, projecting baroque balustrade. The terrace and the steps should not dominate the setting but simply mark off the left-hand side and top left-hand corner of the stage.

For we are not in the house, but in the open air. The steps, the French windows, the walls of the house, the sunniest of which sports a small awning under which stands a little table with various colored telephones and a typewriter, all these are only, as it were, concessions to the "intimate sphere" of the man of command. Opposite the bottom of the steps, in the right foreground, a grassy hillock with a semicircular, eight-legged, white-painted eighteenth-century seat under a tree. No table in front of it. High hedges serve as a demarcation line, stage right, but far from giving a feeling of restraint should rather serve to lead the eye out over the Buckinghamshire landscape of the Chilterns around Princes Risborough on the picture-book projection on the backcloth. The sky is blue to the point of fatuity— nothing indicates any truth in the rumor that the country seat of England's Prime Ministers brings bad luck to its occupants. CHURCHILL, *a superstitious man, only lives there as a duty, perhaps for that reason, since it was here almost exactly three years ago that he received the news that France had laid down her arms before Hitler. On that occasion the weather was particularly fine "as appears often to happen at critical moments of British history," Duff Cooper points out. Nevertheless, it was also here, and also on a Sunday, that the* PRIME MINISTER *received the message that spelled salvation, the news that "that man over there" had at last attacked Russia: at which* CHURCHILL *had an especially good cigar brought on a silver salver to the bedside of his guest the Foreign Secretary.*

After the rise of the curtain the stage remains empty for a moment. Nevertheless, the radio is on and from it comes an announcer's voice:

ANNOUNCER: . . . early hours of this morning the long-expected German offensive on Kursk, in the central sector of the Russian front. Russian units are at present carrying out successful action to adjust their dispositions—reports received at noon today make it clear that the Germans have not succeeded in breaking through.

HELEN *brings* KOCJAN *out of the house onto the terrace. He is ill at ease. She makes sure they are alone, switches off the radio as she passes, looks over the balustrade into the garden, then says quickly:*

HELEN: The Prime Minister wants to speak to you alone!
 (*Quieter, pleading:*)
 Can't you just say you still have to see General Sikorski?
 Then you needn't go till tomorrow evening.
KOCJAN: But he is not in London.
HELEN: But he is coming.
KOCJAN: Where from?

HELEN: That I can't tell you.
> The P.M. called him back, for today.

KOCJAN: Oh—Helen—I'm sorry. But I'm afraid . . .
> my men, will be already on their way to wait for
> me, into the woods.
> It was—so good to be with you, Helen.
> Here is your keys.

HELEN: What for?—keep them.

KOCJAN: Tonight you must come to me. The Captain sends
> a car for me at twenty to one.

HELEN: But not to the hotel—to my flat.

KOCJAN: But what if they notice that I am with you?

HELEN: Why not? Anyway they've known for ages—

KOCJAN (*hurt*): Have you nothing better to do
> than shadowing us Poles in London even?

HELEN: Shadowing?—Shielding!

KOCJAN *takes a card out of the breast pocket of his British army
uniform.*

KOCJAN: Shades of meaning. Here, if you will call me to—
> for changing the car . . . ach, I am so nervous
> about Churchill; when he come?

HELEN (*quickly*): Bohdan—you need an excuse.
> Otherwise he'll keep you here to see the Nelson
> film he shows to all his guests. Then he will
> have you taken direct to Northolt.

KOCJAN: Our last night: *that* I will myself defend
> against the Grand Alliance.

HELEN: And don't shoot, if you're asleep first.
> The one who creeps in beside you
> will be quite unarmed.

KOCJAN: You will never forgive me the pistol in bed, you are
> right.

HELEN *laughs.*

> My nerves are ridiculous, but at least
> in the forest they are useful still,
> in peace no good, kaput. Houses are traps.

HELEN: Mine?

KOCJAN: Yours especial.

HELEN (*helpless, violent*):

You must come back, you must come back,
come back.

She has drawn him over to the wall, he holds her, kisses her hurriedly, uneasy.

She looks once more toward the garden, then at him again. Both of them have tried to avoid this moment and they are still at pains to preserve a relaxed cynicism, thanks to the view that the only reasonable way of life is one based on expectation of life. This conversation, which they had carefully avoided, has now overtaken them, perhaps because their usual escape from it is impossible out here on the terrace. As long as they were able to make love, they could suppress their intimations that this flight of KOCJAN's *will take him further than Poland.*

(Neither of them would ever be able to understand how sexual behavior can be inflated into a problem in peacetime, especially in those countries sheltering happily, if stupidly, to the leeside of history. But where it is not the psychiatrist but Death who stands at the bedside, love is the one surviving thing which is no problem; when it is not neuroses that disturb one's sleep, but the tragic calculation of how long it will be before the body one longs to hold onto will be drawn into the underworld, as surely as the compass needle is drawn to the north. A sentence of Lawrence of Arabia's, written in 1929, seems, even by 1943, a piece of arch-romanticism: "We torment ourselves with inherited pangs of conscience about the lusts of the flesh which are given to us, and concern themselves with paying for them with a life full of pain . . ." This confession is only relevant to the years of the Second World War in that from it one may gather how human were the "sins" of the men in the First. Had the warriors of the Hitler era slaked their thirst for sin in the flesh alone, how humanely the war might have been fought—at any rate behind the front lines, which is where, this time, it was at its worst.)

KOCJAN: Don't be alone, Helen.
It is too difficult in war.
We agreed to this.
HELEN (*ironically*):
Agreed! Of course—I can get my sister to stay with me.
KOCJAN: Nonsense. From yesterday till today: our night,
no one can interfere with that.
What has fidelity to do with bodies?

[HELEN (*irritated*):
    "Her love was eternal; when her husband . . .
    (*She is suddenly horrified at what she was about to quote,
    and quickly bowdlerizes:*)
    . . . when her husband went away,
    she found another."
    (*She is confused, trapped.*)
KOCJAN (*gruesomely amused, also takes her tactlessness not as re-
    ferring to himself. He knows very well that* HELEN *is thinking of
    her dead husband*):
    We know that in Poland too, but you said it wrong:
    Not when he went away, when he died:
    she found another—
    that was not cynical, it was sad.]
    How you live with your husband still.
HELEN (*tears in her eyes. He strokes the back of her neck*):
    Perhaps we wrong the dead,
    by *not* forgetting them, but letting them look on.
    One is always betraying somebody,
    sometimes the very man one is sleeping with.
KOCJAN (*and the melancholy with which he recommends cheer-
    fulness is almost laughable*):
    My father used to say, when I was growing up—
    because I used to go around
    with the sorrows of the world on my head—
    beware of melancholy, my son,
    it is a vice, the only one.
HELEN: Do you think I don't *know*
    what you're going to have to do in Poland?
    Where *is* your father?
KOCJAN (*putting this aside*): Oh—

Telephone.

HELEN: Second Officer MacDonald. The Prime Minister is
    still asleep, your Lordship. Very well—yes,
    I'll make a note. "Duke of York." "Norfolk."
    "Belfast." Convoy JW 55B with fourteen destroyers—
    "Scharn-horst." Thank you, Sir—"Scharnhorst," yes.
    He'll ring you straight away. Thank you, Sir.
    (*To* KOCJAN *after she has hung up:*)
    Before you put the light on, don't forget the blackout.

> The coins for the water heater are in a blue soap dish
> in front of the mirror.

KOCJAN: Thank you, I know.

HELEN: And in the refrigerator—eat it all,
I always have some left over.
I usually eat here or in Downing Street, and . . .
(*Glancing into the garden:*)
He's coming, but not alone.
He's playing with the carp.

KOCJAN: Not alone? Then don't say my name—
call me . . . Karski.
Do you think he is also thinking
something—about you and me?

HELEN (*amused*): Don't worry. Mr. Churchill is interested
exclusively in Mr. Churchill.

*She speaks without bitterness: It is one of the "foibles" which
make him popular since "but for our faults we are all ciphers."
Silence. Voices.*

Now—

She steps off the terrace onto the grass to meet the PRIME MINIS-
TER *and salutes.* CHURCHILL *enters with* DORLAND, *now a Wing
Commander. They are both in RAF uniform,* CHURCHILL *in that
of an Air Commodore, his cap square on his head, in his hand
the Bengal cane with the gold knob and the arms of the House of
Marlborough, a wedding present from Edward VII.*

At HELEN'S *first words he begins to seethe with impatience. He
comes straight onto the terrace, stumping up and down until he is
connected with the Admiralty, yet in no way neglecting his guests.
He draws* KOCJAN *to him at arm's length and shakes his hand
warmly, as he does all his guests, talks to the Pole, introduces him
to* DORLAND, *talks to* DORLAND, *to both of them, and to* HELEN,
*and thinks all the time only about the battleship in the Barents
Straits, passes comments on the artillery duel in the Arctic Sea to
the officers on the terrace while he talks on the telephone to the
First Sea Lord. One feels this septuagenarian who thirty-two years
ago took over the Admiralty for the first time is fretting and
chafing because it is impossible for him to command this battle
too, although he himself was never present at a naval engagement.*

HELEN (*announcing the news, which in "fact," according to the chronology of the war, did not arrive till Christmas of this year*): Sir—a call from the Admiralty.
At nine o'clock this morning the cruiser "Belfast,"
of the convoy escort . . .

P.M.: I know, I know where she is . . . what about her?

HELEN: She established radar contact at thirty miles
with the battleship "Scharnhorst"—

P.M. (*radiant, points to the telephone*):
First Sea Lord.

HELEN (*calmly*): The cruiser "Norfolk" opened fire soon after—
the "Scharnhorst" turned and made headway
in a southwesterly direction.

P.M. (*agitated*): Chased off—Why?

HELEN: No, Prime Minister—radar contact was renewed
at noon.
[The "Belfast," the "Sheffield," and the "Norfolk" attacked again,
scored several hits, the "Norfolk" was hit severely twice,
the "Scharnhorst" headed about again, without having come up with the convoy.]
Meanwhile, however, the Commander-in-Chief
has come up with the "Duke of York"; the range has lessened;
the German cannot get away now . . .
Captain—Karski.

The PRIME MINISTER, *as* HELEN *hurries to the telephone, holds out his hand and draws* KOCJAN *to him. With a movement of his head he invites* DORLAND, *who is still on the lawn, up onto the terrace. All the time he goes on talking:*

P.M.: Has the "Scharnhorst" no destroyer escort?
And where are ours? Asleep?
Ah, Captain . . . is it you? How splendid?
—Wing Commander Dorland: our liaison officer
with the American Eighth Bomber Command.

KOCJAN: Karski.

He bows slightly in DORLAND's *direction.* DORLAND *holds out his hand. Embarrassed by the English custom of not giving his own name, he murmurs: "How do you do?"*

P.M.: What about that, Dorland?
  Incredible, the "Scharnhorst"!—The last heavy vessel
  that man there has.
HELEN (*on the telephone*): The Prime Minister, Sir.
DORLAND: Not the "Tirpitz"?
HELEN (*gives* CHURCHILL *the receiver*):
  The First Sea Lord, Sir.
P.M. (*still to* DORLAND, *then in the receiver*):
  The "Tirpitz"?—We prescribed her a few days in bed
  with midget subs.
  (*Muttering, irritated at having to listen. Then, with great
  urgency:*)
  Nonsense; don't keep her off the convoy—
  use it as bait.
  [Hitler still has torpedo bombers in Narvik.]
  Yes. Give it as my order—the destruction
  of this last operational heavy enemy vessel
  will justify severe losses on our part.
  [If the "Duke of York" does not arrive on time
  the convoy must lessen speed, so that the "Scharnhorst"
  will think there is a genuine chance
  of attacking it.] In no case must the Hun
  be scared off by our three cruisers.
  (*Hangs up.*)
  [It is monstrous that one large ship should tie up
  such a large proportion of the Home Fleet.
  Still, the day of the classic sea battle will soon be over.
DORLAND: You think the aircraft carrier will outdate the battle-
        ship?
P.M.: Since the Japs' torpedo bombers sunk our two largest
  ships in the Pacific in barely three hours, the
  battleship has become a museum piece.]
  (*To* KOCJAN:)
  If this is a victory, Captain Karski, it is
  partisans like yourself we shall have to thank.
  Without the Norwegian Resistance Movement
  we could never have heard in time when Hitler
  was sending his big fish out of their hiding places in the
        fjords.

Telephone. HELEN *answers, takes a message, then hangs up.*

(*Without interruption:*)
Do you understand me, or am I speaking too fast?
(*This is the first sentence which he has not spoken almost in-comprehensibly fast.*)

KOCJAN: Thank you, Prime Minister—I
understood parts very well.

HELEN: Sir, the Bishop of Chichester has just driven up.

P.M. (*annoyed*): Punctual as Nemesis. Dorland—and Helen—
be tough with him. But first
he can amuse himself with Air Marshal Harris;
maybe then I shall be spared his visit altogether.

HELEN *goes out.*

Do you know, Captain Karski—

He points into the garden with his stick, on which, incidentally, he never leans, first, because he walks much too fast to be able to put the stick on the ground; secondly, it is only a toy, light and use-less as a dress sword—useful only for underlining his lavish, ex-pressive gestures.

Dorland, you too—at the shooting range
are a couple of captured German machine guns—
the most vicious secret weapon since radar, I have to say.
(*Cautiously to* DORLAND, *in order to conceal more than to reveal:*)
Captain Karski is from Warsaw and
is to join the Polish Brigade in Africa
tomorrow—we have some things to discuss—
[Dorland, pray, would you be good enough to fetch one of
those inhuman killers?]

DORLAND (*going*): Of course, Prime Minister.

P.M. (*looks about him, then hooks his arm into* KOCJAN's *amicably and brings him forward, blinking*):
What your real name is, I cannot remember:
still, nothing to do with me.

KOCJAN: Bohdan Kocjan, Prime Minister.

P.M.: Bohdan is enough—the rest too much—

He looks around again. HELEN *has just come onto the terrace.*

Helen—see we are not disturbed.
Stay in earshot.

HELEN: Yes, Sir. The Bishop is with Air Marshal Harris.

P.M. (*not pausing*):
Good. You see, Bohdan, before we actually *possess*
one of the rockets, all our defense preparations
—you understand me?—
are based on hypothesis.

KOCJAN: Prime Minister—it will take a long time
before the Germans attack you with rockets.
They only experiment, experiment and experiment,
and always they are losing direction and exploding
in the air—and they cannot yet aim.

P.M.: Aim?—You do not have to *aim*
to hit the largest city in the world somewhere or other.
But how do you propose to do this?
Fantastic!

KOCJAN: I have ten men and women—good.
With bicycles. At night too. You can
see the trails behind the rockets.
The Germans do not find many of them—
we are *in* the woods—the Germans must
first go there when a rocket falls. But
we have seen five times already now how
rockets come down undamaged. The
Germans have made them—not to explode;
we have taken to pieces and brought back.
We will find a complete rocket
quicker—before the Germans, and then
hide him . . .

P.M.: In the ground?

KOCJAN: In ground or the river.
River is better. To throw
him into the Bug—fields there too,
not far from the river, are good for
landing your Dakota.

P.M.: And you will come back with our aircraft,
when you have got the rocket on board?
There is no decoration which can repay
this act of yours. Never forget: by helping us
you are helping Poland. What is happening in the Arctic?
(*Turns away, goes to the balustrade and calls into the garden:*)
Helen; you too, Dorland.

Bohdan, my predecessors were so civilized
as to plant fruit trees here as well;
help yourself, fish, swim, play skittles—
this evening we shall see the Nelson film . . .
Helen, tell the Admiralty I do not expect
them to fail to take action
against the enemies' torpedo carriers.

[HELEN *nods and goes out after giving* KOCJAN *a frightened glance and a signal, on account of the Nelson film.* CHURCHILL, *taking the MG-42 out of* DORLAND's *hand, weighs it in his own and passes it to* KOCJAN.

Take it apart, please.
Dorland, before I forget, from today
carry a toothbrush—sometime, somewhere,
a car will pick you up: You will belong to my
suite if I sail to Washington—or fly. The
President likes courageous young men about the
place. So does the press over there.

DORLAND (*radiant*):
Thank you, Sir. It is—a great surprise.

P.M.: Well—let us hope there won't be any on the journey.
The number of ships the U-boats sank
in March even, is appalling. Since April though
(*laughs grimly*)
we have been slaughtering the sharks
like fishing trout out of a pond for lunch.
The Huns called the mid-Atlantic
the Black Hole.
The submarine pack lurked there in ambush,
because we couldn't give air escort to our ships
as far as that, neither from Canada nor England.
The Black Hole, a wonderful description—
the blackest for some forty German ships.
Forty in barely six weeks.
Bohdan, tell that in Poland, I mean to the Poles—
when you get to Africa tomorrow.

KOCJAN: Yes, Prime Minister.

P.M.: What your fields are to you,
the sea is to us, the provider.

He picks up the band of the MG. KOCJAN *dismantles the weapon with the assurance with which he would use a penknife, and puts in the belt.* DORLAND *imitates him.*

DORLAND: Can that be true?
A thousand rounds a minute?
KOCJAN: More. Thousand five hundred.
Useless for partisans. When have we
thousand five hundred bullets?
The whole machinery is built
for continuous—or for rapid fire.
DORLAND: Doesn't the speed of fire give an enormous coverage?
KOCJAN: Sure—in fixed position, with organized reinforcements,
very fantastic. Especial in winter—
still fires at forty below zero.
And easy to use. After about three hundred rounds
in busts . . .
P.M.: Bursts.
KOCJAN: Thank you, Sir . . . bursts of twenty to thirty rounds
that barrel is not too hot to handle
with a leather glove.
P.M. (*picks up the barrel again, angrily*): Helen, make a note.
DORLAND: She is not here, Sir, shall I . . .
P.M.: Yes, she is to make a note to talk
to Lord Cherwell tomorrow about this material—
astonishing.

KOCJAN *has put the gun together again and sets it on its stand. The* PRIME MINISTER, *like a child, kicks rather than pushes it aside. That he would like to have such a weapon should not lead us to forget how he despises everything that makes of war "a business of attrition," degrading it in the manner of Verdun and the Somme. For this reason he values this weapon no more than he does one of the bad generals of the First World War who had no idea other than to make frontal attacks with measureless loss of blood and proportional lack of point. The great man is unconscious that he himself, the sternest critic of the attrition generals, has fostered in "Bomber" Harris the archetype of them all, equipping him with unique power and even insisting on the "butchery" (at the expense of British aircrews) at a time when many leading men of the RAF, as of other services, believed—by summer, 1944—that the burning of population centers had no*

military value. A man's wrong turnings are all of a piece with the
direct path he follows.

P.M.: A thousand at one blow, this thing is supposed to mow down:
     frightful.
     I always compare the nine hundred thousand wretched
         Britons,
     pointlessly slaughtered in the First War,
     with the hundred and eighty-five who fell at Trafalgar!
     Barely two hundred Englishmen
     snatched world tyranny from Napoleon.
     —You are silent, Dorland?

DORLAND (*smiling*):
     I was thinking, Sir, of the four and a half thousand Frenchmen
     who fell at Trafalgar
     whose names are not inscribed in Notre Dame.

P.M. (*smiling*):
     It never occurred to *me* not to be on the winning side.
     A soldier is a man unweakened by doubt.
     You are a brave man—with so much disbelief.

DORLAND (*embarrassed*):
     A man is only brave at the point of a gun
     not at the trigger.

P.M. (*with sympathy, since he himself always has to conquer his*
     fear):
     The real heroes—yes—
     then there are the others,
     the valorous in God's grace,
     who have no fear of death
     because they lack imagination.
     Happy the army with a majority
     of courageous blockheads: it is invincible.
     It is, moreover, a simple question of age:
     After the First War, Heye, the head
     of the German operations department,
     explained—correctly, I think—the failure of
     the last German offensive in March, 1918,
     by the high average age of the regiments.
     Attacking power, he said, is only found,
     where the main body of the men is under twenty-five.
     Above that age, even soldiers do not want to die.]

While he is speaking, the BISHOP OF CHICHESTER *appears with a suddenness which is in grotesque contrast to the orderly folds of his cassock. No one has announced him—he stands before the* PRIME MINISTER *like an assassin, an impertinence of almost Churchillian dimensions, so much so that* CHURCHILL, *to whom this has never happened before, is at a loss for words—something else that has never happened to him before. The white-haired* BISHOP *is not an old man. He does not stay standing on the terrace—he merely registers that he is in* CHURCHILL'*s presence, and, before* CHURCHILL *can turn round to address him—for the* PRIME MINISTER *had his back to the* BISHOP *and only noticed him from* DORLAND'*s reaction—*BELL *comes down onto the lawn. He leaves the door open, as if he were* CHURCHILL.

BELL (*with an Englishman's unique capacity for speaking quietly at moments of extreme anger, and with biting enunciation*):
    Forgive me, Prime Minister—I can wait perfectly
    well, but not—
    with—I will wait in the garden,
    not with your Bomber Chief,
    with his drumroll of military clichés.

He breaks off and tries to get past CHURCHILL *into the open.*

P.M.: He is after all the expert
    on the problem we have to discuss.
BELL (*calmer, but no friendlier*):
    That I do not believe—since he apparently
    sees in the burning of a city's inhabitants
    a purely technical problem. I shall be glad to wait
    until you—
KOCJAN: May I go now into the garden?
P.M. (*with a friendly glance at* KOCJAN):
    We shall meet this evening.
    (*To* BELL, *almost a threat:*)
    Wing Commander Dorland—Dr. Bell, the Bishop of Chi-
        chester.
    The Wing Commander, Bishop, received the DFC
    this morning at the hands of His Majesty
    in recognition of his leading part
    in the bombing of the dams in Germany.
    (*Almost a shout, a lightning conductor:*)
    Helen! Has the "Duke of York" still not come up?

BELL *shakes* DORLAND's *hand warmly.* HELEN *has appeared in the doorway.*

HELEN: No, Sir—but the position of the "Scharnhorst" leaves no
room for doubt
that Admiral Fraser will be on time.

BELL: My congratulations, Wing Commander—and to you, Prime
Minister,
on this great action. Can the dams be repaired?

DORLAND: I fear so.

P.M.: For the time being the deluge
is come over lands and peoples,
the electricity in the Ruhr, in Kassel,
is paralysed, and with it the factories—

BELL *now lifts up the open newspaper.*

BELL: But why, gentlemen—why then are we doing this?
Here—*Basler Nachrichten,* neutral
eyewitness accounts of the Hamburg tragedy—

P.M. (*screws up his nose as he always has when he wishes to pro-
voke—one of his methods of getting the conversation into his
end of the court*):
Tragedy?—not for the RAF this time, however.
(*Notes* BELL's *reaction with cold satisfaction, and continues:*)
Am I right, Dorland?

DORLAND: Yes, only two point eight per cent losses.

P.M.: *Basler Nachrichten,* well. The
Swedish press states that Gomorrah
has been the most decisive victory
of the RAF since the Battle of Britain.

BELL *has realized that the most persuasive orator of the age has
sublimated his anger at having to take notice of an adversary into
the pleasure of defeating one, even this one—that all of a sudden
he clearly likes having him there. So* BELL *all but turns his back
on the* PRIME MINISTER, *and addresses himself entirely to* DOR-
LAND. CHURCHILL *takes off his cap, lays down the stick, and sits
firmly, knees apart, fists on the seat, in the middle of the bench.*

BELL: Were you too—on the Hamburg raid, Mr. Dorland?

DORLAND: I went over with the Americans once by day.
We tried to knock out the U-boat dockyards.

BELL: With success?

P.M. (*argumentatively*):
Nothing about that in your newspapers, Bishop, is there?
That there is also industry for us to destroy in Hamburg?

BELL: Indeed there is. The reports are detailed;
they point out, though, that burning down a city
does not by any means put an end to her economic existence.

P.M.: Economic existence over there will only be affected
if we "Coventrate" the German cities.
Harris has learned a good lesson from Göring.
Already with the burning of Rostock
fifteen months ago our score with the Huns was even.

BELL: Do you not shrink from actions
which are called murder when Hitler performs them?

P.M. (*with honesty*):
No. The battlefield is at the *enemy's* level.
How otherwise am I to throttle him, stamp him out?
I must struggle with him on the *same* ground,
according to *my* technical capacity.
I could not lay siege to Hamburg, as Hitler has to Leningrad:
There in two years he sentenced
every eighth citizen to death by starvation,
more people probably than we have killed
so far in all our raids on Germany.
From one single city, Amsterdam,
Hitler has carried off one hundred thousand citizens.
Where to? Nothing has been heard of them.

BELL (*with sarcasm*): More people probably than Hitler has killed
so far in all his raids on England,
we kill with Gomorrah in a single night.

The PRIME MINISTER *rises. He is standing higher up than the* BISHOP. *He comes down the little grassy slope, his head sunk in the way in which, even in his thirties, he was having himself photographed, his right shoulder hunched up, his right hand on his hip.*

P.M.: Unavoidable: adversaries in war will use each other's methods and worse besides, each other's qualities.

BELL (*going toward him, interrupting*):
Like every man in England, I thanked God

when in the hour of need *you* took the helm;
but Gomorrah is *not* self-defense.
We are too close to victory—our fury is unworthy.
Wing Commander—I ask you:
Are not these actions a betrayal of the ideals
that impelled us all—unanimously to declare
war on tyranny?

He puts the newspaper down on the bench; it falls to the ground.
Out of his pocket he takes a sheet of paper from which he reads:

Here from various reports—the first estimates
kept secret from the German population:
Forty-five per cent more female casualties than male,
twenty per cent of the dead—under fourteen years of age.
With a corresponding percentage of casualties
of fifty-five and over. Hammerbrook?
A working class area, apparently . . .

P.M.: Those at least we do aim for.
Middle-class districts are too spread out.
Three out of five bombs fall in the gardens.

BELL: I see. In Hammerbrook
every third inhabitant or more was burned to death.
Outside many houses they found the charred bodies
of mothers with children who had tried to escape
from the cellars and had been turned into torches.

P.M. (*grimly, since listening is difficult for him*):
Asphalt plus phosphorus: yes. Firestorm:
Cherwell can explain it.

BELL: In the *Basler Nachrichten* a doctor stated
the incineration in the cellars is often
more complete than in the normal process of cremation.
[Even today, a fortnight later, the
rescue operations are frequently made harder by the heat
in the shelters being so great
that any addition of oxygen causes
further fires.]
Several streets have been walled up on account of epidemics.
(*A question for* DORLAND.)
May I ask you: Is a pilot who bombs
population centers under orders
still to be called a *soldier?*

P.M.: Later—cross-examine Dorland later.
      Helen!—Anything from the "Duke of York"?

While BELL *was reading the last sentence of the Hamburg report,
the* PRIME MINISTER, *listening hostilely, had rung a bell. As* HELEN
appears, CHURCHILL *gives her a signal to wait.*

HELEN: Sir, the German has been heading
       straight for her for the last twenty minutes.
       The Admiralty thinks the "Scharnhorst" is
       sailing without radar.
P.M. (*excited*): Bishop, you see,
       the war has more theaters than Gomorrah.
BELL (*icy*): Is Hamburg a theater of war?
P.M.: Very much so. I want you to understand
       my refusal to regard the saturation bombing
       in isolation. Yesterday I delayed
       sending a cable to the President as
       I learned your visit was announced for
       today. You may listen to it—
       Very well, Helen, to the White House:

HELEN *sits hesitantly on the extreme left-hand edge of the semicircular bench, since* BELL, *at a gesture from* CHURCHILL, *has
taken the right-hand corner. Like any other good secretary, her
face also shows the degree of favor (or disfavor) felt by her boss
for his guest. Her abruptness toward* BELL *is striking, though she
is probably only interested in him as something else to worry the
already overburdened* PRIME MINISTER. CHURCHILL *has picked
up the captured MG once again and bangs the lock back and
forth as he dictates:*

"I have to inform you that in recent months . . .
a flood of reports has reached us, about a
German attack . . . being prepared against London
with extra long-range *rockets,* which, it is conjectured,
weigh sixty tons and carry a warhead
of between ten and twenty tons. On the basis
of these reports we have bombed
the main experimental station at Peenemünde"—Dorland
(don't take this down, Helen) tell the Bishop about that raid.
Harris attacked with five hundred and seventy bombers . . .

DORLAND (*telling the story with more reluctance than his comrades later showed in telling it to the historian David Irving*):
    Defining the target was difficult, as we knew the Jerries
    had blanketed the whole island,
    rocket sites and all, with artificial fog.
    Our apparatus couldn't show the target well enough,
    so we had to go over by moonlight.
    Moonlight, however, gives the night-fighters a sitting target.
    To draw the Germans off, the C.-in-C.
    had routed the main force in the direction of Berlin.
    It worked. We changed course, but
    to see the aiming points we had to go down
    to eight thousand feet. Our bombing caused such damage
    we wouldn't have needed to go over again,
    but by the time we started for home, the Germans
    had tumbled to our deception with Berlin and
    took us on over the Baltic. It was such a shambles,
    I don't even know whether we got
    any of them; anyway we lost forty planes.
    That is . . .
P.M.: That is forty times seven men like Dorland,
    Bishop. Barely three hundred whose sacrifice
    has perhaps saved London for the time being.
    Dorland, tell the Bishop what we don't tell the
    newspapers: what it is like up there when you
    are on fire.—Helen, perhaps you would go
    until I call you.
HELEN: Oh, thank you, Sir, but I do know . . .

The PRIME MINISTER *has nodded kindly to her;* HELEN *waits a moment, then goes all the same.* BELL *turns to* DORLAND, *says to him slowly—the last part however to* CHURCHILL, *hard—*

BELL: My imagination is sufficient to tell me
    it is no easier for a man to die
    in a bomber than in a shelter.
    My admiration for the men who bomb
    targets like Peenemünde is—
P.M.: These are the very same men, my Lord, that bombed
    Gomorrah . . .
BELL: On your orders. That is why I am here.
    (*He gestures to* DORLAND.)

DORLAND: The Prime Minister meant that . . .
a fire in the air often cannot be put out.
The Americans are trying at the moment
to eliminate the German fighters in air engagements.
I was with them over Hanover,
when we shut down the tire factories there.
BELL: By day?
DORLAND: Yes, a target attack. We flew
in very close formation since
we had no fighter escort,
though our defensive armament
was heavy enough, it is true.
BELL: No escort fighters?
DORLAND: They are still being built. What they have
for the present, Thunderbolts,
have to turn back at the German coast
or they don't have enough fuel for the journey back.
None of the American crews survives
more than ten operations, at the moment.
P.M.: You find iniquitous our not aiming at strictly military targets;
I find iniquitous what the Americans ask their young men
to do.
Dorland—

DORLAND *is uneasy at having to chat about such "intimacies" and
speaks with the insensitivity of scar tissue, emphatically anti-
dramatic: without realizing it, his manner alienates him from
the* PRIME MINISTER, *as from the* BISHOP, *and from all noncombatants, whose business this is not.*

DORLAND: Already on the way over two of the Fortresses
were caught in their own slipstream—a maelstrom—
incalculable, like being on a swing. At any rate,
two of them collided and went down.
Then the fighters arrived out of nowhere.
Some of them are masters of the art; they hide
in our condensation trails and suddenly attack.
If their fire is accurate, they can perforate
the hull of a Fortress and tear it off like a stamp.
Where I was, one of the turret gunners was hit,
Sergeant Weaver. He rolled
down the steps onto the floor, his left arm

hanging by a thread, the shoulder joint almost
shot away. His face—just a mouth, but not
screaming—he didn't scream. He fainted in our hands,
green as water. Morphine injection.
They tried to get me on the radio, but the set
was out of action. The bomb aimer yelled for me.
We tried to tie up the artery. No good.
I had to go back to the cockpit; if the pilot
had been hit, we'd all have had it—
the Germans were still all round us.
But the man was bleeding to death, so—"Chuck him out,"
I said, "Chuck him out."

BELL *and* P.M. *together.*

P.M.: ⎫ How could he open his parachute?
BELL: ⎭ Out of the airplane?
DORLAND: We managed to release the pilot chute
before we threw him out. He couldn't put up any more
resistance. We heard three weeks ago via the Red Cross
that he was saved.
BELL (*upset*): How could you count on that?

One can see that CHURCHILL *is somehow irritated by this anecdote
and even more so by the confidence that* DORLAND *seems to put in
German assistance.*

DORLAND: Count? Hope. If a doctor down there had not
taken care of Weaver, then I would—have said
nothing about it. In case of failure, keep your trap shut.
BELL (*putting up defenses against the story, warding it off*):
It is insane—that we are willfully killing people whom we expect
to pick up our men and look after them.
P.M. (*hard, to put an end to the sentimentality to which he has
already fallen victim*):
Insane, Bishop?—Surely it goes without saying
that one should tend a wounded prisoner?
BELL (*with anger*):
For me, yes—I have never denied
that there should be a difference in the treatment
of soldiers and defenseless people.
That is why I am here.

In the cemetery at Darmstadt stood an ordinary bucket
for burial. Contents: bone ash. And a card:
Twenty eight people from No. 11, Kiesstrasse.
Noncombatants, Prime Minister. Do your aerial photographs
show that sort of detail?—Here!

BELL *takes five photographs from his pocket. It is quiet for a long
time as the pictures go from hand to hand, from* DORLAND *to*
CHURCHILL *and back.*

From Sweden. From the men who introduced me to
the two Germans who had the plan to murder Hitler.
P.M. (*grateful for the diversion, but icily*):
Ah yes—we must also talk about
your conspiracy in Sweden.
May I keep these pictures, Bishop?
BELL (*angry*): Would you dare to publish a single one of them—
in your memoirs?
How can His Majesty's Government be answerable
(*he points to* DORLAND)
for sacrificing our best men, in hordes,
in operations about which they will wish to remain silent
after the war is over.
P.M. (*relaxed, quietly*): Politics is what—one does not speak of.
One must be silent about many things
that one has done in war.
[What, pray, Bishop, does it affect? Certainly not victory,
and only the victor writes the history books.
Well, Helen?
HELEN (*who has entered once more*):
The Admiralty announces the convoy is out of range . . .
P.M. (*sulking*): The *convoy,* the convoy.
The convoy is a minor matter today.
HELEN: . . . is out of range of the "Scharnhorst." She is still
heading for the "Duke of York." Admiral Fraser has
ordered his four destroyers to prepare torpedo attack
for 16:17 hours.

The PRIME MINISTER *pulls out his watch and only puts it back
later, after he has paced up and down and given, with enthusiasm,
his explanation . . .*

P.M.: She hasn't seen the "Duke of York" then.
Amazing.
We didn't have it so easy twenty years ago,
the first time I made a "Scharnhorst" food for fishes.
(*Suddenly as angry as* BELL *was a moment ago.*)
My justification for sending men like Dorland,
then, against noncombatants?] Tell me:
how am I to justify the sending of a convoy
to Murmansk, when I *calculate* that it—
and with it, our merchant seamen—
will be annihilated?
The convoy, like the bombing, proves to the Kremlin
that it does not fight alone,
and every man in Russia has a claim to such a proof.
Helen, finish the cable to the White House. [Where was I?

HELEN (*opens her pad, reads*):
" . . . bombarded the main experimental station
at Peenemünde"—

P.M. (*dictates at great speed*):
"Further . . . furthermore we have caused considerable
destruction at various sites in northern France,
where building operations were in progress,
the purpose of which we were unable to ascertain.
At Pas de Calais and the Cotentin Peninsula
there were at least seven such points . . .
Obviously it is in the German interest to encourage
the rumors regarding the new weapons,
to hearten their soldiers and satellites so
it may be that their bark is worse than their bite."]

HELEN: I was to remind you that you wanted to
dictate something for the Poles . . .

P.M. (*angrily*): Not now—not *now*.

HELEN: No, I only learned that the Polish Prime Minister
is expected early tomorrow in London,
and perhaps it would be . . .

P.M. (*extremely agitated. Suddenly he is in a hurry to get away*):
But it has nothing to do with General Sikorski.
(*Looks toward the telephone, then says to* BELL:)
Excuse me, Bishop—
I must attend to the "Scharnhorst" for a moment.
(*Smiling.*)

Mrs. MacDonald has read your leaflets against the bombing—
she has some questions for you.

He goes out, as if he was attacking somebody.
The BISHOP *turns to* HELEN, *who is ill at ease—and* BELL *does little to make her easier. Disturbed by the adroitness with which the* PRIME MINISTER *is continually evading him, he makes no secret of his anger. He begins drily.*

BELL: You said nothing about the photographs.
   What do you think His Majesty's Government will have to say
   to these actions of yours, when the country
   celebrates its victory in Trafalgar Square?
DORLAND (*gloomily*):
   Scant hope, Sir, that the pilots will be present.
HELEN (*with what one feels is an artificial hardness*):
   My Lord—I have never understood your speeches in the Lords,
   but—they concern me too. Might I ask
   how it is permissible for a Christian to kill men,
   but not women and children?
BELL (*irritably*): That a soldier may kill somebody
   who otherwise would kill him:
   that you must surely understand.
HELEN: Forgive me, my Lord. Let us take two brothers.
   Neither ever wanted to be a soldier,
   suddenly it is war, the elder is not asked,
   he is conscripted, sat inside a bomber, he . . . he . . .
   burns to death inside it. Why may he be killed
   and not the younger one,
   who sits, not in the bomber, but the shelter?
   Simply because he is four years younger.
   The child is privileged anyway
   since before his own death he did not have to kill.
   The pilot must perhaps stand before God
   straight after he has destroyed an old people's home.

DORLAND *can so little conceal his satisfaction that he has difficulty in allowing* BELL *to answer.* BELL *begins hesitantly, but soon the conversation gains speed.*

BELL: Let us hold onto one thing straight away;
you make a distinction between pilots who
destroy old people's homes and those who
bomb factories.

HELEN *wants to take it back, but* BELL *does not let her get a word in.*

HELEN: No, you can't . . .
BELL: Hold onto that. You said it without thinking.
But that apart, that you condemn all killing:
I cannot condemn the war,
only its worst inhumanities.
HELEN (*violently*):
War *is* the worst inhumanity.
BELL: How else is mankind to be rid of Hitler?
But children are no enemy.
Whoever neither bears arms nor constructs them,
one may not kill in wartime—do you agree?
DORLAND: But the workers in the factories, men and women?
BELL: I'm afraid so—them one may kill.
HELEN: Sir, that is . . .
BELL: Ruthless, you were going to say?
HELEN: I was going—forgive me—to call it hairsplitting.
My Lord, my sister works, out of uniform, in the head office of
London Transport. [A bomb in the central depot, the garages
destroyed, London without buses, in London five million people
make the bus journeys every day—the Prime Minister was told
lately that one minute lost on every bus journey every day would
mean a loss, over a whole year, equivalent to a nine-hour-day's
work by ten thousand people.] How could the Germans hit us more
effectively—if they could—than by bombing the bus depot? And
to kill my sister, a civilian, at her office or in her home. That would
be murder? But to kill me, because I wear uniform, that is permissible?
BELL: Do *you* think it permissible?
HELEN: Of course I do, Bishop. If murder—war, if you like—
is the watchword then it is just as permissible
as killing Wing Commander Dorland when he flies
over Gomorrah in his Liberator.
The Wing Commander was no more born
expressly to be killed by Germans than I was.

The moment you reduce war and limit its victims,
my Lord—you make it legal, permissible.
[We—in the small circle here, when we saw,
in August, 1940, how the Prime Minister
enticed the German planes away from our
fighter airfields, over Greater London where
they were to bleed to death, we were proud,
in London, that we could make a breathing space
for the men of Fighter Command.]

BELL (*gloomily*): War is a fact, Mrs. MacDonald.

(*Pause.*)

I have never admired Mr. Churchill so much as
during the short speech he made when we declared
war on Germany—when he said: This is no war
for supremacy, for an accretion of power, its sole
aim is to maintain the rights of the individual,
the rebirth of humanity.
Wing Commander, compare those intentions with the
pictures of Gomorrah.

DORLAND: Intentions? War is what outruns our control.

HELEN: What has Hitler not allowed himself?

BELL: Shall what *he* does become the rights of war?
Shooting of hostages, gassing, Rotterdam, Belgrade?
If that is so then we must treat him
and his satraps, when we have vanquished them,
as prisoners instead of hanging them.
Dorland, whatever you are ordered to do,
listen to your instinct, which tells you
there is a difference between the child
burning to death in the shelter
and the airman who so burns him.

DORLAND *is silent, crushed.*

HELEN (*animated*):
And if later the airman himself is burned to death—
in his aircraft?

BELL (*hard*):
Then he atones for his misdeed.
But what has the child in the shelter to atone for?

HELEN (*icy*):
>That is inhuman, Sir, what you are saying.
>Has a pilot to atone, then, for what he does on orders?

BELL: Our military code—Section 3, Article 13,
>protects all British combatants from orders
>the carrying-out of which would make him a criminal.

DORLAND *would like to say something, obviously with regard to* HELEN *since he knows why she is talking in this way, but before he can do so* BELL *continues his line of argument since he is appalled that she, as a woman, can react like this.*

>That you, a woman, should talk like this!
>I am on my own here,
>among soldiers, officers—
>You should be helping on *my* side, as a woman . . .
>Can you not see, even Dorland knows deep down
>my arguments are in accord with military tradition.
>Never before has it been allowed, with us,
>never again will it be understood,
>the shooting of hostages—to demoralize the enemy at the front.
>And shooting of hostages is what it is—
>bombing families, to break the morale
>of the father at the front.
>Mrs. MacDonald, please . . .

She falls back, white as her shirt. BELL *forces her to stay and says, hard to begin with, then sad, persuasive, sincere:*

>A woman like you, with children, fire all around you,
>knowing, seeing them being burned alive—
>Good God!—help me then, tell Dorland that—

HELEN *steps back; before her face crumples and she bursts into tears and runs out, she says convulsively:*

HELEN: I have no children, Sir, I have no husband.

BELL *looks after her, upset at having been the cause of this. Pause.*

DORLAND: Her husband was killed over Cologne,
>on the first thousand-bomber raid,
>May, '42.

BELL (*hostile*): Do you think that was fair . . . ?
    I could have been told.
    (*Directing his reactions at the newspaper, which he picks up,
    folds up. Angrily.*)
    Is it a matter of indifference to *you*
    whether you bomb industry or houses?
DORLAND (*grinning nervously, since grinning is the last thing he feels
    like doing*):
    We only prefer to bomb houses
    because industry is better defended.
    The attack on the dams had the heaviest losses;
    ten aircraft only out of eighteen got back home.
    [We had to fly so low—only fifty feet
    above the water—that five bombers crashed
    on the practice runs alone.
    The surface of the water is like pack ice:
    Two and a half thousand practice hours and even so]
    two of the machines blew themselves up
    by dropping their bombs on the dam instead of in front of it.
BELL (*coming around*):
    [Dorland, I know that the soldier's courage
    will never find an adequate chronicler.]
    But why—when you *can* aim so exactly—
    why residential areas?
DORLAND: Oh, Sir, you are deceiving yourself.
    Do you imagine such an operation costs nothing
    in the way of innocent lives?
    We heard from Sweden that
    several hundred Russian girls, slave laborers,
    were crushed to death in their barrack rooms
    by the avalanche of water in the Eder valley;
    and do not forget the attraction of technique:
    when you attack a target, you simply want . . .
BELL (*cold*): "Simply"?
DORLAND (*uneasy*):
    Yes, to be as *technically* efficient as possible.
    Even when we visit a city . . .
BELL: "Visit"—the word that Harris used to me just now.
    Why can you not "simply" say "wipe out"?
DORLAND (*equally aggressive at the insult*):
    Because it is *not* simple, Sir.

You despise technology. Forgive me,
that is because your own life does not depend on it.
It is in technical efficiency that our hope lies
that we shall not
have to "visit" the same target a second time.
BELL: I beg your pardon—
[Do you never talk about our own dead civilians?
DORLAND: Do you mean "the aiming-points looked at from the
human angle"?
Not if we can help it.
There is a narrow strip of wood
not far from the runway.
Not far enough for us pilots,
we are afraid of the trees on landing—
we hang about there off-duty.
All of us knew a woodman there, with a wife and child,
an invalid ex-miner, they used to sell
sweets, soft drinks and the like.
We called them the Holy Family for a joke—
that's what the three of them looked like,
coming and going, in and out of the wood,
like the Holy Family on the Flight into Egypt.
A pity they didn't go.
A short time ago (it happens every day)
a returning bomber, badly hit, crashed in flames
right into the three of them in their hut.
The pilot and the radio operator were saved—
they went to the funeral of the token coffin.
Later, inevitably—we talked about it
until one of us, worn out, suddenly stood up and said:
Stop making such a bloody fuss—
we are killing people like those three
every night of the week, and a lot more efficiently.
Then he went out and slammed the door.
BELL (*hesitates*): Yes?
DORLAND: In such . . . cases, you feel
you have been caught with your hand in the till.
If you haven't a girl, you get drunk.]
(*Fiercely, with an effort at defiance:*)
All the same, Sir—
BELL: What?

DORLAND: When you attack Mr. Churchill you should think
where we should all be without him.
BELL: It is because I know that I attempt
to speak with him.
DORLAND: Hitler would not allow you to.
BELL (*laughing*):
The comparison is unthinkable.
But the Prime Minister is a great man, Dorland,
and that, in nature, is something terrible.
[Do you know Goethe's definition of genius?
DORLAND: No, Sir. I just burned down his birthplace.
BELL: You? I read about it.
DORLAND: I flew a marker aircraft over Frankfurt.
Weimar was on the list as well,
since the Foreign Secretary asked the Air Ministry
that towns of that size should be destroyed where possible.

Pause.

BELL: Weimar! I was thinking of the bloodbath there would be
in the Nazi camp on a night like that.
Firestorms only serve them as a pretext for their bestiality.
DORLAND: Sir—when we had the Nazi Protector murdered in
Prague
a whole Czech village paid for it.
Is that a reason not to kill a tyrant?
BELL: I do not know. Really: I do not know.
The recent attempt on Hitler's ambassador in Ankara.
DORLAND: Unsuccessful, alas.
BELL: I agree, it is alas. No innocent life
would have needed to atone for his death.
But Prague—I don't know.
DORLAND: But the Prime Minister has to know.
Who would be capable of action, if he thought of all the
consequences?
BELL: I agree. But one must be careful that the war
does not give Mr. Churchill such power
that he ignores them.
We had got on to Goethe, and his house.
If families continue for any length of time,
he wrote, and thinking of this country
I read "peoples" for "families,"

before they die out *one* man appears
who unites in himself all the qualities of his forebears,
exploiting their potential, good and ill.
DORLAND: Before they die out?
BELL: Clearly the climax is the start of the decline.
He is that man.]
In a thousand years, if they speak of England,
they will mean Shakespeare, Churchill—and who else?
The only trouble is, he knows it now.
DORLAND: Wait a minute, now—what about Cromwell, Pitt, Lloyd
George?
BELL: Ah—a Parliament man does not stir the imagination:
Where among them is the adventurer incarnate,
the dilettante of genius, the man who
did not invent the tank but went on asking for it
until it was invented.
The fancy dresser-up, the demagogue,
true to party and platform just as long
as he can be their spokesman,
[chasing after events, like riding to hounds,
not out of hate for the fox,
but he it must be who leads the pack.
And the man who so loves a hunt
will lend a hand in its instigation.
Where is the eternal chronicler of his own deeds,
the monomaniac who for fifty years
has been playing court to fame,
and who admits it, shamelessly as a child?]
The insatiable writer of epics,
and in the end he is *right,* Dorland, that is the point.
[I remember, when he published his history of the First War,
the joke being made that he had once again
extended a chapter of his autobiography
into a history of the universe. But wait and see.]
If he writes an account of this war too,
the history of our *century* will be
one and the same as his autobiography.
That fortune has permitted him to find
just the one enemy who, late as it is,
identifies Churchill's interests with those of the world at large,
that is his destiny.

His opponent in the First War
was just a king among a hundred others,
but Hitler makes mankind his conqueror's debtor.
[And that is Churchill—even if from the soldier's viewpoint
he only holds the front for a single year.
Even as short a time as that will show how great he is.
How could his alliances have been more cunning?
The earliest, most fervent hater of the Communists,
and yet the first to speak comfortable words to Stalin
when Hitler gave him Eastern Poland in 1939.
British policy has always been "Humanity plus five per
    cent"—
Winston takes twenty and still manages
to make the payer grateful to him.]
But none escapes being saddled with the defects
of his qualities in direct proportion.

DORLAND: And Churchill's qualities are tremendous.

BELL *laughs, wryly, and raises his arms in utter resignation.*

DORLAND (*quietly*): You believe that even *he* will be corrupted by
    power?

BELL: As anybody else, for might is mightier than the mighty.
No one who has it senses the moment
when *it* has *him*—the fearful reckoning.
Think of Churchill's technique of attrition,
and how contemptuously *he* described
those generals who, in the First War, practiced
what he himself now practices in the Second
through his pyrotechnician Harris.

DORLAND: Sir, it is not the soldier but the weapon that decides
    the nature of a war.
It is not my fault that I am a bomber rather than a fighter-
    pilot.
That is the luck of my posting:
Only in Essen
have we ever visited a town because of its factories.
Normally we regard the destruction of industry
as a bonus—the targets are
town centers and working-class areas . . .

BELL: You *must* not obey such orders.

P.M. (*within earshot, in the garden, so far unnoticed by the*
    BISHOP, *calls aggressively*):

I am listening, Bishop.

BELL (*coldly*): At last.

P.M. (*softly, threateningly*): Inciting pilots to mutiny.
Bishop, how can you insinuate that attacks
on built-up areas are illegal?
The Red Cross has presented us with so-called laws
to govern warfare on the sea and land,
but none yet for the air, for which God be praised.

[DORLAND (*as* BELL *is speechless*):
My Lord, Air Marshal Harris has pointed out,
albeit with irony, that there is
only one international convention:
It was forbidden at some time or other
to throw explosive devices from gas-filled balloons.]

BELL *speaks with the same irritation with which the C.I.G.S. for
the first and only time in his memoirs mentions the Bomber Chief:
"Bert Harris told us how well he could have won the war if it had
not been for the handicap imposed by the existence of the two
other services."*

BELL: Lawyers make laws. The law is made by God
regardless of the demands of—the judiciary.
Prime Minister—we denigrate our men
if we suggest that they require directives
to tell them that the burning of defenseless persons
is *murder*.

P.M. (*savagely, not looking at* BELL): War is murder.
The murderer is the man who fires first.
That man is Hitler.

BELL: I can well understand that
the thought of *our* civilians
whom Germany has murdered
could give one the anger to bomb Germans.
Revenge may not be humane, but it is human.

DORLAND (*upset that* BELL *should ascribe such motives to him and
that they should again be at cross-purposes*):
Oh—Sir, hardly revenge. What do you think we are?

BELL (*without sarcasm, emptied by a feeling of helplessness*):
Yes—you ... already told me, none of you ...
talk about ...

DORLAND: No—not about our, not about . . . those over there.

P.M. (*wishing to put an end to the sentimentalities, for his own sake as well*):
If you would like to wait inside for the end of the "Scharnhorst" . . . at ten to five the "Duke of York"
surprised her at twelve thousand yards.

DORLAND *is no longer himself. Deeply confused, he looks from one to the other, from the uncritically adored* CHURCHILL *to the* BISHOP, *who his reason tells him is right. He wants to take his leave, but does not know how. He goes, in an unsoldierly fashion, to the door, pulls himself together, and salutes.*

DORLAND: Thank you, Prime Minister . . . of course.
Bishop.

He goes into the house. Silence—now made deeper by the sound of an approaching bomber stream of great size, flying very high, coming slowly nearer then apparently hovering over Chequers, before slowly passing into the distance.

P.M. (*looks at his watch, then up at the sky*):
The first wave is on its way to Germany.

Pause.

BELL: Mr. Eden has said, with regard to
my report from Stockholm, unfortunately—

The P.M. *remembers what occurred to him as necessary to insure* BELL'*s silence, and pretends an interest which only really develops during the course of the conversation.*

P.M.: Stay please—I too have some questions.

BELL (*defensively, does not sit for some time*):
—the Foreign Secretary wrote to me saying
His Majesty's Government must refuse to guarantee
in advance an agreeable peace settlement
to my friends in Germany who wish to overthrow Hitler.

The PRIME MINISTER *stands up suddenly, excited by the subject of resistance. The C.I.G.S. noted eighteen months later, after a meal in Downing Street at which* CHURCHILL *"was not in his usual form and on the flat side," the following: "He said that if he was a German he would get his small daughter to put a bomb under some British bed: he would instruct his wife to wait till some American was bending over his basin washing to strike him on the neck with a chopper whilst he himself sniped at Americans and British indiscriminately."*

P.M. (*interrupting*):
   They murder Hitler? He will most likely kidnap them.
   (*Laughs contemptuously.*)
   Assassins who have first to fly to Berne and Stockholm
   to ask how, and if, their country will be rewarded
   for the assassination of its tyrant? Ha!
   Machiavelli prescribes that no more than four people
   should be let into a conspiracy to murder.
   And quite enough too.
   That man has been in power ten years now
   and only one group to my knowledge has till now
   fought actively in Germany, and been annihilated:
   The armchair Communists in the Berlin Air Ministry,
   seventy men and women round the nephew of von Tirpitz
   —they and the single assassin of Munich, that brave man,
   they actually did something.
   Those students, lately, from Munich University—
   not one single Nazi did they kill.
   [How terrible to have to mount the scaffold
   without at least a couple of Nazis on one's conscience.]
   What else is there?—Leaflets?
   Rich in thought and poor in deed.
   Had Hitler landed here, I would have given the word:
   Take One With You.

BELL: How unjust you are being.
   You have never lived under a dictatorship.
   Do you despise the Russians
   for not having got rid of Stalin
   at the time of the great show-trials?

P.M. (*grins and lays a finger on his lips*): Yes.

BELL: Germany's a prison, one man in every thousand under arrest . . .

P.M.: And the nine hundred and ninety-nine?
   This people has its Hitler because he suits them;
   down to the ground.

[BELL: Do you really believe the priests who are resisting—
or the Munich students—could ever get close to him?
He hasn't yet trusted himself in a single bombed city.

P.M. (*furious*):
Good God, they needn't hit a bull's-eye every time!
They can find criminals who should be disposed of
in every tramcar. Nothing happens.
Not long ago that girl in Russia
who murdered Hitler's Viceroy of the Ukraine
in bed—a Judith—the satrap caressed to death.
If such a patriot arose in Germany, to free his land
the people would bring him to court
for not having a firearms license.

BELL: One must have a talent for assassination.

P.M.: One must be ready to die.

BELL: Do you think we, as a race, have the talent?]

P.M.: Your Berlin friends conspire with generals
who have, for hire, subdued the whole of Europe
for that little Viennese café rat.
Now they send us their best regards and assurances
of their hate of Hitler, because he is bringing
the Red Army to Berlin, via their feudal estates.
Meantime, they wipe out the Jews from land to land . . .

BELL (*roused*):
There I must protest, Prime Minister.
my friends are Bonhoeffer and Niemöller,
The murders, well you know, are the work
of the SS and the Nazi guard.

P.M. (*maliciously*):
The Nazis were able to subjugate Germany, no more.
Even after the fall of France the SS
was barely a hundred thousand strong.
No, the Prussian priesthood is what is to be feared,
the General Staff, the oh-so-honorable old army,
[and you threaten me, Bishop . . .

BELL (*appalled, cuts into the* PRIME MINISTER's *speech*):
Threaten?
Do you call that a threat?
Men of honor, on whose integrity I would stake my life,
ask what peace Great Britain will make with them.

When officers kill a tyrant, it is their *duty*
to demand safety for their country.

P.M. (*coldly, but not cynically*): Not at our expense!
These wretched creatures had the imperial gall
to hint to us in Berne that if the British
would not agree with them they would go
to hawk their wares to Stalin.
Blackmail is what that is, my Lord—blackmail.

BELL (*provoked*): And what would *you* have done?

P.M.: Not that, not that—I would not have threatened
two brothers-in-arms, each of whom has the other to thank
for his continued existence—I would not have threatened
to play off one against the other: the Hun tradition.
(*Laughs amazedly.*)
If they want to play hare and hounds,
I will play too, but not the hare.

BELL: How much British blood—yes, British too—
would there be saved were Hitler shot today?
Is this hope, Sir, not worth any effort?

P.M.: Almost any effort—but not this.
Bishop, understand me, should Stalin hear
that I am negotiating for peace with Germans,
no matter whether Nazis or anti-Nazis,
he will be determined to get in ahead of me . . .

BELL: And if he does? Have you assurances?

P.M.: With Stalin there is no such thing.
If a cable arrived now saying he was dead,
my first thought would be: What does he mean by it?
All the same: when I read your report on the German opposition
which has imperiled our alliance with Russia
almost as much as the Poles in London
with their entire gutter press have done,
I did not think for long—I acted at once,
and, as you know, demanded, with the President,
an *unconditional* surrender.

BELL (*tormented*): —yes, and with that destroyed
my effort at conciliation.

P.M.: This demand is the only way to force Stalin
to a similar *public* utterance.]
Yes? Yes?—what *is* it, Helen?

During the last words, HELEN *has burst into the garden; it is clear she wants to interrupt but can not speak straight away. She stammers and waits till the* PRIME MINISTER, *irritated, asks again:* "Well?"

HELEN: Prime Minister, Prime Minister—
General Sikorski is dead.

CHURCHILL's *eyes blink once, full of tears. He does not say a word. Then, in violent impatience, since* HELEN *thinks she ought to be silent:*

P.M.: Go on. Where, how?
HELEN: In Gibraltar, right after take-off. The aircraft didn't climb, though all four engines were on full throttle—the pilot cut the engines to make a forced landing on the water, came down in a glide, then there was dead silence, they were running over the surface of the water—in the darkness they couldn't see anything from the shore. Then came the crash, and they sank before the first rescue boat could get out to them.
BELL (*instinctively*): An explosion?
HELEN (*shrugs*): —they—only spoke of the *impact,*
but . . .
the alarm sirens were going at the time. The
pilot managed to escape, he was thrown clear,
only the pilot—I've forgotten his name,
something . . .
P.M. (*takes a step toward her, hissing with impatience*):
Stop talking the whole time about the pilot—
he was saved—who was *killed?*
HELEN: Everyone. Everyone else. Sikorski's entire staff. His daughter as well.
P.M. (*in rage*): The daughter? Why—
these damned thoughtless Poles! I warned her—
I don't take my own daughter with me in an airplane.
HELEN: She was an officer, an orderly, like me,
she had to go with him—
Sikorski's entire staff and the member for Chippenham.
[BELL (*looks up, straight at* CHURCHILL): Cazalet!
P.M.: Did he send you too a copy
of the pamphlet he circulated against me last year?

BELL *nods. The* PRIME MINISTER *attempts to neutralize this super-fluous remark with another, of even less interest.*

P.M.: Cazalet had been my liaison man with Sikorski
   for three years, ever since Sikorski arrived.
   (*Angrily, and it helps him:*)
   The daughter too—the daughter too.]
   Get me Madame Sikorska.
   What are you doing? Not now.
HELEN: They've found the body of the Prime Minister,
   horribly mangled.
P.M. (*with irritation*): Arrange for its conveyance to London.
   Tell the Foreign Secretary. We—
   the King must be asked to allow
   the lying-in-state in the Abbey—the General is,
   with the honor of a head of State, who
   as our guest—well, you . . .
   (*He cannot speak.*)

HELEN, *to spare him anything further, is already on her way out, while the* PRIME MINISTER *sits on the bench. She looks at* BELL *as if he should leave too, with her.*

HELEN: I know, Mr. Churchill, I will make the arrangements.
   Shall I—
P.M.: Thank you, Helen.

HELEN *goes.*

[BELL: I've kept you overlong as it is—
   I'll go with . . .
P.M. (*at first only a gesture, then*):
   You are not going to leave me, not just yet:
   I am not at my best for business today.]
BELL: Was Sikorski very close to you personally?
P.M.: Very, very.
   Even in death—most of all in the manner of it—
   he is the embodiment of his unhappy country . . .
   [the embodiment—did you hear,
   terribly mangled; Poland!
BELL (*unsuspecting*): Why should the Polish Generalissimo
   have trusted his life to a Czech?
   Since the Poles divided the Prague booty with Hitler

and gobbled up Teschen like vultures
they must be *hated* in Prague?
P.M.: Warsaw undoubtedly betrayed Prague.]
BELL (*insistently*):
How do you explain it: Everyone killed on impact, after a
glide?
Just by the impact on the water, from so small a height?
And then to sink so quickly, with *no* explosion?

The P.M. *raises his hands and shoulders, lets them sink, and
speaks with increasing assurance, faster and faster, without looking for a word of explanation, or answer, as he is soon to do in
the Commons.*

P.M.: Do you think *I* fly without misgivings?
[A short time ago in the desert, we needed a day's rest,
everything was prepared for a flight to the Siwa Oasis,
when I suddenly said to Alexander: No.
Is the pleasure worth the risk?
I do not know what the Generals can have thought
about their Minister of Defense.]
With flying machines and with the Kremlin
one should only have dealings
when absolutely necessary.
BELL: The Kremlin?
P.M. (*smiling wryly*): Why—ah, I see. Of course, they will hardly
be flying the flags at half-mast there.
Just when I was striving—in vain—
to postpone the discovery of the truth
about the officers in Katyn . . .
Sikorski was not a politician.
BELL: Will you postpone the truth here too—about Sikorski's
crash?
P.M.: To govern, my dear Bishop, one must treat
truth as the mariner treats the Pole Star:
Never let it out of your sight,
but do not head straight for it.
BELL: But the General was your friend—will you not
attempt, for Poland, the furtherance of
his aims with the Kremlin?
P.M.: No, no, no. No, certainly not.
I see Stalin's demand for the re-extension

of Russia's frontiers to the Curzon Line
as moderate and reasonable—a good deal more so
than what Sikorski wanted to get for Poland.

BELL *emphasizes the word "friend," seeking from the* PRIME
MINISTER *a counterassurance against a horrifying idea which has
occurred to him.*

BELL: But you said Sikorski was your friend.
P.M.: I believe it was you who said that.
Men may be bound by friendship, nations only by interest:
a discovery which makes the greater man
the lesser human being:
[Clear skies and smiling leaders are not to be trusted.]
(*What he says now makes him much calmer.*)
But does my office not oblige me still,
each day to send young men
who wish for nothing but to go on living
to battle and to death.
And you can see—friendship is . . .
an entirely private arrangement.
I am tired, Bishop, it *disgusts* me . . .

He sits once more, pulls out his handkerchief, mops his face, neck,
and eyes.
Pause.

BELL: Mr. Churchill, you *could* never have wished it otherwise.
[Who would have heard of Hector, had Troy remained at
peace?
You have described the envy with which you,
at twenty, regarded the men born a century earlier,
just in time to find fame in Napoleon's campaigns.]
You realized early it is not the man
who prevents a war, who goes down in history,
but the man who wins one.

The P.M. in profound agreement, protests mildly. BELL fills a pipe.

P.M.: Did I discover Hitler?
BELL: No, the First War did that.
That too was our nemesis, that we should liberate
the thrones of Berlin and Vienna for the Beast from the
Abyss . . .

[P.M. (*firmly*): It was also the result of German policy.
 I am not speaking of guilt—grace and good fortune
 have tides of ebb and flow, no other cause.
 Nevertheless, the Bismarcks, *père et fils,*
 declined for two decades to make common cause
 with us against Russia.
 How diligently my father and Lord Salisbury
 stood cooling their heels in outer offices—
 and later even Joseph Chamberlain did so—
 He was the one who said—
 Sine Germania nulla salus.
 But not even Vienna could achieve more in Berlin
 than a promise of support in the case of Russian *aggression.*
 In addition we gave the sincere warning
 Great Britain would eventually compound
 her differences with Russia if Prince Bismarck
 continued his attempts to divert Russia
 toward the Dardanelles and Asia at our expense.
BELL: Was he not bound to try it?
 Had Bismarck, with our assistance,
 wrenched Poland, and the Baltic states from Russia,
 his *cauchemar de coalition*
 would have been more oppressive still.
P.M.: We wanted it as well, we had to want it.
BELL: Well then—Bismarck had to keep his peace with Russia!
P.M.: No!
 He had to make his decision—Britain or Russia—
 but fear of war robbed him of the power to do so.
 He wanted what one can never have:
 a perpetuation of the status quo.
 But that belongs to God—and to the Swiss—
 and not to sinful man.
 Old men are war-shy—
 Bismarck should have marched alongside of us:
 Since he could not, moreover, trust the Russians,
 he would have had to set a Hapsburg up
 in Warsaw, king of a free Poland:
 At least it would have prevented
 the Russian cavalry entering East Prussia
 three days after the outbreak of war in 1914;
 and we would not then have had the frightful difficulties

of reconciling ourselves
with the archplague of the Foreign Office, the French,
as some kind of de Gaulle we have with us always.

BELL (*with sympathy*): He appears to see in himself
the rebirth of Joan of Arc.

P.M.: The afterbirth more like.
This little cross of Lorraine I have to bear
Marlborough had in Louis XIV, the plague of Europe.
Later Napoleon. And even my father could write officially,
France must be *écrasée*.
But the Bismarcks forced us
to make peace with Paris and St. Petersburg—and
to bring the Czar and the République Française together.
That of course was something only the Holy Father could
      manage.
When there was no other help for it,
Salisbury despatched his papist crony, Norfolk,
to Leo XIII—who contrived somehow
to get the Czar to stand for the "Marseillaise."
Beforehand it had been punishable with imprisonment
even to whistle such a tune in Russia.

BELL (*ironically*): With some reason—one can hardly say
the hymn of revolution agreed with the Czar,
nor with the Vatican, nor, I fear, with us.

P.M. (*flatly*): We see that now, I know, but at the time
Rome could see only in an anti-German alliance
a hope of turning at least the north Germans
against the Protestant inventiveness
of Luther and Bismarck.
The British, though—are absolutely guiltless.
My father and Lord Salisbury, and King Edward,
were only following tradition in their efforts
to counteract that war after 1870.
The strongest power in Europe—
that was not Germany, nor Russia, and not Austria,
it was the alliance of three.
And Bismarck knew he could not tolerate it.
What could have seemed more favorable
than to make the Germans,
the nation of the Queen's son-in-law,
our partners against Russia?

The Germans would have got the Western provinces
or, since Bismarck was already glutted with land,
they would have had Poland as a buffer state—
and we would have insured perpetual enmity
between Germany and Russia.
But that slipped through my father's hands.
He said at the end to Bismarck *fils*
that the two of us could rule the world between us
but Bismarck senior only wrote, with an irony
that has cost them dear: "Not enough."
Bismarck was as cunning as Theseus and Odysseus together—
and yet blind
when he switched the points to lead to a war on three fronts
that put his country on the rack in 1914.]
History is what eludes our grasp,
Poland's autonomy—our *casus belli.*
But when the guns are silent, who will then
be able to raise his voice in Poland?
History is what eludes our grasp.
[Bismarck's failure is a warning—
the miracle of his founding of a kingdom
put the fear of God into him.
He reacted after the robbery of Lorraine
like the *visitor* of Polycrates.
But it was no use: he had to be brought down.
And my life's work, Bishop—mine as well.]
Whenever I am on top, glutted with victory, gorged with
    flesh,
I ask myself quietly where is the hook, the snag,
which of the hostile corpses is the poisoned one,
the bait of Hell. The horoscope of history
is cast in the sign of the Hydra.
BELL: Oedipus—in the day of victory is thine end conceived.
P.M.: There you are: with Sikorski, too.
The Russians, whom, twenty years ago, he put to flight
on the Vistula now stand about his coffin.
And I?—I am leading Britain from the brink
of total defeat on a *via triumphalis*—
British legions march out of Africa
from the old Carthage to the new—Berlin.
And yet this victory will only help

to trample down the balance of Europe
for whose preservation we went to war.
The greatest victories in English history—result:
We sink,
sink under my leadership to a second-rate power.
BELL (*passionately*):
No, no—to see things in this way, Mr. Churchill,
is to underestimate what you have done with this island.
In 1940 you saved the freedom of the world!
[P.M.: Partially and temporarily—let us hope.
Nor shall I give up, but lay about me till I drop
for Poland's freedom and the constitution
of an anti-Russian federation of the Danube states;
I shall be in Budapest *before* Stalin.
But tell me, as a theologian,
why has the Creator set the machine
to bring about the destruction of His creatures?
BELL: Is not this process one of complete logic?
Wisdom, to be worthy of the name,
must range herself against Humanity.
(*As* CHURCHILL, *for the first time, looks at him helplessly.*)
The behavior of men, when they become a mighty nation
forces the Creator periodically
to strike them down with the thunderbolt of war.
P.M. (*lost in thought*): Is that why we couldn't march alongside the
Germans at the end of the last century?
It was so close. Our sovereigns were first cousins,
we by sea, the Hun on land: invincible.
Nothing that man could think of spoke against it.
BELL: Precisely: nothing that man could think of.
P.M. (*taking no notice*):
But the demons are neither fussy nor refined:
They use a common cancer of the throat
to topple the Queen's son-in-law
prematurely from his throne.
It is unthinkable that Britain should have been
the enemy of that most liberal of all Germans.
BELL: Demons?—Say simply:
Ecology, nature preserving her own balance,
she must frustrate the alliance of the strongest.
You see how victory makes the Germans brutes.

And us—in Ireland then, in Hamburg now?
Intolerable for the other nations if the near in blood,
who are also the strongest, should unite.
Would new powers ever have been able to enter the arena
if Briton and Teuton had mounted common guard?
Not Russia, not America, let alone France
and China would have stayed a colony
like Africa or India: no nation,
urbi et orbi, could even have raised its voice in protest.
That, however, nature does not even allow
in the founding of a species—read your Schopenhauer.
Why does the specially well-favored man
usually marry a much plainer girl and vice versa,
the healthy stock weaken itself instinctively
in alliance with an oversensitive, decaying family?
Teuton and Gaul—how near was their alliance:
But, as their interests both spoke *against* war,
that is why they had to wage it.
Age stills the urge to aggression in man,
exhaustion stills it in a nation.

P.M. (*looks up questioningly*):
History then—a stratagem of nature?
The men of action blind, so they may work its purpose?

BELL: Blind—were you blind?

P.M.: Yes—error, blood, lust, hysteria,
the sum of all those things that makes man blind.
I envisaged Wilhelm's ships in the Solent,
the Germans saw the Home Fleet in the Bight, by Hamburg:
none of all this took place.
What took place, none had seen:
no more than an Athenian, or a Spartan,
as they rent each other, noticed the Macedonian,
the laughing, lurking third man, tomorrow's master.]
They say, whom God will destroy—
and is there anyone whom He will *not* destroy!
Why else, upon the crimson stream of history
flowing for millennia, is there not
one house, one city, or one bridge left standing?
Why? A man who makes *mistakes,* who merely comes to
grief
does not elicit from us the feeling that history awakens in us.

What does divination in the bowels of the ages show
but thwarted men of action?
The silent sacrifices dumfound us
(tragic Sikorski),
we rear up, to strike
before thought holds our arm,
but when a deed for once does not miscarry—
then it can be permitted to endure.
The Empire—how long did it last?
My father could still say, when in office,
we Britons are not Europeans but Asiatics:
Bombay seemed to him as indivisible
from us as Edinburgh—and nearer than Paris or Vienna . . .
No. All that endures is the panorama
of ruined empires, telling us we are sand before the wind.

[BELL: You call it ruination but it is, at any rate,
organic and not tragic, except for the individual
whose heart struggles against indifferent Nature,
who sweeps his achievements away from him.
Even your achievement will disappear—but not your fame—

P.M. (*relaxed*):
That will become legend—undisturbed by truth.

Silence.

Your notion of the tides of history
makes nonsense of our old British sagacity.
Our fathers acted for four centuries
in the natural belief that they should fight *against,*
not with, any power that threatened
to upset the balance of the Continent.
Now for the first time, in my hands, it miscarries
since it is obvious that we have no more
to fear from the Teutonic forests;
but from the icefields of Siberia,
where the mammoth will break loose . . .
and is it not I who have invoked him?

BELL (*firm*): No, no—Hitler, not you!
And Russia too will find her subjugator,
perhaps in America, perhaps in Asia,
let us hope within herself.
—And who can say that it will be the Russians

who will drive out the spirit of old Europe
and not America?
Whether one worships the Golden Calf
or the Red Flag, or Christ,
it is not this or that religion,
but its power that makes pigs of the pious.

P.M. (*grins in agreement*):
Oh, I have not forgotten how the Americans
with the rapacity of an Oriental despot
sent a battleship to Capetown in winter, 1940,
to commandeer our last gold reserves . . . and other things.
What if the tamer of the Russian Bear
should not arise till too late—for the rest of Europe?

BELL: This fear is the price the Continent pays
for the destruction of Hitler—not too great a price
when one considers what the man is.

P.M.: Thank you, Bishop.]

HELEN *enters.*

HELEN: An announcement from the Admiralty—
P.M. (*relieved*): At last—all quiet in the Arctic Sea,
the "Scharnhorst" finished?
HELEN: No, Sir, not the "Scharnhorst"—
P.M.: What?
HELEN: There is no news from the north as yet.
But in the Mediterranean: German torpedo bombers
early this morning destroyed the entire convoy
of the HMS "Duchess of York" not far from the Spanish
coast,
sunk to the last ship . . . only a few survivors.
That's why the news is so late.

The P.M.*'s distress changes at once to anger—the reason why
disaster always roused rather than paralyzed him. He dictates at
an almost incomprehensible speed, speaking with hissing articula-
tion, and very quietly.*

P.M.: On the coast!
How many times—have I warned against operation within the range
of the Focke-Wulfs? Take this down: "To the First Sea Lord. I hear,
with great dismay, of the annihilation of the convoy under HMS
'Duchess of York.' Will you let me have a copy of the signal from

the C.-in-C. Mediterranean warning us of the intolerable dangers of
the air attack on this route too near the Spanish coast? [The loss of
these large ships will spoil our monthly record, which anyhow is
burdened with operational casualties.] Where did the aircraft come
from? If the enemy was able to reach the convoy, why could not our
aircraft in Gibraltar protect it? [How far off-shore was it? Pray let
me know what will be done to avoid this form of air attack in the
future?] Report to me this evening."

(*As he dictates, he stumbles against the machine gun: his fury
flames up.*)

Get that bloody Boche blunderbuss out of my sight.

HELEN *returns, without a word, and removes the piece.*

BELL (*seeking to pacify him*):
Air raids are hardly in the tradition
of the Royal Navy [—poor chaps.]
P.M.: Traditions?—The Royal Navy has only three:
Rum, sodomy, and the lash.

The P.M. *smiles now with an ironic satisfaction at playing the
wicked uncle in the fairy tale, rather as he grumbled once, when
Brendan Bracken—"that inexplicable Grey Eminence"—lit his
cigarette at* CHURCHILL's *cigar-end, "I have murdered men for less
than that."*

P.M.: We shall break up—tradition or not—
every big ship they have—other than the carriers.
The airplane decides the war on land as well.
Top secret: Harris hopes that in nine months,
by April, '44,
the destruction by fire of the city of Berlin
will bring victory within our grasp.
BELL (*mocking*): Victory?
P.M.: Yes, there is the suicide-wish in the character of every
German.
We shall set Berlin on fire, night after night,
until it is like Carthage, dust and ashes.
BELL (*with mounting anger*):
Verdun—the strategy of attrition—
only this time directed at civilians—
so, even *less* decisive for the war.
P.M.: Wait and see. Every night we shall go over,

every night the weather lets us—
including Christmas Eve; a death knell for the German spirit.

BELL (*who actually did insure that on Christmas Eve, 1943, the
British pilots were relieved of their orders, which they already
had in their pockets, to bomb Berlin*):
As I am an Englishman—they will *not* bomb on Christmas
Eve.
Even if it is high treason, I shall give
the alarm to the American press.
They will *not* bomb on Christmas Eve.

*He speaks as if he was cutting each single word into the rockface.
For the first time, and not by force of argument, he is stronger
than* CHURCHILL, *whom this disconcerts.*

P.M. (*with an utterly unsuccessful try to disarming amusement*):
Bishop, you seem to think the Germans are still a pious flock.
If I was not going to let you *talk* with me,
I should not have invited you here.
As far as I am concerned, agreed:
Our airmen may enjoy their Christmas Eve in peace.

CHURCHILL *has conceded this without wishing to:* BELL, *by his
quiet strength, has released something akin to shame in* CHURCH-
ILL. *This cannot be indicated logically, only portrayed illogically.
The feeling does not last. The* PRIME MINISTER *is discomposed for
a moment by the knowledge that someone is stronger than he is;
he argues in self-justification, but he quickly recovers at the sound
of his own voice:*

But you must realize—Harris assures us that no
more than four or five thousand British airmen will
pay for this victory.
How many on the other hand will die—
on the first day alone—
if we are forced to land in France!
Dunkirk is something we shall not allow again.
[This time God has given us the bombers—
BELL (*annoyed, warding him off*):
As a priest one knows too much of God
to know only good of Him;
but if it really is He who gave you them,
then He was exposing you to a temptation

in every way as much to be feared
as your own power as Prime Minister.

P.M. (*coolly*): I have never knowingly abused power.
I have accomplished my mission.
I know the very hour when I received it:
October, 1911, in Scotland, coming back from golf,
the Prime Minister said, "Winston, take the Admiralty."
I saw in the fading light two ships of the line
slowly sailing out of the Firth of Forth . . .
and saw the terrible power of Germany before me
shining harshly in the sun of their Empire.
And they were laying the keels of still more warships.
I thought about the thoroughness of the Hun
about their scientific triumphs, and their General Staff . . .

BELL (*ironically*): . . . and about *our* Fleet.

P.M.: . . . In my room I found the book I seldom read;
I opened it at random:
"Thou art to pass over Jordan this day,
to go in to possess nations greater and mightier than thy-
self . . .
Understand therefore this day, that the Lord
thy God is He which goeth over before thee; as a consuming
fire.
He shall destroy them, and bring them down
before thy face; so shalt thou drive them out and destroy
them quickly
as the Lord has said unto thee."

BELL (*irritated*): Prime Minister—happy the nation whose leader
has an extra ace permanently up his sleeve.
But woe to us if he thinks God put it there.
You believe in a connection between these words of the Bible
and your command to reduce to ashes
the fifty largest towns in Germany.
Nevertheless, I . . .

P.M.: No "buts," Bishop,
when the Admiralty came to me for the second time,
and a short time after that, the power to command the
bombers
—"Thy God goeth before thee, a consuming fire."—
did I not have to obey?

BELL (*sarcastic*):

Maybe the Catholics are right to forbid the Bible.

P.M. (*shakes this off, but concedes*):
It's true the Commons have never seen
my fight against the Hun in quite the same light
as Israel's standing before the children of Anak.
However, as early as 1915, Fisher, the First Sea Lord,
wrote to me after Gallipoli to console me:
We shall certainly win, we are
the ten lost tribes of Israel.
I gave my warning *in time,* and that acquits me.
—The burning of Hamburg: eighteen years ago
I wrote it, clear as daylight, on the wall.
Copyright, Winston Churchill—there for all the world to see.

BELL (*shocked*):
Hitler had not been heard of eighteen years ago.

P.M. (*cool*): He could still read. So could his Germans.
I warned that next time we would deliver
fire to their homes, free, gratis, and for nothing:
I said that had the First War lasted one more year
I would, as Minister of Munitions,
have sacked Berlin. I wrote that Death
was standing in readiness to reduce civilization to dust.
Nations that feel their existence to be threatened
will not be shy of using any measures.
We know how closely that man over there
took my warning to heart.

BELL: How—do you know?

P.M. (*sarcastic*):
From his impotent appeals to the Red Cross
to have air warfare against towns forbidden—
efforts with which Great Britain's pacifists—
men who let others do the fighting for them—
were so impressed he very nearly succeeded
in striking the only weapon from our hands
which would have been left to an island without infantry.
And the imponderable factors—those you forget.
A decisive battle can also be like this:
In November, 1940, our Intelligence
reported that Molotov was going to see Hitler.
Let us divide the world between us, he suggested,
take India, the British are *kaput.*

That sounded attractive, but—
just as the Russian decided to retire
(a day spent talking with Hitler must exhaust one),
just then we came! A nightcap.
Molotov had to get up and bundle down to the shelter,
rigorously taken care of by the lackeys of the Nazi Foreign
    Office.
Stalin confirmed immediately
what effect *that* had had.

BELL: But today: Has not the victory in Africa
proved that we can defeat the Germans
on land as easily?]

P.M.: If Hitler, instead of defending his towns,
digs in his guns—in thousands—on the coast,
how will a single one of our tanks be able
to get sand under its tracks?
How many workers will not appear on Monday morning
to fill grenades—because their houses
fell in about their heads on Sunday night?
A people that has made "scorched earth" of Eastern Europe
must be left with nothing but their eyes
with which to bewail the war.

BELL: Scorched cities for scorched earth: but why
has your Air Minister been telling lies for years
in Parliament?

[P.M.: That will stop now. The strong can afford to be honest:
In the New Year a book will be allowed to be published—
Bombing Vindicated, which coolly claims the credit
for Great Britain for having *chosen*
to decide the war by the bombing of cities.

BELL (*angrily*): Do not shift the blame onto the British people.

The PRIME MINISTER *speaks with an assurance he was first to forfeit when he was able to study the world reaction to the destruction of Dresden.*

There was too much enthusiasm in the British press as well in November, 1943, during the unsuccessful Berlin offensive: Hitler's Propaganda Minister noted dispiritedly—since he was the only Nazi leader whose family lived within the range of the British bombers—that they were saying in London that a million Berliners had been killed in the bombing. Goebbels: "That is a lot of non-

sense: the casualty figures in all three heavy raids veer between three and four thousand. But this exaggeration of the English will not be denied. The sooner the English believe that life in Berlin is extinct, the better for us."

P.M.: No, the people are the only beneficiary.
   Mr. Spaight can show you the manuscript,
   he is the Deputy Permanent Under-Secretary to the Air
       Ministry.
   Spaight reminds us of the Somme.
   Graveyards like that shall not disturb my sleep.

BELL: That does you honor. But what would you have done
   had Hitler not begun the bombing
   in Rotterdam and Warsaw?

P.M. (*blinking, ferociously*):
   No, Bishop, the fact that the man overran
   Poland and Holland, and Belgrade,
   these things too are crimes for which he shall hang.
   But Rotterdam and Warsaw were *not* open cities;
   both were declared citadels and both of them
   were urged, repeatedly, to surrender
   before the Huns sent in their air power.

BELL: Then why—are we assured the opposite?]

P.M.: Because the myth is mightier than the sword.
   Do you imagine in a struggle for life and death—
   I shall try first to justify
   anything that will bring Hitler down?
   [(*A laugh of vexation. He is bitterly amused. He does not
       understand* BELL *at all.*)
   Geneva is a fair city . . .
   but had the Germans landed on our shores,
   we would have wiped them out with mustard gas.

HELEN *has silently handed him a note, which he reads and then speaks without triumph as he crumples it and flicks it with quiet satisfaction onto the grass.*

   (*To* HELEN:)
   Release it for the BBC and the newspapers.
   (*To* BELL:)
   The "Scharnhorst" has ceased fire.

BELL (*to break the pause as the* PRIME MINISTER *is clearly no
       longer "with us"*): Sunk?

P.M.: —mm? No, that will be taken care of with torpedoes.
 But her turrets are silent.
 The "Duke of York," the victor, is already heading for home.]
 You ask *me* so many questions, now I ask you:
 What did *you* achieve
 as the first foreigner to protest
 against Hitler's race laws—when?—
BELL: [In '34—Hindenburg was still there.
 Our curious government at the time condemned it
 as intervention in German internal affairs.]
 Achieved—I achieved nothing.
P.M.: And later you made a protest to Hitler
 against the imprisonment of Niemöller—
 you killed no one, you helped no one.
 I kill because there is no other help for it.
BELL (*with profound sincerity*):
 Kill the enemy—kill the enemy—not his family.
 How is it that you will not understand me—
P.M.: One can only choose to do what one is able to do.
 Against the greatest land force in the world,
 I had no infantry.
 Against the greatest city in the world,
 that man had only fighters and short-range bombers.
 (He had to withdraw the famous Stukas
 from the battle after a week.)
 Udet had persuaded him that as possessor
 of such breach-busting armored forces, he need not build
 long-range heavy bombers.
BELL: If he could not do it, why
 did he try to "rub out" London?
P.M. (*simply*): I wanted him to try.
BELL: You?—Sir.
P.M.: Yes, I—since *we* had seen in the Spanish war
 that hooligans could destroy market villages like Guernica
 with its ninety-eight dead
 but that great cities could not be "rubbed out"
 by combat aircraft. Bloody cheek.
 The Romans were before me with the idea:
 "If you are a great general," said Pompaedius Silo
 to Marius, "come down and fight."

"If you are a great general," came the celebrated answer,
"get me to fight against my will."
I had to throw him the rope;
the hanging he could manage on his own.
Hitler was bombing docks and airfields
and fighter factories to make a breach for the invasion.
In more than forty raids he killed
barely fourteen hundred—but our *fighters,*
they were nearly finished.
I had to make a breathing space for them,
to trick Hitler away from Dowding's fighter airfields.
I told the House: our city of eight million souls
on the Thames is like a colossal prehistoric monster:
it cannot be killed if it bleeds from a thousand wounds.
At last that sick creature over there
became the darling of misfortune:
One or two machines went off their course;
the bombs fell on London,
only nine people were killed, possibly a mistake.
But now I was able to
send eighty bombers over Berlin.
But Hitler did not come.
He had no thought of bombing London.
Once more I went to Berlin,
but Hitler did not come.
He ranted, screamed revenge,
puffed up with vanity, he gnashed his teeth,
wailing about hearth and home and heritage,
threatening to destroy us.
But still he did not come.
Our own performance was wretched—but at last,
after our sixth attack upon Berlin,
he struck back, our airfields were left in peace,
Dowding's fighters caught their breath—
and then we slit the throats of Göring's clumsy cows
as Harris called them
and disembowelled them over our cities.
BELL (*not without a shudder of admiration*):
Then it was a stroke of genius on your part—
the stratagem of reason that saved the freedom of the world.
The freedom, now, to say, "Enough."

[P.M.: Why? I said in 1935 that
every German aircraft that attacked our cities
would be unwillingly withheld from other duties;
today, too, it is my aim, I wrote to Stalin in March,
to tempt Hitler's other fighting machines,
with which he is lying in wait for us in France,
to tempt them over our cities.
The legendary morale of the people
encourages me to lay this on their shoulders,
once again, as in 1940.
Humiliating enough, Bishop,
that Hitler can entice us to the duel;
the choice of weapons, however, rests with me.
Ha—the man to whom Vienna, Prague,
Oslo, and Brussels, even Paris, have fallen,
without a broken windowpane, that man must dream
of ravishing an untouched London,
as he has violated the shameless beauty on the Seine.
Cities are stumbling stones of the highest order!
Well, we have not broken with the tradition
of a thousand years
that enemies only come to *London* as prisoners.
Hitler's howling about open cities,
in the summer of 1940 even,
while his Prussians, armed to the teeth,
crouched in Boulogne ready for the spring;
all this only meant: open for his infantry.
He must have been confusing us with Luxembourg.
Amazing.]

BELL *goes up to the* PRIME MINISTER, *speaks quickly and quietly.*
The PRIME MINISTER *listens patiently, since the talk is of fame.*

BELL: Prime Minister—you cherish the opinion of posterity.
In twenty years, forty years, the *Herrenvolk,*
with its extermination factories
will no longer be the bomber's target.
The targets change—but what will stay the same
is the writing upon the wall, put there by you eighteen years
ago:
The killing of the defenseless from the air.
Every conquerer is a founder.

[Think of this country, lying in the sea,
defenseless as Manhattan.
What if a time should come when there should be
an explosive material which would make
the Doctrine of the Four Last Things a fact?]
What will you found as conqueror, Mr. Churchill?
You know yourself, as an *homme de lettres,*
ideas survive actions.
Don't let the Churchill era pass away
without one idea to survive its greatest action:
Hitler's destruction.
[(*Smiles.*)
You said before, and you have often written:
the Romans had stolen all your best ideas.
Virgil despised Homer for seeing
the purpose of war simply in the destruction
of all one's enemies and nothing else.
Virgil has Diomedes denigrate the Trojan campaign
as a primitive show of force.
Roman political instinct demanded more than that:
totum sub leges submitteret orbem—
a universal society at peace under the law.

P.M. (*darkly, with pomp*):
And the British are, of course, the Romans.
Milton did not say, "We are founding a new Rome."
He said, "We are founding Rome new."
But, Bishop, all foundations, even Rome's,
are built on murder—
fratricide. As Cain slew Abel,
Romulus slew Remus
so that he could found his city.
Am I to found this liberation—without killing?

BELL (*insistently*): No. But without murder!
You have already made a beginning.
Your order that in air attacks on Hitler's satellite states
and occupied territories such as France, every care
must be taken to avoid killing civilians:
this order is the beginning. Extend it
to include civilians within Hitler's borders too.
That would be an order that would surpass

even the fame of the deeds of your bombers . . .
I speak of fame, since I am building all my hopes
upon your quite legitimate love of it.

P.M. (*quite naturally*): Of course—what else can a man love
other than fame and freedom?

BELL (*drily*): His fellow men—I would suggest.

P.M. (*mocking*): To a leader of them—you would suggest
to an old man, one who has grown old among them,
that he should love his fellows? Clemenceau
held the view that one must debase a man
before one can master him.

BELL (*objective*): I agree, but mastery is not fame.
On the contrary, fame is forever—mastery *cannot* last.
That it cannot do so is what makes the world
tolerable, every now and then.
Clemenceau—is a useful example:
He had no *ideas*. And where is his fame now?
(*Laughs with contempt.*)
The left bank of the Rhine for France—and on the right
live twenty million men too many—
that may be strategy. But nothing can be founded on it,
and therefore not fame either.
But you, Sir, are a great soldier.]
Be a great founder, like Augustus, Constantine,
bring forth an idea, as Napoleon or Lenin
brought forth the spirit of the revolution.
Since you are not a revolutionary,
then preserve something:
insure the inviolability of the defenseless.
And the honor of the soldier—
who is not a criminal, only so long as he protects the child.
[The whirlwind of these years has swept away
so many taboos: cannot you, the conservative,
set one up again?
Posit this:]
Only the *number* of his victims—
differentiates that moral criminal, who,
hiding behind his uniform [and his orders,]
murders civilians, from the one
who kills *one* seventeen-year-old girl in the park at night.

The PRIME MINISTER *has stood up at the words "moral criminal."*
*When he has heard the sentence out—*BELL *has spoken hurriedly*
and vehemently—he is white with rage, speechless. Then he
speaks, loudly because he has only words to express himself:

P.M.: Bishop—for that comparison I despise you.
I protest in the name of the men of all bomber forces
—even those of the enemy.
I reject, with the utmost contempt . . .

BELL, *comes closer, which increases the* PRIME MINISTER'S *anger*
—then confidentially, as only the stronger man can be toward the
weaker, he speaks with cool imperturbability.

BELL: Sir, what is an anti-social man compared with an officer
who persuades himself and his men, by whatever argument,
to aim at cities—to annihilate them?
[The chances of survival for mankind
lie in the personal choice of every man,
each single individual—who on his own instinct,
or as a mercenary—purposely takes the lives
of noncombatants.
The reason does not bear discussion—
a reason can always be found.
P.M.: I would have left you standing here long since—
I am only speaking to you still
to defend men like Dorland.
Do his *motives* count for nothing?
BELL: You mean his orders?
Yes, they count—but they do not acquit.
They count for the criminal only—not his victim.
I too am speaking for Dorland.
I recognize myself in him;
had I been an airman in this Second War too—
I would have been equally, criminally thoughtless:
done the dishonorable alongside the most honorable.
For what the bomber pilot does is still
not his subjective guilt but that of our *society.*
We have first to reawaken the consciousness
of what is a criminal deed.
And then threaten its doers with the harshest punishment.]
Dorland himself hinted at the cold elation

produced by the—I don't know—satisfaction
of the technical, statistical, achievement
of overpowering a whole city
in a single night,
at a single stroke.

P.M. (*laughs maliciously*):
Of course, in war! Are we to call that perverted?

BELL: Not with dams, refineries, and bridges—no.
But cities are feminine:
It is obscene that German schoolchildren roar themselves
hoarse
with a song called "Bombs over England."
It is obscene that the official name
of the RAF's heaviest bomb should be "Blockbuster."
[Let us not examine the backwash of our instincts.
Psychology is a private matter, and accordingly
without interest. But—]
when the city is the bomber's target
and therefore the maternity hospital too,
then the man who aims *must* submit
to people estimating him
according to the *results* of his actions;
and those are photographically identical
with those of a sex murderer.

P.M. (*turns brusquely away, to* HELEN):
Helen—a car for the Bishop. At once.

HELEN (*not moving, then pointing to the terrace, uneasy*):
It has been waiting for some time, Sir.

BELL, *as* CHURCHILL *is obviously wanting to get by and away from him, pointedly ignores* HELEN'*s answer and stands right in the* PRIME MINISTER'*s way with an assurance that shows nevertheless that he does not wish to give the impression that he is doing it on purpose. After taking a couple of steps,* CHURCHILL *too is once again the man who does not yield, who believes he owes it, as it were, professionally to himself—and to the country—always to be the last one left on the stage.*

BELL: [You have written that all actions,
like the moon, have an unseen hemisphere.
Think if the night-side of *your* fame were such

that the engineers who shall destroy the Ten Command-
ments—
the *future* practitioners of Harris's area-bombing—
should use your name as precedent.]
Our country has already sent into the world
an angel who fought that war might hold its hand
from those who could not fight or who could fight no longer.
And now we have sent you into the world
to save its freedom.
Save what an Englishwoman brought into being,
take your stand by the legacy of Florence Nightingale.

*He turns away, he is forced to, overcome by despair and the
trembling in his voice. Victor as long as he was the attacker, he is
victor no longer since he began to plead—and his voice fades
like that of mankind in the tumult of the massacre of history. To
hide his despair, he makes an effort to regain some sort of composure—but composure won at the cost of an effort is never very
complete. So he says to* HELEN, *who is standing holding the door
open, as coldly and strongly as he can, apparently with frozen
amusement:*

Now, Mrs. MacDonald—I must be going.

She follows him at a distance: the door remains open. CHURCHILL,
*alone, sunk in thought, gives himself up, unobserved, to the im-
pression* BELL *has made on him. He is therefore relieved when*
HELEN *returns almost at once, having given* BELL *into the care
of a servant in the house, picks up the paper* BELL *left lying, puts
it away, and then rouses* CHURCHILL *purposely from his reverie by
ostentatiously taking out her dictation pad and approaching him
as if, after a completely fruitless interruption, they could finally
get back to their work.*

HELEN: Sir—for the Poles, you wanted to dictate something?
Or would you like to rest now?
At seven o'clock the BBC is announcing
that the "Scharnhorst" has ceased firing.
P.M.: Both: It is restful to *do* something.
Very well: To the C.I.G.S.
"The time has come to bring the Polish troops from Persia into the
Mediterranean theater. Politically, this is highly desirable, and the

men wish to fight, and once engaged will worry less about their own
—(*he falters*)—tragic affairs . . . we should also draw on the
Polish Armored Division in Great Britain." Paragraph. "The Soviet
government is inclined to mistrust"—no, just put, "is inclined to be
skeptical about this Polish Corps—and suspect that it is being held
back and nursed so as to be employed against the Russians in defense of Polish rights. If, however, the Polish Corps enters the line
against the Germans and begins to fight this view will be dissipated."
That's all. [Listen and see
what the BBC says about the "Scharnhorst."]
HELEN: You know Sir Alan is coming at seven—
and Lord Cherwell?
P.M.: [They can pick me up at the shooting-range.]
Will it rain?

HELEN *goes to the typewriter and puts in a sheet of paper as the*
PRIME MINISTER, *taking his cap and stick, disappears into the*
darkening garden.

HELEN: I hope so—it's too clear for Kocjan's flight.

The PRIME MINISTER *is already out of earshot and has turned on*
the radio. After she has lit a cigarette, she starts typing.
The radio plays a Scottish song. HELEN *turns the volume*
down. CHERWELL *enters.*

CHERWELL: Well—did the P.M.
silence the old demagogue?
At the shooting-range?—
HELEN (*sighs, smiles*):
If *he* ever got to be Archbishop of Canterbury . . . !
CHERWELL: I expect that will be taken care of.

A *burst of fire has been heard and now there is another. The door*
opens. CHERWELL, *about to go into the garden, waits for* BROOKE,
whom DORLAND *ushers onto the terrace.* BROOKE *raises his swagger*
stick to his cap; one can see he is excited, but before he has time
to speak CHERWELL, *with unusual energy, opens one discussion as*
if he wished to avoid another.

CHERWELL: Did you follow all that? Such extravagance—
all for the "Scharnhorst."
[That not only battleships, but two destroyers as well
have to lie up in Scapa to look after

the precarious health of the "Tirpitz."
Dorland—if you and Gibson were able to destroy the dams,
surely with a dozen twelve-thousand pounders you could—
well?
DORLAND: The "Tirpitz" would put up a smoke screen,
though if we could fly over Sweden—]
HELEN (*to* BROOKE, *who is standing coldly disinterested*):
I am just typing something for you, Sir Alan.

The musical introduction to a victory announcement and the
strokes of Big Ben. HELEN *turns the radio down, so as not to*
disturb the speakers. We see that she is taking down the radio
announcement. BROOKE *looks over her shoulder at the page in*
her typewriter, then frostily interrupts CHERWELL, [*who is speaking*
with remarkable eloquence to DORLAND:

CHERWELL: Fly over Sweden and put down the bombs
next to her. A near miss in the shallow fjord—
and pfft! She'll turn turtle—
her own anchor chains will keep her face down.

He promises no more this time than Harris is later to perform.]

BROOKE (*brusquer than usual*):
Cherwell, I brought the Wing Commander along with me—
I thought you wanted to ask him how Sikorski—
Dorland being a Liberator pilot . . .
CHERWELL (*as if disturbed*):
Of course—do you actually know anything yet?
DORLAND (*slowly, shaking his head*):
No—no, Sir. Sir Alan was astonished
that the aircraft sank so quickly,
so near the coast, even before the speedboat
managed to get to her.
I wasn't so surprised—when you come down hard,
Liberators break up amidships more often than others.
CHERWELL (*interrupting quickly*):
That it should have sunk immediately, then, is not surprising?
DORLAND (*more warily*):
—I should not say so, no. But what is inexplicable,
quite inexplicable,
is that the joystick should ever have stuck:

I never heard of a case of it before;
we feel as safe as the Bank of England in those things . . .

CHERWELL (*interrupts with mounting impatience and irritation*):
—"safe." Of course the Liberator is "safe,"
or we would have given Sikorski something else,
but that was Anthony's—was Eden's aircraft;
(*resigned, as if he wanted to avoid saying what he now says*)
but not, alas, I now hear, Eden's pilot.

DORLAND (*quickly, while* BROOKE, *with an unashamed attempt to catch* CHERWELL's *eye, proves that on occasion the eye is more voluble than the tongue*):
I would not put it quite as directly as that, Sir—
but in point of fact, just *how*
he escaped alive, the only one to do so,
I shall never understand.

CHERWELL (*to* BROOKE, *whose glance is difficult for him to bear*):
What do *you* say?

BROOKE (*with contempt*):
I?—I am just a poor bloody infantryman—
The P.M. is waiting—

He goes quickly into the garden. DORLAND *makes to follow him but* CHERWELL *puts a hand on his arm and they go out together at a slower pace than* BROOKE's. *What they say need no longer be clearly audible.*

CHERWELL: May I, Dorland, ask the P.M. to put *you* onto the "Tirpitz"?

HELEN *had already turned up the radio as* BROOKE *went out and we hear* . . . *"Admiral Fraser's victory has cost the German navy her last currently operational heavy vessel."*
They are out of sight and earshot.

HELEN *has typed three lines when* KOCJAN *enters, not from the garden but from inside the house. She starts and goes to him. He is a changed man; he cannot speak.*

We are not including here the conversations held by the Governor, Mason MacFarlane, with Madame Sikorska and others, only because they took place some weeks later. He came especially to London, not to carry out an order, but on a call of conscience, a man spiritually broken by the tragedy which occurred in his sphere of command. He told the widow, with tears in his eyes, that he had begged first Sikorski, and, when that was no use, his daughter, not to board the aircraft. He assured General Kukiel: "The Russians could not have done it"; and the widow: "It cannot have been an accident."

HELEN: I wanted to tell you myself,
   but *first* I couldn't get away,
   and then I couldn't find you in the garden.
KOCJAN (*who is only submitting to the touch of her hand on his arm, looks at her, then away, speaks tonelessly*) :
   I see why well enough. [You have a great deal to do, it is clear.]
   You *knew.*
   You killed him. Admit it.
HELEN (*releases him, amazed*) :
   Killed? You don't mean—you can't—
KOCJAN (*all the despair of his downtrodden race breaks out, anger and hate make his speech clearer, his words are like knives, cutting through the Elgar march now coming from the radio*) :
   Yes—Sikorski!
   You murdered him—we Poles,
   everywhere we are in enemy territory.
   No one wants us, everyone uses us—
   like the Jews, a people without a country,
   abandoned, crushed—and yet
   the avalanche shall crush the Germans
   who have set it rolling.

HELEN *is about to say something, but* KOCJAN's *desperation so frightens her that she cannot get far with it.*

HELEN: You are mad!
KOCJAN (*laughs*) :
   Mad. Tomorrow I die at the hands of the Gestapo,
   fighting for Great Britain,
   or even today at the hands of the British Secret Service,
   fighting for Poland—like Sikorski.
   It is the same—all the same . . .
   Madness is—for Poles, the normal thing.
HELEN (*firmly now*) :
   Bohdan—there is not a word of truth in what you're saying.

Now it is she who pushes him away.

KOCJAN: Do not *you* lie—to me.
   I *cannot* defend myself against that.

HELEN (*despising his every word, forces herself to speak to him*):
Lie? It is only because you can't be sent away like this—
that I'm still talking to you.
(*Since Intelligence has never stopped a woman from be-
lieving what she wants.*)
The Prime Minister cried.

KOCJAN *laughs. He is unwilling to believe that* HELEN *is lying to
him, and unable to believe she cannot see through the nonsense she
is talking.*

He has sat himself on the balustrade and pulls HELEN *savagely by
the wrist; she resists, but her gaze does not falter before his. He
speaks quietly, as an inquisitor:*

What about the pilot?
HELEN: He survived.
KOCJAN: I know that. The only one.
HELEN (*ironically, bitterly*): Circumstantial evidence for you.
He was wounded. Ask him.
KOCJAN (*laughs*): What is he called, Helen?—His name!
HELEN: A Czech—
A Czech name. How should I know . . .
KOCJAN: It's enough. I just—wanted—
had to hear that again.
(*Again the sickened laugh.*)
A Czech!
How many Polish pilots in the RAF?
There *must* be thousands.
But when the Supreme Commander of the Polish Forces
goes on a tour of inspection, lasting weeks—
the pilot of *your* aircraft has to be
a Czech.

He laughs, unnerved, as people sometimes laugh at funerals.
HELEN, *a patriotic Englishwoman who sometimes, albeit with the
difficulty of all widows and mothers whose children have been
killed, manages to transmute her violent feelings into a kind of
pride, can hardly defend herself any longer from the fear she is
feeling. She feels she could not bear to believe what* KOCJAN *is
saying. He is standing closer to her than he knows and closer than
she, for the whole of the rest of the war, will want a man to stand
to her. But she idolizes the* PRIME MINISTER. *The most that*
KOCJAN *might achieve—although he is only speaking, not trying*

to "achieve" anything—would be HELEN's *belief in what he is saying. But that would only add a shudder to her admiration for the Old Man—the ultimate heightening of adoration.*

HELEN *(labored)*: He is not the *only* Czech in British uniform.
Both Masaryk's grandsons
were killed over Germany in a British bomber.
KOCJAN *(again contorted with mistrust, quietly)*:
How well-informed you are—
HELEN: Because the Prime Minister sent a message of
sympathy when the second one was killed.
(No longer trying to hide her distaste, and that she thinks he is mad—infected by his sarcasm, contemptuous.)
Your proofs! First you were oh so sure
I knew all about it—that was horrible!
Now you are oh so sure the Czech is one of us.
Why in that case did we let him survive?
KOCJAN *(laughs)*: Because only a Czech who is sole survivor
is able to draw suspicion to Czechs.
If the Czech is also killed—people will say:
Secret Service. [If the pilot survives—
he *must* swear engine trouble.
HELEN *(contemptuous)*:
Oh, who is going to believe what a pilot says
who is the only one to escape
out of a dozen people in the aircraft?
KOCJAN *(smiles)*:
You see? Your disbelief shows just how right
the calculation was: the world should not
completely believe all that the Czech says.]
The world should say, poor, unsuspecting British,
they too were much deceived about the pilot.

He has said this so unpleasantly that at this moment she really hates him, and her contradiction is proportionally weak to the force and pride with which she utters it.

HELEN: What you are hinting is appalling. This is England!
KOCJAN: Oh, yes, and black men start at Calais.
Only my kind come from Poland. Then let me tell you—
(maliciously)
unless, of course, you are already informed of it,

    —this was not in England, but in Edinburgh—
    Lieutenant Colonel Kleczynski, a Battle of Britain hero,
    the man who found a time fuse in Sikorski's aircraft
    on the way to Washington, and dismantled it,
    was conveniently run over and killed.

HELEN: I don't believe it.

KOCJAN: Doubtless the best way.
    [Nothing is more expedient than a street accident:
    take it from a professional.
    Do you think the Empire has been drummed together
    just by playing the game?

HELEN (*woundingly, since she herself is wounded*):
    I am well aware that we have probably thrown it all away
    —without the annexation of a single village—
    for Poland's sake.]

KOCJAN: One last thing, Helen—between us,
    not another word about Sikorski.
    I don't want you to lie to *me,*
    and more you must not say.
    Don't leave me alone today.
    I must go to Madame Sikorska.

HELEN *speaks consolingly, with the intimacy they use at night
—she escapes from what he has said to her into the "mission" of
worrying about him, rather than his unbearable accusation.*

HELEN: Yes . . . Bohdan, for your own peace of mind
    stop trying to persuade yourself . . .
    this disgusting nonsense is true.

KOCJAN (*hard; he shuts himself like a door*):
    Here are your keys—I do not come—

HELEN (*does not take the keys. Tears*):
    Don't go—don't go now, please.

[KOCJAN (*unyielding*):
    Will you be keeping your uniform on in bed,
    to prove to Poland the integrity
    of His Majesty's Government?
    Stop it.

HELEN: Don't you see—I have a certainty
    stronger than all your so-called evidence.
    Two years of working in his presence
    refute you!]

In the distance, in the garden, men's voices are heard laughing.

[Hasn't he saved Poland too?
KOCJAN (*disconsolate, as if he was referring the laughter to his own words*):
Saved us? He *treated* us.
You pay the doctor for the treatment, not the cure.
He cannot help it if the patient dies.]

Pulls HELEN *into his arms. Suddenly agitated once more by a new and terrible thought, he speaks to her urgently, persuasively, as if his peace of mind and not merely his despair depended on her agreement.*

Helen, once and for all, believe me.
The attempt in Montreal—
on his journey to Roosevelt . . .

HELEN *frees herself, glances into the garden, but says quite quietly and frankly to* KOCJAN:

HELEN: Attempt in Montreal? I know nothing about it.
KOCJAN (*now almost unable to speak, he is so affected*):
—not about the "special" aircraft crashing in Montreal—?
All four engines failed at the same time.
Too soon though.
HELEN (*agitated*): Too soon—what does that mean?
KOCJAN (*sarcastic*): Only the machine was damaged.
People—only shocked, shaken.
The engines failed too low.
HELEN: Bohdan, *believe* me—never,
I have never heard about it.
KOCJAN: [Yes. I believe you. It's horrible.
In the Prime Minister's house it is never mentioned
that *that* airplane crashed, the one that was lent
to the Prime Minister of Poland,
just like today . . . Sikorski's death
was the *fourth* . . . incident in an aircraft
provided by Downing Street.

HELEN *can say nothing.*]

(*Crushed.*)
Helen, since the incident with the fuse

he has not traveled out of England *once*
without an attempt being made on his life:
Three journeys, one after another—
three "accidents," one after another.
Roosevelt was never in any doubt
that it was sabotage in Montreal.

HELEN: Why can you not conclude the obvious?
It was the Germans or the Russians killed him?

KOCJAN: Now *that* you *do* know: procedure for surveillance
of aircraft of important people.
Always two on watch inside the machine
and two outside it, *all the time,* night and day.
Stalin?
As long as Poland was governed
by the man who had accused him
of the rape of Eastern Poland and
of the massacre of Katyn
he had no need to speak to Poles of Poland,
only with the jackals
who would hand our country over to the Kremlin.
And Hitler? Don't you see, he would trade a victory
to bring Sikorski back to life again?—
At last, a man in the heart of the Allied Staff
demanding extreme measures against Stalin.

In the garden, a long way off, the voices are heard laughing again.

HELEN (*as if she were going to be sick*):
Oh, Bohdan—if [that were so.
But *why* did Sikorski go so far as to . . .

KOCJAN: Was it *Sikorski* who cut Poland in two?
Shot her officers in the neck?

HELEN: But—no.
And yet if] a man has to send thousands . . .
to their deaths, hundreds of thousands,
all innocent,
like my husband . . .

KOCJAN: Like myself.

HELEN (*close to him*): No—don't—[don't say that.

KOCJAN: Sikorski had misgivings at the end. Everyone was
begging him before this journey, only to fly with

Polish crews. He said—no, it is when we mistrust
the British that we must put ourselves in their hands.
Then they will be obligated to . . . oh, it is dreadful.
(*He breaks down.*)]

The laughter sounds again, no longer distant. She breaks from him.

HELEN: He's coming. Go!

She wipes her eyes, points to the door, and goes quickly to her typewriter. She has said "Go," more automatically than thinkingly, but KOCJAN *is hurt by the brusqueness and comes ostentatiously to the middle of the terrace and hisses, hostilely:*

KOCJAN: *Go?* Why?

Voices. Footsteps. And high, high above them, approaching very slowly, the second bomber wave, destination Germany. At the final word of the scene, the dull roar of the aircraft reaches its most threatening pitch, seeming to hang motionless over Chequers.

CHURCHILL *enters quickly, head down as usual, accompanied, surrounded by* LORD CHERWELL, *the* CHIEF OF THE IMPERIAL GENERAL STAFF, *and* WING COMMANDER DORLAND. *The* PRIME MINISTER *is surprised to see the Pole still there. He looks at* HELEN, *who has stayed where she is. Now, not coming too close, he turns to the Pole.*

P.M.: Captain—ah, you are still here.
    Then I can . . .

He raises his hand to his cap, in a military salute. Apart from LORD CHERWELL, *who raises his bowler hat and holds it in front of his chest, the other men of his entourage, one after the other, raise their right hands in salute.* HELEN *has stood, but she does not salute. She stares at the stone floor, then closes her eyes for a long while.*

(*Shattered.*)
. . . express my deepest sympathy
and the condolences of the entire British people
to you, as representative of your nation and . . .
the courageous army of Poland, the unconquerable,
on the—tragic loss of your Commander-in-Chief
and Prime Minister.

He lowers his hand. He takes a step toward KOCJAN *but something seems to warn him not to extend his hand to him.* KOCJAN *says nothing. With unnatural rigidity, he holds his hands to his trouser seams as if this escape into a military "attitude" could give him support from within as well.*

CHURCHILL, *it is clear, wishes the Pole would turn and go. As he does not,* CHURCHILL *continues, extraordinarily clumsily, as he is to do the next day in the House and a week later over the radio to* SIKORSKI's *soldiers. It does him good to talk, since it is only by means of words, quite unlike his usual style, but completely honest, that he regains his balance, which he had nearly lost.*

> General Sikorski—Captain, [up to the moment of his death]
> lived in the conviction that everything must be
> subordinated to the—necessities of the common struggle.
> Now he is gone: yet were he at my side,
> he would, I think . . . have . . . wished, that—
> I should say to you . . . [what—I now say
> from my heart:] soldiers must die,
> but by their death . . . they nourish
> the nation that gave them birth.

KOCJAN (*using his last reserves of energy to keep control of himself*):
> —at all events, that nation
> whose guests we are,
> Sir—and . . . the Allies.

He turns without saluting and hurries out. From the discomfiture of the others, which makes them more motionless than ever, one may see what has been going on inside KOCJAN *more easily than from his own behavior.*

Silence.

CHERWELL's *face alone remains smooth as a monument.* BROOKE *glances at* CHERWELL. DORLAND *avoids looking up.* HELEN *leans back against the balustrade. No one dares look at the* PRIME MINISTER.

CURTAIN

EPILOGUE

The curtain is drawn up again at once. All the actors have disappeared and the stage is in a harsh working-light.
The STAGE MANAGER *and two* STAGEHANDS *enter and begin to strike the scenery.*
DORLAND *enters and beckons to the* STAGE MANAGER.

DORLAND (*slight irony*): Tell everyone, notes in the vestry in ten
    minutes.
STAGE MANAGER (*going out*): O.K.

The STAGEHANDS *roll up the white screen, from which the projection of the garden has disappeared, and the wall of the ruined cathedral—up to now only indicated right and left of the setting—becomes the real background of the stage.*

SCULPTOR (*approaching* DORLAND):
    Dorland, I think you'll have to
    say something to cool your son down.
DORLAND (*drily*): Really—him too?
SCULPTOR: To be expected. Our young lions
    still have an appetite for meat—
    only they don't wish to admit
    that one must kill a beast to get it.

The SON *appears in the background, brandishing a telegram:*

SON: Thank you so much, Father—
    a wire from the Air Ministry:

He hands the telegram to the SCULPTOR, *while his irritation subsides into irony.*

SON: I am summoned to Group Captain MacIntosh
    tomorrow morning: [you have effectively
    made my name mud in that quarter, Father dear.
DORLAND: You can put your Ministry's mind at rest
    about my expectation of life—
    corroboration available on demand . . .
SCULPTOR: Peter, the time's perhaps not so far off
    when you will no longer regret
    having been removed from a Strategic Air Command.
SON: They don't need to kick me out—
    they just have to pass me over, that's enough.]
DORLAND: Amazing to see my own son, so young,

    reacting just like Marshal Harris already—
    taking offense on a *personal* level
    in the presence of a problem which might
    be thought of slightly more importance
    than our own worthy selves.

The SCULPTOR *has handed the telegram to* DORLAND, *who reads it and returns it to* PETER, *who puts it back in his pocket.*

SON (*changing the subject, disturbed*):
    Personal? No—the insult is to the Air Force and to Churchill.
    I do not understand you anymore:
    Whenever I wanted to show off at school,
    I used to bring out your photograph,
    the one with Churchill at High Wycombe.
SCULPTOR: I hope you'll go on doing so.
SON (*points at his father*):
    After he has made such an imputation?
DORLAND: I have not pronounced sentence . . .
SON: No, you've carried it out on the spot.
SCULPTOR: I thought *you* were the one who wasn't showing
    his picture of Churchill around anymore.
    Why? Does that imply that he . . .
    could have acted better or otherwise, in your opinion?
SON (*quietly*): My father has imputed an assassination to him.
DORLAND (*icy*): "Hardly cricket, what?" I mean
    "people don't do such things."
    And that is perfectly true—for people like us.
    It is no coincidence that not you,
    (*he points at* PETER, *then at the* SCULPTOR, *then
    at himself*)
    not him, not I—but Churchill
    led the country to victory.
    Greatness has its own dimensions.
    How can you have the gall to condemn an action,
    simply because you could not have performed it?
[SCULPTOR: I was thinking of what he said in his essay on
    Asquith—it might have been a self-portrait . . .
    "Loyal as he was to his colleagues, he never
    shrank, when public need required it, from putting
    them aside once and for all . . . But how else can
    states be governed?"

DORLAND (*following on*):
"What sort of villains would we be, if we did,
for our own benefit, the things we do for our
country?"
SON (*mulish, impatient*): You're both hiding behind quotations.]
Did he kill Sikorski?
DORLAND (*firmly*): If he thought it necessary, yes.
If not, no.
SON: Do *you* think he thought it necessary?
DORLAND: Three successive journeys in VIP machines:
three "incidents," one after the other.
Without a doubt he thought it necessary
to save the alliance that saved the world.
SON (*disparaging*): And I thought you—humane, like him.
Oh, I know a thing only becomes serious
when one makes sacrifices for it, but
he did not sacrifice himself.
DORLAND: That would have been as pointless as if
he had sat himself in a bomber or a tank—
[to send others to death was, for a man
who feared death as little as Churchill,
harder than dying.
SCULPTOR: I saw him at Sikorski's funeral:
as shattered as the widow.
SON (*hard, decisive*): But that he should have sacrificed a *Pole!*
SCULPTOR: For Poland, yes—which is today
larger than Sikorski ever dreamed.]
To be sure, when Churchill said, during the war,
he was fighting not for Poland's frontiers
but Poland's freedom—the end, here too,
only shows that history is
the disproportion between intention and result.
Poland's frontiers he has extended
further than ever before:
her freedom though, as he understood the word,
he was unable to restore to her.
DORLAND: The life of every great man of action
closes, I am convinced, with the parable
of the sorcerer's apprentice—only without the happy ending
since it is not just a story, but history.

Think of Churchill's last call to arms as Prime Minister,
the Bermuda Conference in 1953:
He pressed in vain for a law to protect open cities.
But he was grown old, the sorcerer of power.
The sorcerer's apprentices of today
(*he points at his son*)
just smiled at him.

The AMERICAN *enters hurriedly between the* STAGEHANDS, *looking for the banner: 1864 First Geneva Convention 1964* . . . (*He may either look vainly for it here, because it is fixed to the street side of the ruin; or better perhaps, if it has been nailed up* inside *the ruins, has been hidden by the stage settings, and is now once more to be seen.*) *The three men in the foreground have not noticed him at first, while they are still talking—now he lurches toward them, less drunk than tired:*

AMERICAN: 'Evening—could you please help me:
    they're taking everything away; only for God's
    sake,
    not the poster: Hundred years of Red Cross!
    That's a collector's item: my mother is a collector.
SCULPTOR (*as* DORLAND *says nothing*):
    What is he talking about?
DORLAND: He means the Red Cross funeral ribbons there:
    all right, we'll keep them safe for you.
AMERICAN: I'll be happy to pay for it—money no object.
    It's historical, you might say. Did *you* write it?
DORLAND: The banner?
AMERICAN: No, I heard they're going to act some play here,
    against the atom bomb. I'm all for it.
DORLAND: The bomb?
AMERICAN: No, the play—against the bomb.
    The atom bomb is robbing us
    of all freedom of negotiation.
    (*To the* SON:)
    RAF!—you'll understand me.
    The bomb is just one great big piece of dog.
    On March 10, 1945, I was over Tokyo,
    B-29, a whole three months before Hiroshima.
    We—not them over Hiroshima and Nagasaki—
    we were the ones who did the most economical job.

One hundred twenty thousand Nips in a single night
—nothing left but the chemical elements,
68 per cent water, 20 per cent albumen,
2.5 per cent fat, and 9 or 10 per cent . . .
I dunno . . . mineral salts or sump'n.
General Curtis E. LeMay, back on the job once more now,
he said, right after the Thanksgiving service,
"We bombed them right back into the Stone Age."
What for, I ask you, do we *need* the Bomb?
It only gives the military a bad name.
The scientists have stolen the victory from us—
sitting at home on their butts—they . . . the winners!
[SCULPTOR (*in a changed voice, as if he were chipping every word
out of granite*):
"When you see something that is technically
sweet, you go ahead and do it, and you argue what to
do with it only after your technical success . . . "
AMERICAN: Very right too. What's that?
SCULPTOR (*continuing*):
"We wanted to have it done before the war
was over and nothing could be done."
There is the real explanation of Robert Oppenheimer
for the dropping of the two atomic bombs.]

SON *speaks to* DORLAND, *who, during the conversation about
Tokyo, has gone upstage to a* POLICEMAN *who has appeared in
the background and given him a telegram, which* DORLAND *has
opened.*

SON: Anything special?
DORLAND (*offhand*): Only in a negative way:
the play has been banned in England.

THE END